M000317329

ANTIETAM

ANTIETAM
THE LOST ORDER

DONALD R. JERMANN

PELICAN PUBLISHING COMPANY

GRETNA 2006

Copyright © 2006
By Donald R. Jermann
All rights reserved

*The word "Pelican" and the depiction of a pelican are
trademarks of Pelican Publishing Company, Inc.,
and are registered in the U.S. Patent and Trademark Office.*

Library of Congress Cataloging-in-Publication Data

Jermann, Donald R.
  Antietam : the lost order / Donald R. Jermann.
     p. cm.
  Includes bibliographical references and index.
  ISBN-13: 978-1-58980-366-4 (hardcover : alk. paper)
  1. Antietam, Battle of, Md., 1862. 2. Lee, Robert E. (Robert
Edward), 1807-1870—Military leadership. 3. McClellan, George
Brinton, 1826-1885—Military leadership. I. Title.

  E474.65.J37 2006
  973.7'336—dc22

                                        2006017726

*Photographs courtesy of Massachusetts Commandery, Military Order of
the Loyal Legion and the U.S. Army Military History Institute*

Printed in the United States of America

Published by Pelican Publishing Company, Inc.
1000 Burmaster Street, Gretna, Louisiana 70053

To my wife, Florence

Contents

Acknowledgments

I would like to thank my entire family for their encouragement and support. In particular, I am grateful to my daughter Mary, who handled the typing and initial proofreading, turned my maps into publishable illustrations, and helped navigate us through the murky waters that stand between a manuscript and a book; to my daughter Lucy, who did a final editing that made publishers realize they were dealing with pros; to my son Peter, who prepared the manuscript for publication, created the index, and used his computer expertise to bring my (and his) ideas for the cover into the real world; to my son David, an accomplished artist, who created sketches for the cover; and to my son Paul, also an accomplished artist, who provided finished cover ideas.

I would also like to thank Earl McElfresh who read the manuscript and steered us in the right direction to get it published.

Introduction

When the Confederates under Gen. Robert E. Lee invaded Maryland in September 1862, the invasion force passed squarely between the main Union army under Gen. George B. McClellan in Washington and the large Union garrison at Harpers Ferry. General Lee decided to take a risk and divide his army into four parts, first surround and then capture the Harpers Ferry garrison, and then reunite his army before McClellan knew what was going on.

By a fantastic set of circumstances, a copy of Lee's secret plan fell into McClellan's hands. McClellan then knew exactly what Lee's intentions were, where each of the pieces of Lee's divided army was, and where all of them were going. This provided McClellan with an unparalleled opportunity to destroy Lee's army before the pieces could reunite. When McClellan read Lee's plan, he exclaimed, "Here is a paper with which if I cannot whip Bobbie Lee, I will be willing to go home."

From the time McClellan read the plan, the clock became king. There were only so many hours available to him before Lee's army reunited and the opportunity to destroy it in detail, and possibly end the war in 1862, was gone for good. This book covers those hours. As it turned out, it was a photo finish.

The area of conflict is shown in map 1.

Map 1
Perspective Map

Area of Conflict ⭕

MILES 0   50   100

Chapter 1

The Nature of War in September 1862

In order to understand the events in Maryland in mid-September 1862, it is necessary to have some understanding of the nature of war in America at that time. We will start with a primer of war in the Eastern states in 1862.

Armies on the Move

In September 1862, Union general George B. McClellan's Mobile Army of the Potomac had approximately 90,000 troops present, 3,219 wagons, 315 ambulances, and 32,885 horses and mules. If he put the whole army on a single road, it would extend for more than forty miles; and if the front were attacked, it could not be reinforced from the rear for more than two days. The answer was to divide the army into corps.

A corps consisted of two or more divisions and contained its own contingent of cavalry, artillery, transport, and administration. In effect, it was a small, self-contained army. Union army corps contained ten to twenty thousand men. When the army was on the march, the various corps could be assigned different routes to avoid clogging the roads and extending the column too long. The general idea was for the corps to separate to subsist, advance, or retreat, but to unite to fight.

An army commander's principal assistants were his corps commanders, and it was normally to them and to his cavalry commander that he gave his orders.

If the commander wanted to move faster and keep the roads as unclogged as possible, he might order that each man carry three days' rations on his person, and that all supply wagons (except those carrying ammunition) and ambulances be moved off the road.

If two opposing armies were headed for a battle, the one with the road layout that allowed the quickest concentration of forces enjoyed the advantage.

Moving armies were "screened" by their cavalry. Each army's cavalry operated between it and its enemy. If a group of Union cavalrymen tried to see if the Confederates occupied the next town down the road, they would encounter a group of Confederate cavalrymen who would block their access. The Confederate cavalry at this time, under its redoubtable commander, Maj. Gen. Jeb Stuart, was particularly efficient at screening, and generally dominated the Union cavalry.

When only the cavalry were in contact, casualties were generally very light. There was a saying among infantrymen that no one had ever seen a dead cavalryman. To cite an example, Confederate general D. H. Hill, when writing of the Union casualties at the battle of South Mountain, mentioned Union losses of 1,812 infantry and artillery and one cavalryman, and then added, "how killed is not explained."[1]

When the two moving armies desired to contest a location, a battle involving the infantry and artillery ensued. Each cavalry then took up position on the flanks of its own army. The battles resulted in major bloodletting, but usually lasted no more than a day or two.

Tactics

When troops were on the move, they normally marched in a column of fours. However, to fight, they deployed into what was known as a "line of battle." A line of battle was perpendicular to the line of march and consisted of two rows of troops, shoulder to shoulder, one row right in front of the other, facing the enemy. The officers stood behind the troops. The rifles were single shot and had to be loaded through the muzzle. The troops would fire in volleys, the first row shooting while the second row was loading, and then would reverse positions.

The action usually began when the enemy was one hundred to three hundred yards away. The tactics were designed for the era of the musket. Muskets were short-range weapons and notoriously inaccurate. The rifles the troops now carried were not. They could kill at half a mile, and they were deadly accurate. The outdated tactics resulted in frightful casualties. More casualties were suffered in one day in the battle of Antietam than the country had experienced in the Revolutionary War and the War of 1812 combined.

When an army approached the battlefield where the enemy was located in force, it could often see little of the enemy, if in fact anything at all. Only hills, woods, cornfields, or orchards might be visible, concealing the enemy. Consequently, before committing the entire line of battle, "skirmishers" were employed. Skirmishers consisted of a thin line of troops that were not restricted to a formation when advancing, but were permitted to take advantage of the features of the terrain, such as crouching behind rocks or trees. It was their function to determine where the enemy was, how he was deployed, and in what strength. When they had served their purpose, a line of battle was oriented, and they withdrew through the line of battle.

The artillery of the time could fire shot, shell, or canister. Shot was simply solid, non-exploding spheres that bounced along the ground. A soldier's head would not significantly slow up a bounce. Shell contained exploding charges. Canister was simply cans full of pellets equivalent to heavy buckshot. Shot and shell were used at long range. A bombardment of shot and shell could be an unnerving experience, but usually did not inflict many casualties. Canister was used only at short range against advancing infantry and was deadly.

In general, cavalry was not intended or expected to engage in stand-up fights with infantry; that is, unless the cavalry occupied an especially advantageous feature, such as a mountain pass. Cavalry was equipped only with carbines and pistols (as well as sabers) and hence was at a disadvantage when fighting with infantry, which was equipped with rifles. When cavalry did fight with infantry, it was always dismounted, with the horses a safe distance behind. The horses were considered too valuable to risk.

Intelligence

In a word, intelligence, or information on the enemy's size, movements, and intentions, was awful. There was no formal intelligence service in the armies in September 1862 as there is today. General McClellan, recognizing the problem and being the enterprising type that he was, contracted with the Pinkerton Detective Agency to serve this function for him. The Pinkertons proved to be to military intelligence what the Keystone Cops were to law enforcement. It is said that they employed such scientific strategies as peering out cellar windows and counting the legs marching by—and then forgetting to divide by two. In any event, McClellan could have gotten far better estimates of the numbers of enemy facing him if he had just counted his own troops and multiplied by two.

When a moving army moved through enemy territory, as the Confederates were doing in September 1862, they would cut any telegraph wires connecting the area with its own army. There was no aerial reconnaissance and no radio; if an invading army was covered by a cavalry screen, as the Confederate army was in September 1862, the opposing army, in this case the Union army, had few means of finding out how many of the enemy there were, where they were, what they were doing, or where they were going. To gain information, the defending army had to depend on reports from its cavalry or friendly civilians passing through the area, or on reports from outposts on the perimeter of the area of operations that still maintained communications.

Reports by friendly, even intelligent and conscientious civilians, were likely to be gross exaggerations, as well as misleading. An individual who had never experienced ten horsemen galloping past his house and who now saw a thousand, or who watched an infantry column march past from dawn to dusk, was likely to be enormously impressed and greatly exaggerate the number. Furthermore, if his house was on the Frederick-Hagerstown turnpike, and the troops were headed in the direction of Hagerstown, he was likely to say they were going to Hagerstown, even though they may have turned off at the next intersection. Reports based on civilians who had mingled with enemy soldiers were also usually wrong, inasmuch as the enemy soldiers normally did not know either their own strength or their destination. The Confederate general, Stonewall Jackson, not only kept his intentions from his closest associates, but purposely created false information in anticipation of it being passed to the enemy.

One of the best sources of intelligence for an invading army was the newspapers, and the leaders eagerly purchased and read the latest periodicals of the area as they advanced. The ultimate example of bad intelligence came somewhat later, in late June to early July 1863, when the Confederate cavalry commander, Gen. Jeb Stuart, despite access to all the latest newspapers, was unable to find his own army.

In mid-September 1862, intelligence on the Confederates' numbers, location, and intentions was such that confusion reigned at the Union headquarters.

Generals and Troops

In 1861, before the outset of the Civil War, the United States Army, authorized by Congress, consisted of 12,689 enlisted men plus officers. The officers included twenty-two colonels and fewer than ten generals. By 1865, more than two million men had served in the Union and Confederate armies, and there were 1,988 Union and 344 Confederate generals. (There were thirty-eight General Smiths.) Where did all these generals come from?

Since the War of 1812, the United States had participated in only one foreign war. That was the War with Mexico in 1846-47. The war had lasted less than twenty-one months and had involved fewer than 100,000 Americans. This was the experience pool for the Civil War.

The senior officers of the Civil War consisted primarily of officers who had served in the peacetime army, veterans of the Mexican War, graduates of West Point or the Virginia Military Institute, or connected politicians wishing to serve. In this regard, West Point graduated fewer than fifty per year, on average, in the twenty years preceding the war, and VMI even fewer. If a person could combine any two qualifications from the aforementioned list, such as being a West Point graduate with Mexican War experience, or a politician with Mexican War experience, he could count on at least a colonelcy at the outset.

Another source of senior officers in the North was the leaders of the ethnic communities, the votes of which the administration was anxious to secure. The largest ethnic community of 1860 was the German-American community. They were the Hispanics of the time. If an individual was a leader of this community, his prospects of a colonelcy were excellent. If he was a leader with military training and experience in the "Old Country," his prospects were even brighter. For example, Franz Sigel, who came to the United States for the first time in 1852, was a community leader who had attended the military academy at Karlsruhe. He was a major general in the Union army by 1862.

Then there were political generals who had sufficient political clout that they were given their commissions with no military experience at all. It is said that some had to learn which end of the gun the bullet came out.

Major General George B. McClellan, who commanded the
Army of the Potomac, was a thirty-five-year-old graduate of West
Point. Four of his seven senior generals were also young men
under forty who had graduated from West Point in the years 1845-
47, the last years in which they could participate in the Mexican
War. None of them had risen higher than the rank of captain in
the peacetime army and hence, up to 1861, had never commanded
more than a hundred men. With the outbreak of the war in 1861,
they jumped rank up to colonel, or major general in the case of
McClellan, with nothing in between. In contrast to the McClellan
team, fifty-five-year-old Robert E. Lee had risen through each rank
in the peacetime army to colonel, and then to general in the
Confederate army. Furthermore, Gen. Winfield Scott, the general
in chief of the peacetime army, considered Lee the best officer in
the army. Thus, in September 1862, the contest between Lee and
McClellan and his ilk was, in a sense, a contest between an
experienced professional and amateurs who were still learning.

In the North, the tradition that no officer could be senior to
George Washington still prevailed. Inasmuch as George
Washington was a lieutenant general and not a full general,
Union officers bunched up at the rank of major general. Division
commanders, corps commanders, and army commanders were all
major generals. The Confederacy did not adhere to this tradition,
and army commanders, such as Lee, were full generals.

As for the troops, by September 1862, most, but not all, were
in for the duration. At the outset of the war, everyone expected
a short war, and troops were enlisted for as little as ninety days.
There were still some short-term enlistees in the army in
September 1862. There is an old saying that no one wants to be
the last man killed in a war. When an enlistee could count the
days until he was to get out and walk safely and unmaimed back
to his home, he was unlikely to take any risks. Panic in combat is
contagious, and one bad (short-term) regiment could determine the outcome of a battle. In general, short-term regiments
were assigned to what were believed to be the backwash areas of
the war—such as Harpers Ferry.

The West Point Clique

Although both armies contained numerous political generals,
the top posts in both went to West Pointers. In fact, the number

of West Point graduates in top posts went beyond all logic. In the South, this might be explained in part by the fact that the president of the Confederacy, Jefferson Davis, was himself a West Point graduate. However, there was no comparable explanation for the North. If these leaders consisted primarily of professionals who had chosen a military career, attended and graduated from the military academy, remained in the peacetime army and rose in rank to lieutenant colonel or colonel, their preponderance in top leadership posts might be logical. This, however, was usually not the case. Many had served only a short time after graduation, then had resigned as junior officers and pursued civilian careers. Others had graduated only five years or less before the war and sometimes, as in the case of Gen. George Armstrong Custer, less than one year. Most Civil War West Point generals had never risen higher in the peacetime army than captain and had never commanded more than a hundred men. It almost seemed that the magic four years itself was all that was required.

The preponderance of West Point generals in top positions in both armies was even more remarkable when one considers that, at the time, West Point was primarily an engineering school. The top graduates usually entered the topographical engineers, rather than the combat arms of infantry, artillery, or cavalry. The topographical engineers, although in the army, were involved in all government construction, including such things as lighthouses and even the capitol building. Consequently, they often acquired little to no experience in combat or troop command.

To cite an example of the wartime promotion potential of West Pointers, of the class of 1846, twenty-three members served in the Civil War. Of these, twenty rose to the rank of general and two to the rank of colonel; at least one of the colonels probably would have risen to general had he not died prematurely. Of the twenty generals from the class, ten served the Union, and ten the Confederacy.

In the prewar years, the graduating class at West Point usually contained fewer than fifty members. Thus, the generals on both sides who were classmates were likely to be well acquainted. Often, they had forged friendships that endured a lifetime. To cite some examples, Gen. Ulysses S. Grant, ultimately the general in chief of the Union armies, and Gen. James Longstreet, the Confederate general second in command to Lee, were not only classmates, but lifelong friends. Grant had married Longstreet's cousin, and Longstreet was best man at the wedding. After the war, President Grant appointed Longstreet to important posts in his administration. Union general McClellan and Confederate general Jackson were four-year classmates and graduated together in 1846. Friendship between Union and Confederate general classmates often continued during the war. Union general George Armstrong Custer and Confederate general Thomas Lafayette Rosser were known to picnic together during the war. When Confederate general George Pickett married, his Union army friends forwarded him a silver tea service through the lines.

When the Confederate army invaded Maryland in September 1862, its commanding general, both corps commanders, cavalry commander, and seven of its nine division commanders were West Point graduates. The corresponding head of the Union army, General McClellan, his cavalry commander, and five of his six corps commanders were all West Point graduates. Most of these generals on both sides knew each other from West Point days.

All eight Confederates who acquired the rank of full general were West Point graduates, as were all Union generals who commanded the Army of the Potomac or were general in chief, other than the first, and probably the best, Gen. Winfield Scott.

Were these West Point graduates the most talented people available for top command? Possibly not. As the war turned against the South, others, who had attended no military academy, began rising to the top, based solely on their accomplishments. These included Generals Nathan Bedford Forrest, Richard Taylor, John B. Gordon, Wade Hampton, and Patrick Cleburne. Forrest was a slave trader, and Taylor and Hampton were plantation owners—the natural leaders of the Old South. Gordon was a lawyer, and Cleburne was an Irish émigré and lawyer.

Organization

The basic organizational building block of the military during the Civil War was the regiment. A regiment, at the time of formation, consisted of ten companies. Each company contained a hundred men and was headed by a captain. The regimental commander was a colonel, and his deputy a lieutenant colonel. Regiments were normally recruited in a single area, and many of its members were likely to know one another. The colonel might be a congressman from the area or some other political notable.

The regiments were usually recruited by state and bore their state's name throughout their existence. For example, the first infantry regiment recruited in Indiana would be forever known as the First Indiana Infantry, the second as the Second Indiana Infantry, and so on. The colonel and lieutenant colonel were usually appointed by the governor. The other officers were often elected. When a regiment was formed, the members often signed up for a given obligated period of service; when that time expired, they expected to go home, regardless of the situation then prevailing.

In the North, there was a tendency not to replenish losses a regiment might incur due to illness or casualties, but rather to create more new regiments. This practice provided for greater political patronage.

Two or more regiments formed a brigade, which was commanded by a brigadier general. Two or more brigades formed a division, which was commanded by a major general. Two or more divisions formed a corps, which was commanded by a major general in the North or a lieutenant general (after 1862) in the South. Two or more corps formed an army, which was commanded by a major general in the North or a full general in the South. A battalion consisted of a number of companies less than a regiment and, in most cases, was not a fixed administrative organization but one created temporarily for a special situation. A battalion was commanded by a major.

The basic unit of artillery was the battery. A battery consisted of four or six cannons of the same caliber. In the early phases of the war, batteries were distributed to the brigades. However, as the war progressed, there was a tendency to concentrate the artillery directly under the corps commanders, with a reserve directly under the command of the army commander. Next to the cavalry, the artillery was the biggest user of horses. It took six horses or mules to move each cannon.

Communications

If intelligence was awful in September 1862, communications were merely very bad. Telegraph, which was invented in 1844, was already widespread. Telegraphic communications required a wire from the sender to the receiver. An enemy reaching the wire at any place along the line could monitor the signal, intrude, and send his own signal, or simply cut the wire and terminate any possibility of communications. Telegraphy used Morse Code—that is, dots and dashes. The skill of a telegrapher was such that it could not be acquired in a few days. It was like playing the piano—it took time to get good. Consequently, most of the operators during the Civil War were civilians. The speed of transmission on any line was determined by the poorest operator. If one could send and receive at thirty-six words per minute, and the other at twenty words per minute, the top speed was limited to twenty words per minute.

Each Union corps had a special telegraphic wagon with operators that it hoped to connect to the nearest line.

Delays of several hours in the receipt of telegraphic messages were common. The transmission of the message itself took time. A message of three hundred words might require fifteen minutes. Then there was the time of delivery. The intended recipient of the message was likely to be an important person who was usually not at the telegraphic terminal. Telegraphic communications were not suitable for conferencing or discussions, so messages had to be carefully phrased to avoid misunderstandings and confusion.

In addition to telegraphic communications, both sides used visual signaling. This entailed the use of a single large signal flag (four feet square) by day, or a torch by night. At night, rockets were used to gain the attention of the other station. In modern signal flag systems, two flags are used, and a single posture of the two flags denotes a letter. In the Civil War system, only one flag was used, and the signaler had to move the flag or torch four times to denote a single letter. The speed of visual signaling (as now) depended upon the skill of the sender and receiver, but because of the system then in use, it was very slow at best. With a spy glass, visual signaling could be used up to a distance of about fifteen miles.

Visual signal stations demanded height to obtain distance. Stations might be set up on a mountain, in a church steeple, or on a wooden platform constructed for the purpose. Because of the height and field of view, the same station was used as an observation post, and the signaler could originate his own messages depending on what he could see.

Because of the exposed position of the signaler, the station could not be close to the front. It was not considered a good idea to be standing atop a platform waving a big flag when an enemy rifleman was within a couple hundred feet, contemplating who he was going to shoot next.

Logistics and Transportation

To understand the events of September 1862, it is necessary to have some understanding of logistics and transportation as it existed at that time: an army, to exist and to move, required supplies. This included food and medical supplies for the troops, ammunition, and last, but certainly not least, feed and fodder for the horses and mules. The experiences of World War I showed that as late as 1915, supplying the horses and mules with feed and fodder required 50 percent more tonnage than supplying the troops with food. In fact, the amount of horse feed and fodder that the United Kingdom shipped to its expeditionary force in 1914 and 1915 exceeded the tonnage of the ammunition shipped.

There were three ways to transport supplies in 1862. These were by horse (or mule) and wagon, by railroad, or by water. Water was by far the most efficient, and horse and wagon by far the least efficient. A supply wagon was pulled by up to six horses (or mules). As of 1914, the average army ration for a man weighed 1.7 kilograms, and that for a horse, 10 kilograms. A horse, then, required almost six times the ration of a man. Thus, if six horses pulled one wagon, they consumed the equivalent rations of thirty-six men.

If a two-day trip was required for a wagon to travel from the supply depot to the front, instead of a one-day trip, twice as many horses and wagons would be required, since now, for every wagon reaching the unloading point, a second one would just be reaching the halfway point. Furthermore, the farther the wagons were required to travel, the greater the percentage of their cargo would be consumed by the horses pulling it. For a one-day trip to the front, six horses would consume thirty-six equivalent man rations on the trip out, and an additional thirty-six on the way back. For a two-day trip, they would consume seventy-two equivalent man rations out, and seventy-two back. As the supply line lengthened, ever more horses and wagons would be required, and the horses would consume an ever-greater proportion of what each wagon could carry. Thus, it was imperative that an army keep the horse and wagon part of its supply line as short as possible, and that it rely on rail or water to the maximum degree possible.

There was yet another consideration. Any wagon train or railroad, particularly if passing through or near enemy territory, was subject to surprise attack by enemy cavalry. Thus, it had to be protected, which required still more feed and fodder. Inasmuch as an attack could take place at any point and at any time, protection had to be provided at all points and at all times. Considering this situation, all other factors being equal, an army moving away from its supply base receded in strength, and one moving toward its base grew in strength.

In September 1862, the very poverty of the Southern army provided it an advantage of sorts. Each Southern soldier expected less, received less, and could make do with less. In addition, Southern armies of the time displayed a greater capability to feed themselves off the land they passed through.

There was one area where the Union possessed an absolute superiority over the Confederates, and that was in the matter of navies and waterway control. In general, the Union exercised near complete control over the high seas, as well as any contested inland waterways. The Union was thus able to use this safe and cheap means of transport to a degree that the Confederacy could not. General McClellan was one of the first to recognize this advantage and hence initiated his Peninsula campaign to seize Richmond, wherein his supply line was largely via water, rather than over land.

Lee's invasion of the North in September 1862 was governed by two logistics and transportation considerations. First, Lee had to secure his own supply line. This he proposed to do by transferring it from the direct route to Richmond to the Shenandoah Valley, which was not only safer, but made better use of available railroads. Second, Lee's major objective of the invasion was not to capture Washington, as commonly believed, but to severely damage the enemy's transport system. One of the most vulnerable parts of a rail line was where it crossed a major river. In his invasion, Lee hoped to destroy the bridge carrying the Pennsylvania Railroad over the Susquehanna River and the bridge carrying the Baltimore and Ohio Railroad over the Potomac River. In addition, he hoped to destroy the aqueduct carrying the Chesapeake and Ohio Canal over the

Monocacy River. If successful, he would cut three of the major transportation arteries linking the East with the West—which would severely affect Union operations in both theaters.

Nomenclature

There are two names for every battle in the Civil War. The Confederates named a battle after the nearest town, while the Union named it after the nearest stream. Thus, there are the battles of Manassas and Bull Run, Sharpsburg and Antietam. Likewise, the Union named its armies after rivers, and the Confederates after states. Thus, there are the Union Army of the Potomac and the Confederate Army of Northern Virginia.

Union corps, divisions, and brigades were usually referred to by their numerical designations. However, the Confederate corps, divisions, and brigades were almost always referred to by the name of their first commanders. Thus, there was Kershaw's brigade in McLaws's division in Longstreet's corps. The original names usually prevailed, even though the unit might be under a new commander.

A Gentleman's War

Winston Churchill said that the U.S. Civil War was the last gentleman's war. This was still true in September 1862, although things did deteriorate after that time. In September 1862, civilians were usually not harmed, property was usually respected, women were not raped, and, even in enemy country, soldiers watched their language in the presence of women, and officers tipped their hats to them. Men were still considered as good as their word.

When one side captured troops of the enemy, they were usually released or "paroled" after surrendering their rifles, if they promised not to fight again until they were formally exchanged by their governments for an equal number of prisoners from the other side. Captured officers were usually not even asked to surrender their sidearms. However, if an officer who had been paroled returned to combat without an exchange, he was considered no gentleman and might be subject to execution if recaptured.

After a surrender, the winners and losers often chatted amicably, exchanged newspapers, and bartered coffee for tobacco or anything else, until the losers marched off under their own officers to their own territory.

In the summer of 1862, the two sides formalized the granting of paroles with the conclusion of the so-called Dix-Hill Cartel. It held that all prisoners held by the North or South would be paroled within ten days of capture and sent to their own lines to await a formal paper exchange, when they would be freed to rejoin the fighting.

With the parole system, it seems that the losers often fared better than the winners. While the winners marched off to their next battle where they could be killed or maimed, the losers marched off to a safe haven in their own territory.

In the North, it was decided that it was not a good thing to be too easy on those of its own men who had surrendered and were awaiting exchange. There had to be some onus attached to the fact of surrender. Consequently, it set up special camps to hold parolees awaiting exchange. The conditions in these camps were less than ideal, and there were restrictions, such as no alcohol.

Paroled prisoners generally took their status seriously. On September 12, 1862, Union colonel Augustus Moor was captured by the Confederates in a cavalry clash in Frederick, Maryland. Two days later, as the Union troops advanced toward the Confederate position on South Mountain, they encountered Colonel Moor walking down the road toward them from the Confederate position. They asked him if the mountain pass was strongly fortified. Moor replied that he could not tell them, inasmuch as he had been paroled, but then as an afterthought added, "My God! Be careful!"[2]

In September 1862, Union and Confederate army commanders were still commonly exchanging courteous messages with each other relating to humanitarian and other matters. At the battle of Chantilly in August 1862, Union general Philip Kearny was killed, and his body fell into the hands of the Confederates. General Lee of the Confederate army sent the following message to General McClellan of the Union army:

> Headquarters Army of Northern Virginia
> Oct. 4, 1862

Mjr. Gen. George B. McClellan,
Commanding Army of the Potomac

General: I have the honor to inclose a letter to Mrs. Philip Kearny, and at the same time commit to your care the sword, horse, and saddle of Major-General Kearny, which fell into our hands at the time of his death. Mrs. Kearny expressed a great desire to obtain the sword and horse of her husband, and I beg leave to hope that it may be convenient to you to forward them to her.

The horse has accompanied the march of the army since its capture, and may have suffered from the journey. The bridle was either lost at the time of the capture or has not been recovered.

I am, most respectfully, your obedient servant,

R.E. Lee
General, Commanding[3]

McClellan replied as follows:

Headquarters Army of the Potomac
October 5, 1862

General R.E. Lee
Commanding Army of Northern Virginia:

General: I have the honor to acknowledge the receipt of your letter of the 4th instant, inclosing a letter to Mrs. Philip Kearny, and, at the same time, committing to my care the sword, horse and saddle of Major-General Kearny, to the end that, in accordance with the expressed wish of Mrs. Kearny, they may be placed in her keeping. The articles have been received, and, with the letter, will be forwarded to Mrs. Kearny by the earliest opportunity. I beg you to accept my thanks for your courteous and humane attention to the request of the widow of this lamented officer. I shall be happy to reciprocate the courtesy when circumstances place it in my power to do so.

Very respectfully, your obedient servant,

Gen. B. McClellan
Major-General, Commanding[4]

When the Union surrendered Harpers Ferry, Confederate general A. P. Hill, who accepted the surrender and paroled the garrison, agreed to lend the surrendered Union officers twenty-seven wagons and the corresponding teams of mules to cart off their personal possessions, with the understanding that the wagons and teams would be returned at the earliest opportunity.

Apparently, this was not done quickly enough, and General Lee sent General McClellan the following message:

> Headquarters Army of Northern Virginia
> October 2, 1862

Maj. General George B. McClellan
Commanding U.S. Forces on the Potomac

General: Maj. Gen. A. P. Hill of the C.S. Army, who had charge of the arrangements connected with the paroling of the prisoners at Harpers Ferry on the 15th ultimo, permitted General White to have the use of 27 wagons and teams, to carry the private baggage of the officers to some point convenient for transportation.

It was agreed between these two officers that these wagons and teams should be returned within our lines at Winchester in a few days, or, if that place should be in the hands of United States forces, then to the nearest Confederate post. I think proper to make known to you the above agreement, in order that some arrangement may be made for the return of the wagons and teams.

I am, most respectfully, your obedient servant,

R.E. Lee
General, Commanding[5]

McClellan answered Lee's message as follows:

> Headquarters Army of the Potomac
> October 6, 1862

General R.E. Lee
Commanding Army of Northern Virginia

General: I have the honor to acknowledge the receipt of your letter 2nd instant, in regard to the return of 27 wagons and teams, furnished by Maj. Gen. A. P. Hill for the use of certain paroled officers of the United States Army. These wagons and their teams are now on their return from Washington, and are expected here in two days. Upon their arrival, I will send them immediately to such place as you in the mean time be pleased to designate.

I am, General, very respectfully your obedient servant,

Gen. B. McClellan
Maj. Gen., Commanding[6]

And so it went.

Major General George B. McClellan USV
The "Young Napoleon"

Chapter 2

The Situation on Tuesday, September 9, 1862

Old General Winfield Scott retired as general in chief of the U.S. Army on November 1, 1861. In accordance with President Abraham Lincoln's decree of November 1, thirty-five-year-old George Brinton McClellan became general in chief of the army on November 5, 1861. McClellan was born for success. He was handsome, charismatic, and smart, and he generated an intense loyalty in his subordinates. However, he was also egotistical, intolerant of criticism, and a difficult subordinate.

McClellan graduated from West Point in 1846, second in his class. His classmates included Thomas (later "Stonewall") Jackson, A. P. Hill, and other generals-to-be. He distinguished himself in the Mexican War, which further enhanced his reputation as a "comer." After the war, he received the enviable assignment of an observer to the Crimean War. McClellan resigned from the army as a captain in 1857 and achieved immediate success as a civilian. He first became a vice president of the Illinois Central Railroad and then president of the Ohio and Mississippi Railroad. Among his other accomplishments was the invention of the McClellan saddle, which became a mainstay in the cavalry right up to the time the horse cavalry was finally abolished.

McClellan reentered the army in 1861 as a major general. After some minor but highly touted (largely by himself) successes in West Virginia, he was called to Washington to set matters right after the Bull Run fiasco. By this time, McClellan was known as the "young Napoleon." Young he was, but Napoleon he wasn't.

He immediately set about with his usual vigor and undoubted organizational skills in organizing and polishing the Army of the Potomac and, in fact, can justly be called its father. Once he had it, however, he appeared extremely reluctant to use it where it could be harmed. After much prodding by Lincoln, he finally came up with a plan. The plan was for a combined sea-land campaign to attack Richmond from the east and south via the York

29

Map 2
McClellan's Plan

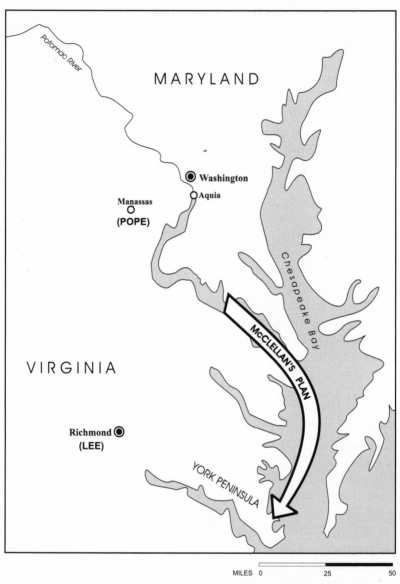

MILES 0   25   50

Peninsula (see map 2). In retrospect, it was not a bad idea. In fact, it was ultimately a variant of this plan that worked for Grant. The plan just might have worked had it not been for the interference of Abraham Lincoln and, later, Henry Halleck.

Why was the plan a good one? Because it capitalized on the Union's greatest advantage over the Confederacy—sea control. When an army advances overland through enemy territory, as the Union would have to do to reach Richmond overland, the advancing army has an ever-lengthening vulnerable supply line, and thus must leave behind an ever-growing part of its strength for its protection. An advancing army must continually sacrifice teeth for tail, and theoretically, could end up all tail and no teeth. Under McClellan's plan, all of his supply line would be by sea, enabling him to bring all of his teeth before Richmond.

Lincoln and Secretary of War Edwin Stanton, however, could only see the negative. They could only see that McClellan's plan would leave the Confederate army between McClellan and Washington, and in their eyes, make Washington vulnerable. McClellan correctly understood that if the Confederate army was pinned down defending Richmond, it could not be advancing on Washington. If the Confederates did send a force against Washington, McClellan could send back forces to confront it by sea more quickly than the Confederates could get there by land. In fact, this is precisely what happened in 1864, later in the war.

The Union troops began to embark on March 13, 1862, for what was subsequently known as the Peninsula campaign. The meddling started before the last soldier embarked. Lincoln, ever fearful for the safety of Washington, directed that Gen. Irvin McDowell's corps remain behind. This was one-sixth of McClellan's army.

On March 11, 1862, just before the troops embarked, Lincoln relieved McClellan as commander in chief of the army. Lincoln explained that this was not a rebuff; rather, it was an act to permit McClellan to devote his full energies to his position as commanding general, Army of the Potomac, during the pending campaign.

On July 11, 1862, Lincoln appointed Henry Wager Halleck as general in chief of the U.S. Army. However, it was understood that this was now an administrative position in Washington and not a field command. Halleck was to serve as a buffer between Lincoln and Secretary of War Stanton, and all the armies.

Halleck was born in 1816, attended West Point, and graduated third in the class of 1839. He published a book entitled *The Elements of Military Art and Science* and several other obscure works that garnered him the nickname "Old Brains." Actually, he wasn't very old, and another of his nicknames was "Old Wooden Head."

Halleck had a good record in the Mexican War and ultimately resigned in 1854 with the rank of captain. He then found his true calling in the law and became senior partner in one of the largest law firms in California. At the outbreak of the war he received a commission as major general. In November 1861, he succeeded John C. Fremont in command of the Western department. His subordinates now included Ulysses S. Grant.

Among Halleck's other qualities, he was not above taking cheap shots at subordinates who acquired too much success or fame. On March 23, 1862, while Grant was basking in fame for the victories at Forts Henry and Donelson justly attributed to him, he received the following message from Halleck:

> You will place Maj. Gen. C.F. Smith in command of expedition and remain yourself at Fort Henry. Why do you not obey my orders to report strength and positions of your command?[1]

Grant didn't even know what orders Halleck was talking about, but now faced arrest and disgrace. However, when Halleck perceived that Lincoln liked Grant, he made an about-face, reinstated Grant, and convinced Grant, using all his lawyerly skills, that Grant's problem originated elsewhere, and that he, Henry Halleck, was the one who saved him.

Later, in September 1862, McClellan, who was now Halleck's subordinate and was receiving wide acclaim for his victories at South Mountain and Antietam, was accused by Halleck of being responsible for the loss of Harpers Ferry. In fact, it was none other than Henry Halleck himself who was responsible for the loss, having twice peremptorily refused McClellan's request to evacuate the garrison while there was still time. But more about that subject later.

On April 11, 1862, after the battle of Shiloh, Halleck took field command of the armies of the West in the Corinth campaign and proceeded to demonstrate his total lack of aptitude for field command.

Halleck's modus operandi was to make tiny advances followed by extensive digging in, and then repeating the process. If the motto of Woody Hayes, football coach of Ohio State, was "three yards and a cloud of dust," Halleck's was "two yards and a cloud of dust," with no one apparently explaining to him that it was necessary to make ten yards in four tries to get a first down. If Halleck had been left to his own devices, the war could still be going on. However, as so often is the case, having demonstrated his lack of capability in small matters, he was called to Washington to decide on large matters.

It is not known what qualities Lincoln saw in Halleck, but his performance was apparently satisfactory, and he survived in Washington until the end of the war, even though his position changed from general in chief to chief of staff to Grant on March 9, 1864.

The arrangement between Halleck and McClellan was somewhat unusual. Halleck had served under McClellan when McClellan was general in chief. In fact, even after Halleck's appointment, McClellan was above him on the seniority list. Only *ex officio* was Halleck McClellan's boss. These factors did not, however, deter Halleck in the least from treating McClellan as if he, Henry Halleck, was superintendent of schools, and George McClellan was a junior member of the Head Start class.

On June 17, 1862, while McClellan was battling on the peninsula, President Lincoln and Secretary of War Stanton, always unduly fearful for the safety of Washington, created a new army to operate between Richmond and Washington. This was called the Army of Virginia. It brought together the two small armies that had been operating in the Shenandoah Valley and McDowell's corps that Lincoln had withheld from McClellan. Major General John Pope from the West was selected for command.

General Pope, like McClellan, was a blowhard—but without McClellan's charisma. Like McClellan, he had trumpeted his own modest successes in another theater to solicit a higher command in the East. In one instance, Pope, to convey the impression of dynamic action, signed an order "Headquarters in the Saddle." This caused one wag to comment that Pope's headquarters were where his hindquarters ought to be. However, Pope was aggressive, and Lincoln expected great things from him. Pope's army consisted of the corps of Irvin McDowell, Nathaniel Banks, and Franz Sigel.

By July 7, 1862, it appeared that things were not going well on the peninsula, and Lincoln set sail to confer with McClellan and assess the situation firsthand. This visit by Lincoln was followed by a visit from Halleck. It was ultimately decided by the powers-to-be

that the Peninsula campaign was a failure, that the Army of the
Potomac should be withdrawn, and that its troops should be
turned over to Pope. Pope, it was expected, would prosecute the
war more vigorously, and, in any event, his army would be
between the Confederate army and Washington.

On August 3, 1862, McClellan received a message from
Halleck peremptorily ordering him to withdraw his troops from
the peninsula to Aquia Landing (see map 2) just south of
Washington, from whence they would march to reinforce Pope.
McClellan dutifully began the withdrawal. It was a monumental
sea-land operation that produced much confusion. For instance,
the artillery might be on one ship, and the horses to move it on
another. It was ultimately agreed that Sumner's Second Corps,
Heintzelman's Third Corps, Porter's Fifth Corps, and Franklin's
Sixth Corps would be removed, and Keyes's Fourth Corps would
remain for the time being.

As each corps arrived in the Washington area, it set out to join
Pope. Lee, who was now in command of the Confederates, was
no fool. When he detected the withdrawals, he realized that his
presence was no longer required to protect Richmond, and that
if he was going to "suppress Pope," as he phrased it, he had better do so before Pope was reinforced with all of McClellan's
troops. He did it just in time.

On August 29 and 30, after Pope had been reinforced by
Heintzelman's, Porter's, and Burnside's corps, but before he
had been reinforced by Franklin's and Sumner's corps, Lee
defeated Pope decisively in the battle of Second Bull Run. Lee's
third in command, General Jackson, never willing to let a suck-
er off the hook, intercepted the fleeing Federals just outside
Washington at a place called Chantilly, and defeated them again.

Now, to Lincoln and Stanton's horror, the war had moved
from the distant peninsula to less than twenty miles from the
White House—and there was no organized Federal army left
between the Confederates and Washington.

Wild rumors hit Washington as retreating, disorganized troops
poured in. Lincoln and Stanton feared that the Confederates were
about to seize the city. In the streets, innumerable herds of stragglers mingled with an endless stream of wagons and ambulances.
Disorder reigned unchecked, and confusion was everywhere. The
government ordered the arms and ammunition at the arsenal and
the money in the treasury to be shipped to New York. The banks

followed the example. A gunboat with steam up lay in the Potomac as near as it could get to the White House as if to announce to the inhabitants the impending flight of the president.

McClellan was now a general without an army, having shipped off all his troops to Pope. On September 1, McClellan met Halleck in his office. Halleck verbally ordered him to take charge of Washington and its defenses, but expressly prohibited him from exercising any control of the troops under Pope. McClellan said that he had heard that things were going badly with Pope and suggested that Halleck go personally to the front and see for himself. Halleck declined but sent Colonel John C. Kelton of his staff. When Colonel Kelton returned, he convinced Halleck, Lincoln, and Stanton that no matter how bad they thought things were, they were actually worse.

On the morning of September 2, 1862, Lincoln and Halleck came hat-in-hand to McClellan's house on H Street while McClellan was at breakfast. The president informed McClellan that Kelton had represented the condition of affairs worse than supposed, that there were thirty thousand stragglers on the road, that the army was entirely defeated and pulling back on Washington in confusion, that he (Lincoln) regarded Washington as lost, and asked McClellan if he would accept command of all of the forces. Note that this offer did not exclude the forces of Pope as had Halleck's offer of the previous day. McClellan accepted with alacrity and "guaranteed" the president that *he*, George B. McClellan, would save Washington.

Lincoln's offer was followed up by a written order from Halleck that read as follows:

> Major General McClellan will have command of the fortifications of Washington and of all of the troops for the defense of the capital.

By order of
Maj General Halleck
General-in-Chief [2]

Note that this written order restricted McClellan's task to the defense of the capital and was less eclectic than Lincoln's verbal offer on the morning of the second.

This written order was the only one that McClellan was to

Major General Henry Halleck USV
General in Chief
"Old Brains"

receive and was to cause much uncertainty and anxiety on his part in the future. In any event, McClellan set out with his usual energy to straighten things out, and Halleck did what he could to exacerbate the confusion.

There were now eight army corps crowded into the environs of Washington. These included the three from Pope's Army of Virginia, the four withdrawn from McClellan's Army of the Potomac while on the peninsula, and Burnside's corps that had been a part of neither. In addition, there were almost thirty thousand other troops, including garrison and miscellaneous units.

McClellan's first task was to sort out from the masses a mobile field army that would be the successor to the Army of the Potomac. When he announced to Halleck that he had ordered three corps across the Potomac as a nucleus of a field army and that he was going to take command himself, Halleck countered that McClellan's orders included only the defenses of Washington and did not extend to any column that moved out beyond the line of Washington's works. He repeated the same on more than one occasion as McClellan took command of the field army and moved ever farther away from Washington.

Thus, McClellan felt continual anxiety as to the legality of his position. He believed that he was treading in uncertain legal territory, that if anything went wrong the authorities (e.g., Halleck) would turn on him, and he could end up in prison or worse. However, as McClellan gradually moved off with the field army, Lincoln began sending personal messages to him asking him how things were going. This action must have presented *prima facie* evidence to Halleck's lawyerly mind that Lincoln had accepted McClellan's position as head of the field army, and he did not further contest McClellan's position.

During the period that McClellan was sorting out the mobile army from the forces to be left behind to defend Washington, organizational confusion reigned. Apparently, no one thought to tell Pope that he no longer had an army. On September 5, Pope sent the following message to Halleck:

> I have just received an order from General McClellan to have my command in readiness to march with three days rations and further details of the march. What is my command and where is it? McClellan has scattered it about in all directions, and has not informed me of the position of a single regiment. Am I to take the field under McClellan's orders?[3]

So Pope wanted to know what his command was and where it was. Halleck placated him by ordering him off to Minnesota to fight Indians. However, before Pope left, he filed formal charges against two of McClellan's corps commanders, Fitz John Porter and William B. Franklin, for disobedience of orders during the Second Bull Run campaign. These were serious charges, and each officer could have faced dismissal from the army or worse. Halleck informed McClellan that both officers would be relieved from their commands until the charges were resolved. Porter and Franklin were two of McClellan's favorites, and McClellan requested that this action be deferred until the resolution of the present crisis. The request was granted, but the charges hanging over their heads could not help but affect the morale and performance of the two.

By September 3, the Confederate army had disappeared from before Washington, and between the fourth and seventh, there were reports that it was crossing the Potomac into Maryland in the vicinity of White's Ford, almost thirty miles northwest of Washington. This movement put the Confederates squarely between McClellan's forces in Washington and the large Union garrison at Harpers Ferry, some fifty miles upriver from Washington (see map 3). Sometime after McClellan was given command of the Washington forces on the second, but before he set out for Rockville on the seventh to put the new mobile army in motion, the matter of Harpers Ferry came up. He decided that the garrison at Harpers Ferry was vulnerable, and he must do something about it. Let us see what transpired in McClellan's own words:

> Secretary Seward came to my quarters one evening and asked my opinion of the condition of affairs at Harpers Ferry, remarking that he was not at ease on the subject. Harpers Ferry was not at that time in any sense under my control, but I told Mr. Seward that I regarded the arrangements there as exceedingly dangerous; that in my opinion the proper course was to abandon the position and unite the garrison (about ten thousand men) to the main army of operations, for the reason that its presence at Harpers Ferry would not hinder the enemy from crossing the Potomac; that if we were unsuccessful in the approaching battle, Harpers Ferry would be of no use to us and its garrison necessarily would be lost; that if we were successful we would immediately recover the post without any difficulty, while the addition of ten thousand men to the active army would be an important factor in securing success. I added that if it were determined to hold the position the existing arrangements

Map 3
The Confederate Invasion

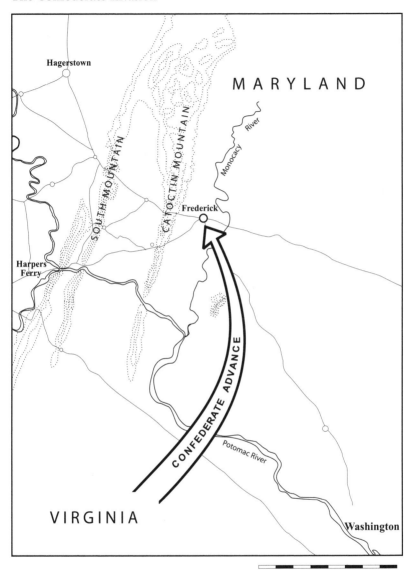

Hagerstown

MARYLAND

Monocacy River

SOUTH MOUNTAIN

CATOCTIN MOUNTAIN

Frederick

Harpers
Ferry

CONFEDERATE ADVANCE

Potomac River

VIRGINIA

Washington

MILES 0 2 4 6 8 10 12 14 16

were all wrong, as it would be easy for the enemy to surround and capture the garrison, and that the garrison ought at least to be withdrawn to the Maryland Heights where they could resist attack until relieved.

The Secretary was much impressed by what I said, and asked me to accompany him to General Halleck and repeat my statement to him. I acquiesced, and we went together to General Halleck's quarters, where we found that he had retired for the night. But he received us in his bedroom, when, after a preliminary explanation by the Secretary as to the interview being at his request, I said to Halleck precisely what I had stated to Mr. Seward.

Halleck received my statement with ill-concealed contempt— said that everything was all right as it was; that my views were entirely erroneous, etc. and soon bowed us out, leaving matters at Harpers Ferry precisely as they were.[4]

On September 7, McClellan departed for Rockville (twelve miles northwest of the White House) to take command of the new field army and to put it in motion to assume a position between the invading Confederates and Baltimore and Washington. In describing the new mobile army, it is necessary to first point out that the Army of Virginia had been disbanded and its three corps incorporated into the new Army of the Potomac. The Third Corps of the Army of Virginia became the First Corps of the Army of the Potomac, the First the Eleventh Corps, and the Second the Twelfth Corps. The new mobile army now temporarily consisted of five of the eight corps available in the Washington area with the remaining three being left behind to assist the garrison. The five corps taken consisted of the First (Hooker's), Second (Sumner's), Sixth (Franklin's), Ninth (Reno's), and Twelfth (Mansfield's).

McClellan divided his mobile force into three wings. The northern wing, consisting of the First and Ninth Corps, he placed under his good friend Ambrose Burnside. Burnside had relinquished his position as Ninth Corps commander to Gen. Jesse L. Reno for the purpose of assuming the position of wing commander. The center wing consisted of the Second and Twelfth Corps and was under the command of Gen. Edmund Voss Sumner. The southern wing consisted of the Sixth Corps and one division of the Fourth Corps that had been withdrawn from the peninsula and was under the command of General Franklin.

The army that McClellan moved out with was vastly different from the one he had so recently commanded on the peninsula. Three of the five corps had not been on the peninsula, and three of his six principal subordinates had not been on the peninsula. As the army moved out, no one suspected that within ten days, two of the five corps commanders would be dead and one seriously wounded.

McClellan left three corps behind to assist the garrison in the defense of Washington. These were the Third, Fifth, and Eleventh headed by Heintzelman, Porter, and Sigel. The total troops left behind were the following:

Army Corps

General Heintzelman	16,000
General Porter	21,000
General Sigel	9,800
	46,800

In Garrison

General Abercrombie	1,335
Lieutenant Colonel Senges	266
Colonel Tyler	1,056
Lieutenant Colonel Haskin	6,458
General Woodbury	4,000
	13,115

Metropolitan Guard

General Wadsworth	4,000
General Slough	2,500
	6,500

Provisional Brigades

General Casey	4,500
TOTAL	70,915

Including 120 cannon

Confusion was rampant in Washington as McClellan moved out. Dispatches flew among the moguls moving a brigade here and a division or corps there. Many of these dispatches were signed by one Richard B. Irwin. Now the reader may justly ask, "Who is Richard B. Irwin?" He was, in fact, a twenty-two-year-old captain on McClellan's staff.

As McClellan was departing for Rockville on the seventh to take command of the mobile army, at the last minute he directed Captain Irwin to stay behind at McClellan's Washington headquarters to remain in charge of the adjutant general's department, to issue orders in his name, and "to prevent the tail of the army from being cut off."[5] When McClellan reached Rockville, he sent a message to Major General Banks, who was sick in bed in Washington, directing him to take charge of the defenses of Washington in his absence. Banks accepted on the eighth, but inasmuch as he had no staff at present and no knowledge of the situation, asked McClellan permission to take on Irwin as his assistant adjutant general. McClellan agreed. Thus, Irwin continued as the de facto generalissimo, first issuing orders under McClellan's authority, and then under Banks's authority.

As McClellan began moving to the west on September 7, all he knew for certain was that a large number of Confederates had crossed the Potomac into Maryland and were between him and Harpers Ferry. The numbers were wildly exaggerated. One hundred and ten thousand were reported near Frederick, Maryland. In addition, Gen. Braxton Bragg of the Western armies was reported to be moving up the Shenandoah Valley with forty thousand more. The destination of the Confederate armies was variously reported as Washington, Baltimore, Philadelphia, Hagerstown, and Harrisburg.

McClellan placed Burnside's two corps on his right flank centered on the Baltimore Pike, the center two corps under Sumner centered on the Washington Pike, and the corps of Franklin centered on the River Road and anchored on the Potomac (see map 4). Thus, the five corps presented a north-south front from the Potomac to the B & O Railroad north of the Baltimore Pike and covered both Baltimore and Washington.

McClellan explained that he was advancing on five roads to make a broad, continuous front. What he failed to mention was that four of the five roads converged at a single point— Frederick, Maryland. McClellan was thus advancing at the rate of about six miles a day to an ultimate concentration at Frederick, about fifty miles from Washington and about fifty miles from Baltimore. Not bad, because this was where the Confederate army was actually concentrated. The only forces contesting McClellan's advance consisted of three brigades of Stuart's cavalry—Gen. Fitz Lee's to the north, Gen. Wade Hampton's in the center, and Col. Thomas Munford's to the south. The actual strength of the Confederate army was about

Map 4
McClellan's Advance

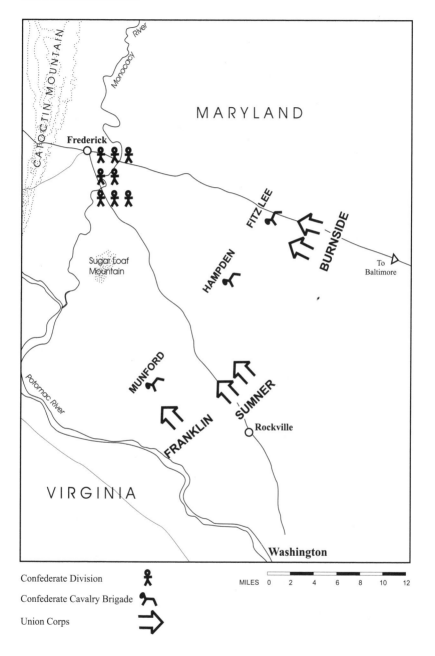

MARYLAND

CATOCTIN MOUNTAIN

Monocacy River

Frederick

FITZ LEE

BURNSIDE

To Baltimore

Sugar Loaf Mountain

HAMPDEN

MUNFORD

Potomac River

FRANKLIN

SUMNER

Rockville

VIRGINIA

Washington

Confederate Division

Confederate Cavalry Brigade

Union Corps

MILES 0 2 4 6 8 10 12

forty thousand. The actual strength of McClellan's mobile army was about ninety thousand.

The belt of land through which McClellan was advancing between Baltimore and Washington and the mountains beyond Frederick is flat to low-rolling hills with one exception. That exception is Sugar Loaf Mountain, a high, isolated mountain eleven miles southeast of Frederick (see map 4). It controls no vital road and in itself was of no strategic significance. However, its crest provided an outstanding observation and visual communications point. From the peak, it was possible to observe the entire field of operations up to the mountain range. It was the next best thing to aerial reconnaissance. Unfortunately, by the time the Union seized it and set up an observation post on the top of it, the activity was receding beyond the mountains to the west of Frederick. The situation that existed at the close of September 9 is as indicated in map 4.

During the period of McClellan's slow advance, Halleck was busier than a chaplain on Good Friday. He responded, mostly constructively, to McClellan's requests; he arranged the numerous changes of command; he fulfilled his duties to the other theaters of war; and, most important of all, he mollified the panic-stricken politicians of Pennsylvania. In brief, he was short-circuiting annoyances for Lincoln and Stanton, and that was what they were paying him to do.

What were Lee's intentions when he invaded Maryland? He was not trying to capture Washington. He had multiple objectives. First, he wanted to move the theater of operations out of war-ravaged Virginia. Second, since Maryland was a border state with strong Southern sympathies, Lee hoped both to induce it to join the Confederacy and to recruit new troops from it. Third, he hoped to draw the Union mobile army away from the defenses of Washington, defeat it on Northern territory, and thus encourage the European powers to recognize and aid the Confederacy. And last, he hoped to cut the vital rail lines and canal linking the East with the West.

Unfortunately for Lee, the Confederate army was very poorly equipped and provisioned and not suited for offensive operations. Much of Lee's army was barefoot, literally dressed in rags, and poorly fed. The farther he marched, the more the weak were unable to keep up and fell by the wayside. As he moved into Maryland, his army was melting away. By the time he made his headquarters in Frederick, he had lost more than ten thousand stragglers, and his army numbered barely more than forty thousand.

McClellan, however, could only see his own problems and continued to believe that Lee's army vastly outnumbered his.

Lee did have assets, however. The weak had been culled from his ranks, and now he had only the strong. Man for man, as events later proved, his army was more than a match for the Union army. Lee had another great advantage, and that was leadership. While McClellan surrounded himself with cronies of limited to no competence in generalship, Lee was supported by individuals of the highest military competence. He accepted the opinionated and difficult Longstreet and the taciturn, shabby, and eccentric Jackson as they were, and formed a harmonious, working relationship. Both Longstreet and Jackson were masterful tacticians and inspired leaders—far superior to anyone in McClellan's army.

Now that Lee was at least momentarily stationary at Frederick, he engaged in voluminous correspondence with Richmond. Among the subjects discussed was the problem of straggling, which was ruining his army. Lee considered that additional legal means were required to more promptly and more severely punish those guilty. Lee also suggested that the time was now propitious to offer the North peace terms, with the sole condition being that the North recognize the independence of the Southern states. With the Southern army implanted on Northern territory, this would look more like a magnanimous gesture of the strong, rather than a desperate plea of the weak. If the North rejected the gesture, he contended, its leaders would, in the eyes of the electorate, be held responsible for the continuing carnage, and the Northern politicians would be called to account at the next election.

Among other things, President Davis suggested that he travel to confer with Lee in person. Lee dissuaded Davis, as he considered this journey too dangerous under the present circumstances. Davis recommended that Lee, in order to gain the support of Marylanders, issue a proclamation to the citizens of the state declaring the purpose of the presence of the Southern army in Maryland. Lee issued the following on September 8:

To the People of Maryland:

It is right that you should know the purpose that brought the army under my command within the limits of your State, so far as that purpose concerns yourselves. The people of the Confederate States have long watched with the deepest sympathy the wrongs and outrages that have been inflicted upon the citizens of a commonwealth allied to the States of the South by the strongest social, political, and commercial ties. They have seen with profound indignation their sister state deprived of every right and reduced to the condition of a conquered province. Under the pretense of supporting the Constitution, but in violation of its most valuable provisions, your citizens have been arrested and imprisoned upon no charge and contrary to all form of law. The faithful and manly protest against this outrage made by the venerable and illustrious Marylander, to whom in better days no citizen appealed for right in vain, was treated with scorn and contempt; the government of your chief city has been usurped by armed strangers; your legislature has been dissolved by the unlawful arrest of its members; freedom of the press and of speech has been suppressed; words have been declared offenses by an arbitrary decree of the Federal Executive, and citizens ordered to be tried by a military commission for what they may dare to speak. Believing that the people of Maryland possessed a spirit too lofty to submit to such a government, the people of the South have long wished to aid you in throwing off this foreign yoke, to enable you to again enjoy the inalienable rights of freemen, and restore independence and sovereignty to your state. In obedience to this wish, our army has come among you, and is prepared to assist you with the power of its arms in regaining the rights of which you have been despoiled.

This, citizens of Maryland, is our mission, so far as you are concerned. No constraint upon your free will is intended; no intimidation will be allowed within the limits of this army, at least. Marylanders shall once more enjoy their ancient freedom of thought and speech.

We know no enemies among you, and will protect all, of every opinion. It is for you to decide your destiny freely and without constraint. This army will respect your choice, whatever it may be; and while the Southern people will rejoice to welcome you to your natural position among them, they will only welcome you when you come of your own free will.

R. E. Lee
General, Command[6]

Unfortunately for Lee, he was in the wrong part of the state. It was the east of the state that was the most rabidly pro-Confederate—and Lee was in the west. The east remained firmly under the thumb of the Union, and the west failed to rally to the cause of the Confederacy.

As Lee's forces moved north across Maryland, he expected that the Union garrison at Harpers Ferry, which was becoming ever more vulnerable, would be evacuated. To his great surprise, it was not.

Chapter 3

Harpers Ferry

Harpers Ferry is a small city in the Shenandoah Valley on the south side of the Potomac at the confluence of the Potomac and Shenandoah Rivers. It is about fifty miles upriver from Washington. This is where it all started in 1859 with John Brown's raid. At that time, it was a bustling city that was important on a number of fronts. It was here that the Baltimore and Ohio Railroad crossed the Potomac, proceeded westward across the valley, and exited the valley at Martinsburg. A spur ran off the Baltimore and Ohio at Harpers Ferry to Winchester, thirty-two miles to the southwest. The Chesapeake and Ohio Canal, another important east-west freight artery, ran by Harpers Ferry on the north side of the Potomac. Thus, Harpers Ferry was an important transportation choke point. In addition, it was an important military-industrial center. It contained a major armory, a rifle factory, and a mill.

At the outbreak of the Civil War, West Virginia had not yet broken off from Virginia. Hence, Harpers Ferry was in Virginia. It was occupied by the Confederates under the command of Col. Thomas (later Gen. Stonewall) Jackson. When Jackson withdrew from the city in June 1861, he blew up the railroad bridge; ripped up thirty miles of tracks; demolished the railroad repair shops at Martinsburg; destroyed the armory, rifle factory, and mill; blocked the canal; and carried off all the rolling stock he could get his hands on.

From the time of Jackson's withdrawal until February 1862, Harpers Ferry was largely a no-man's-land and suffered depredations by both sides. By February 1862 the population had been reduced to about three hundred.

From February 1862 onward, a Union garrison moved in to stay. Order and stability were restored, and rebuilding commenced. By the summer of 1862, the B & O main line, the Winchester spur, and the canal were all back in operation. The garrisons at Harpers Ferry and Martinsburg were primarily to protect the railroads and canal from cavalry raids. However, they also served another purpose. They shut off the Shenandoah Valley as an invasion route to the North.

The Shenandoah and Cumberland Valley, as it is known north of the Potomac, provided a natural avenue for the South to invade the North (see map 5). The valleys were bounded by two north-south mountain ridges, about twenty miles apart and a thousand feet high, that extended all the way from Roanoke in southern Virginia to Harrisburg, Pennsylvania, on the Susquehanna River.

The valleys served as a protected supply route for an invading army that could debouch at a number of points to threaten Washington, Baltimore, or Philadelphia, or continue to the Susquehanna and seize Harrisburg and cut the vital Pennsylvania Railroad east-west link where it crossed the Susquehanna.

The Shenandoah River enters the Potomac at Harpers Ferry from the southwest, and Harpers Ferry is in the triangle between the two rivers. The city consisted of a lower town that contained the industrial areas, an abrupt hill, and an upper town that contained the residential areas (see map 6). The railroad bridge terminated at the apex of the triangle in the lower town. In addition, the Federals had constructed a pontoon bridge over the Potomac that was slightly upriver from the railroad bridge.

Any attack on the landward side of Harpers Ferry would have to come from the west or southwest and hit the hypotenuse of the triangle. There were no water or mountain obstructions to an attack from this direction. The first logical point for a defense was a low eminence in the upper town called Bolivar Heights. Bolivar Heights was a little more than two miles from the apex of the town at the confluence of the rivers. One problem with Bolivar Heights was that it did not run all the way from the Potomac to the Shenandoah River. It ran only halfway, terminating at the Charlestown Road, which ran east-west and bisected the hypotenuse as it entered Harpers Ferry. Furthermore, even if Bolivar Heights extended all the way from river to river, the distance would be more than three miles and therefore too long for a strong defense by the available garrison. Thus, if Bolivar Heights were selected for a defense on the landward side, it would require a refused (angled back) left flank.

The next logical point for a defense on the landward side was at a military camp called Camp Hill. Camp Hill was right at the

Map 5
The Valley Route to Harrisburg

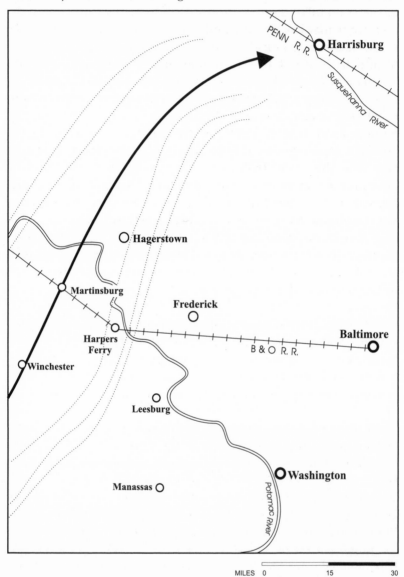

crest of the hill leading from the lower town to the upper town and less than a mile from the apex of the town at the confluence of the rivers. The distance across the hypotenuse at this point is only three-fifths of a mile, and thus, at this point, both flanks could be anchored on the rivers. However, there were two huge factors that affected the selection of either of these defense lines. Their names were Maryland Heights and Loudoun Heights.

A high ridge commenced twelve miles to the north of the Potomac and came abruptly down to the river at the bridge. Just enough room had been blasted from the face of the ridge to permit the passage of the road, railroad, and canal between its base and the river. This ridge was called Elk Ridge, and its prominence that towered fourteen hundred feet over the river was called Maryland Heights. The river below Maryland Heights was just four hundred yards wide, so that Maryland Heights towered over the city and looked down its throat. From its top, one could easily see the rear of any line defending Bolivar Heights and could look nearly straight down at Camp Hill. In the words of Confederate Maj. Gen. Lafayette McLaws:

> Harpers Ferry was entirely commanded by Maryland Heights, from which a plunging fire of even musketry can be made into the place . . . So long as Maryland Heights was occupied by the enemy, Harpers Ferry could never be occupied by us. If we gained possession, the town was no longer tenable to them.[1]

Elk Ridge rose up abruptly again on the south side of the Potomac and continued its run to the south. The eminence on the south of the river, which was somewhat lower than Maryland Heights, was called Loudoun Heights. If an enemy occupied Maryland and Loudoun Heights and contested the refused line on Bolivar Heights, every foot of the town would be subjected to artillery fire from all four cardinal points of the compass.

The defenders of Harpers Ferry had easy access to Maryland Heights. Near the bridge, a steep road that ascended to the top had been carved into the rock; access to the Heights by an attacker was less readily available. An attacker had to ascend Elk Ridge via a depression called Solomon's Gap that was six miles north of the river.

In September 1862, the bridges at Harpers Ferry were particularly important because the other bridges on the upper

Map 6
Harpers Ferry and Surroundings

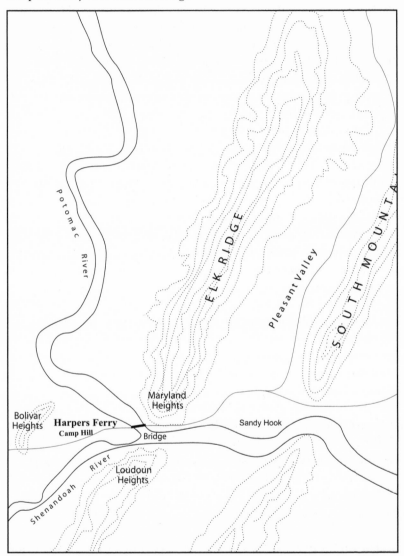

Potomac were down. Other than at Harpers Ferry, the only way to cross the Potomac was at fords. The Potomac was fickle. While crossing a ford might be easy one day, it could be impossible two days later. An army divided by the Potomac was at the mercy of Mother Nature. In mid-September 1862, the Potomac was low and could even be crossed at places not known as fords. The fords that played a part in the Antietam campaign are indicated in map 7. The ford that the Confederates used for their invasion between September 4 and 6 is the one known as White's Ford.

In September 1862, Harpers Ferry was commanded by Col. Dixon Miles. In 1860, at the onset of the rebellion, there was every reason to believe that Colonel Miles was destined to play a leading part and become one of the top Union generals. He was a native Marylander, born in 1804, and had graduated from West Point in 1824. This was two years before Albert Sydney Johnston, four years before Jefferson Davis, and five years before Robert E. Lee and Joseph Johnston. Miles, unlike later West Point graduates, such as Henry Halleck (1839), William Tecumseh Sherman (1840), Ulysses S. Grant (1843), and George B. McClellan (1846), remained in the army continuously until the outbreak of the war. In 1860, he was one of only twenty-two colonels in the regular army. Among the others were Robert E. Lee, Edmund Voss Sumner, and Joseph Mansfield. While Miles had risen to the rank of colonel in the peacetime army, McClellan, Grant, and Halleck had never risen higher than captain.

Miles had extensive combat experience. In the Mexican War, he was brevetted major for "Gallant and Distinguished Conduct" in the defense of Fort Brown, and then was brevetted lieutenant colonel for "Gallant and Meritorious Conduct" in the battles around Monterey. He also saw combat against the Indians in the Gila River Campaign of 1857 and in the Navajo Expedition of 1858.

At the battle of First Bull Run, July 16, 1861, Miles was already a division commander, normally a major general's billet, and a sure sign that he was on track for promotion to general. While Miles was a division commander, other soon-to-be luminaries participating in the battle, such as William Sherman, Ambrose Burnside, William B. Franklin, and Oliver O. Howard, were mere brigade commanders. Miles's future looked unclouded. But then things began to go awry.

Miles was formally charged with being intoxicated during

Map 7
Principal Fords of the Potomac

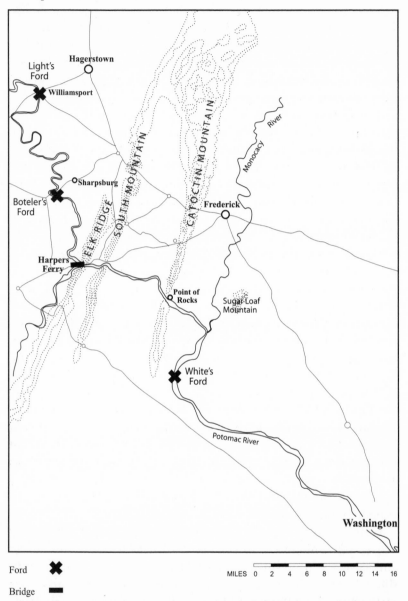

Ford   ✖

Bridge   ▬

MILES   0   2   4   6   8   10   12   14   16

the battle. The person making the charge was Col. Israel B.
Richardson, who was to play a major role in the Antietam campaign. Miles's unlikely defense was that he was just following
doctor's orders in taking small but frequent drinks to break a

drinking habit. For unknown reasons, Miles was not court-
martialed and cashiered, but his reputation was permanently
sullied, and he was relegated to what was then thought to be
the backwashes of the war. He was detailed to Harpers Ferry.

Miles arrived at Harpers Ferry in March 1862. At the moment,
the main theater of war in the East was far away on the peninsula opposite Richmond, and Miles's main task was to protect the
B & O Railroad against cavalry raids. However, things changed as
Stonewall Jackson began his famous Valley campaign. With success after success, Jackson approached closer and closer to
Martinsburg and Harpers Ferry. Lincoln and Stanton, misassess-
ing Jackson's campaign from the diversion it was to a possible
major attempt to seize Maryland and Washington, sent Brig.
Gen. Rufus Saxton from Washington to Harpers Ferry to bring
reinforcements and to take charge. This was the beginning of
Miles's humiliation.

Saxton was thirty-seven years old, young enough to be Miles's
son. He had graduated from West Point in 1849, twenty-five
years after Miles. Worse yet, he had been promoted to brigadier
general over Colonel Miles just six weeks before taking command from Miles on May 25, 1862. Worse was to follow. Major
General Franz Sigel arrived after Brigadier General Saxton.
Sigel, like Saxton, was also thirty-seven years old but, unlike
Saxton, was not a graduate of West Point. In fact, he was not a
graduate of any American school. He entered America for the
first time in 1850 from what is now Germany and still spoke with
an accent. As recently as 1860, when Miles was already a colonel,
Sigel was a civilian and director of a St. Louis school. Sigel did,
however, have a lot of political clout in the German-American
community.

Things quieted down in the valley, however, and Sigel left on
June 4, 1862, leaving Miles in command again.

Miles's fortunes now took a decided turn for the better. On
June 2, 1862, Maj. Gen. John Wool took command of the Middle
Department. The Middle Department covered essentially all of
Maryland and the slice of northern Virginia in which Harpers
Ferry and Martinsburg were located. It did not, however, include
the Washington defense forces or McClellan's Mobile Army of
the Potomac. Thus, the Middle Department encompassed sub-
stantially all the territory of the Antietam campaign; all garrisons
within it, except for the aforementioned, were under Wool.

Middle Department headquarters were in Baltimore.

Major General Wool was a relic from the past. At the time, he was seventy-eight years old. He had served continuously in the army since the War of 1812. By the end of the War of 1812, he was already a lieutenant colonel and had received citations for gallantry in the battles of Queenstown and Plattsburg. He was promoted to brevet brigadier general on April 26, 1826, the same year in which McClellan was born. He was one of the three most prominent generals of the Mexican War, being eclipsed only by Gen. Winfield Scott and future president Gen. Zachary Taylor. In 1854, he received the thanks of Congress and a ceremonial sword for his many contributions. By the beginning of the Civil War, he was already a national icon beyond criticism.

When Wool looked over his new command, he noted that it contained only one senior officer from the old army, and that was Miles. Obviously an old army colonel had superior military capabilities to any of the political ninnies now donning generals' uniforms. Wool considered Miles the best officer in his command and began expanding his authority and responsibilities. First, reinforcements were sent to Harpers Ferry. These included four regiments of infantry and a battery of artillery. Then, on August 8, 1862, Wool placed all the troops at Williamsport, Hagerstown, and Frederick under Miles. Miles was, in fact, now a theater commander. Then another political general showed up at Harpers Ferry.

Brigadier General Julius White was commanding officer of the troops at Winchester, thirty-two miles southwest of Harpers Ferry and not in Wool's department. White, a friend of Lincoln's, was born in 1816, and was, as of 1860, the collector of customs in Chicago. At the outset of the war, he helped recruit the Thirty-seventh Illinois and was appointed its colonel in September 1861, despite a total lack of prior military experience. Colonel White was sent to the West where he participated in the battle of Pea Ridge, Arkansas. White did well and was promoted to brigadier general. He was then ordered to take command at Winchester. Despite his lack of experience, he learned quickly, showed considerable promise, and earned the respect of his men. On September 2, 1862, upon the approach of superior Confederate forces, White and his command of some two thousand were compelled to abandon Winchester and retreated along the rail line to Harpers Ferry.

Under the existing rules of military discipline then and now,

Brigadier General Julius White USV
A Politician in Uniform

Brigadier General White, upon his arrival at Harpers Ferry on September 3, 1862, should have assumed command from Colonel Miles. However, General Wool would have none of it. On September 4, he sent the following message to Miles at Harpers Ferry:

> General White will either repair to this place or join the Army of the Potomac, but his troops and supplies will remain at Harpers Ferry and you will dispose of it.[2]

This message was almost immediately cancelled and followed by another as follows:

> The order making disposition of Brigadier-General White is countermanded. He is ordered to repair to Martinsburg and take command of all the troops in and about that place, guarding the railroad and defending that place to the last extremity. Answer immediately.
>
> John E. Wool
> Major-General[3]

White knew an insult when he saw one. Wool obviously considered Colonel Miles better qualified than Brigadier General White and wanted White off the scene. White dutifully proceeded to Martinsburg without his troops and took command of the garrison there, which consisted of about three thousand infantry and cavalry. This was not the last Miles was to see of White. With the accretion of White's troops, Miles's garrison now swelled to more than ten thousand.

Whatever Miles's qualities were, he was not noted for his intelligence. He graduated from West Point twenty-seventh out of thirty-one. In the military commission that was later convened after the loss of Harpers Ferry, subordinates testified to his "stupidity" and the commission found that "Col. Miles incapacity, amounting to almost imbecility, led to the shameful surrender of this important post."[4] However, we are getting ahead of our story, and this situation was not yet evident.

Colonel Miles had demonstrated his incapacity to lead a division at the battle of Bull Run. Now, in September 1862, he was in charge of what was becoming the equivalent of a corps. He had demonstrated impaired judgment at Bull Run and thus was removed to the backwaters of the conflict. Now the center of the conflict moved to him. He had become the central figure who would make decisions on which the fate of the Union hung. Furthermore, when he was to make these decisions, he was effectively cut off from communications with any higher authority.

When the Confederates began to cross the Potomac on September 4 at White's Ford, Miles's widely deployed forces were among the first to notice and report. At 8:20 p.m.,

September 4, Miles telegraphed the following message to Halleck and Wool:

> Col. Banning at Point of Rocks, reports that the enemy has passed the Potomac south of him in force and [is] advancing on him.[5]

This was followed at 10:00 p.m. with the following dispatch:

> Col. Banning, 3 miles west of Point of Rocks, reports that he has abandoned the place: that 30,000 of the enemy have crossed the Potomac, and are marching on him. I have ordered him to halt and obstruct the road and that I would support him.[6]

At 10:15 a.m. on September 5, he wired the following report to General Wool:

> I have already telegraphed you this morning, but fear the enemy has possession. This will be sent in cipher and also via Wheeling. Col. Banning reports A. P. Hill's division (30,000) crossed the Potomac before dark last night; kept crossing all night, and are now crossing at a higher ford, about 3 miles from Point of Rocks. They have cut the canal at seven-mile level. As Banning's force would be cut off if he staid [*sic*] longer, I have ordered him to retreat slowly.[7]

Up to the time of the Confederate invasion, Miles had regular telegraphic communications with his chief, General Wool in Baltimore, and with Washington via direct wires to the east. He also had a visual signal flag station on Maryland Heights that was in regular contact with a flag station at Point of Rocks. When the Confederates crossed the Potomac, they cut the wires. The last message Miles received via the wires to the east was on September 6, and it was from the Confederates. It read: "How are you General Pope? From general Jackson's Army."[8]

The Confederates also seized the Union signal flag station at Point of Rocks. When Captain Fortesque, Miles's flag signal officer on Maryland Heights, found that he could not reach anyone anymore, he considered his services no longer required and, with Miles's permission, left the area, not to return.

Miles managed to maintain intermittent telegraphic communications with Washington via an intricate patchwork through Martinsburg and points west; but by the end of September 11, all communications were cut off for good. Miles was on his own.

The last order Miles received from General Wool was on September 5 and was as follows:

> The position on the Heights ought to enable you to punish the enemy passing up the road in the direction of Harpers Ferry. Have your wits about you, and do all you can to annoy the rebels should they advance on you. Activity energy and decision must be used. You will not abandon Harpers Ferry without defending it to the last extremity.[9]

On September 7, Miles received the following order from Halleck. This was the last order he received:

> Our army is in motion. It is important that Harpers Ferry be held to the last moment. The government has the utmost confidence in you, and is ready to give you full credit for the defense it expects you to make.[10]

After the Confederates passed between Harpers Ferry and McClellan between September 4 and 7, it was becoming increasingly evident that Harpers Ferry was either going to have to be evacuated or to put up a fight.

After the accretion of White's troops on the third, Miles commanded a not inconsiderable force. In addition to cavalry and artillery, he had eleven regiments of infantry. On September 5, he reorganized his forces into four brigades. He placed Brigades One and Two under Colonels Frederick D'Utassy and William H. Trimble on Bolivar Heights, Brigade Three under Col. Thomas H. Ford on Maryland Heights, and kept Brigade Four, under Col. William G. Ward at Camp Hill, in reserve. Brigade Four was composed almost entirely of short-term troops that were anxious to get safely home (see map 8).

Between September 5 and 9, Miles was joined by three more regiments falling back from advanced positions. These were Col. William P. Maulsby's First Maryland Potomac Home Brigade regiment, Col. Henry Blackstone Banning's Eighty-seventh Ohio Volunteers, and Lt. Col. Stephen Downey's Third Maryland Potomac Home Brigade regiment. Miles assigned Downey to the

Map 8
Harpers Ferry Defenses

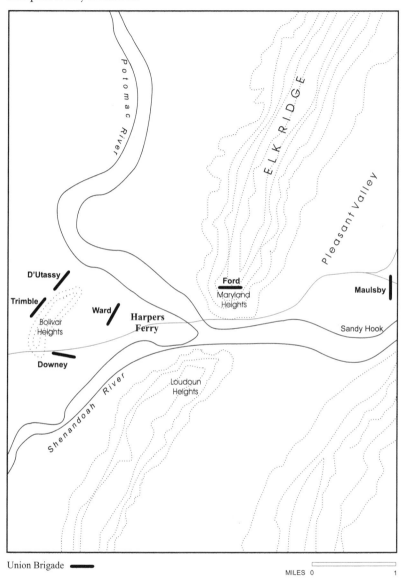

Union Brigade ▬▬▬

MILES 0   1

refused flank, Banning (who had short-term troops) to Ward's
Fourth Brigade, and retained Maulsby's regiment as an independent command and assigned it to protect the river road on the other
side of the Potomac in order to protect Harpers Ferry from an
attack from the east. Miles elected not to garrison Loudoun

Heights. He now had all the troops he was going to get—that is, until General White showed up again like a bad penny.

Miles's force contained a large number of Marylanders. Considering that Miles's fiefdom included most of western Maryland, this is not surprising. In addition to the First and Third Infantry regiments of the Maryland Potomac Home Brigade, commanded by Colonels Maulsby and Downey, Miles's force included three Maryland cavalry units. These were the battalion attached to the Maryland Potomac Home Brigade called "Cole's Cavalry," commanded by Maj. Henry Cole, and companies H and I of the First Maryland Cavalry, commanded by Captains William Grifflin and Charles Russell.

As Miles's outlying troops gradually fell back on Harpers Ferry as the Confederate invasion progressed, Miles tended to assign the Marylanders to the defenses on the north side of the Potomac at Maryland Heights and Sandy Hook—that is, on the Maryland side. Thus, the Marylanders were defending their own state and, in some instances, their own neighborhoods. This fact presumably provided them added motivation. The Marylanders already had an added motivation for not becoming prisoners. Maryland was a border state that provided troops to both sides. Many communities, and even families, were divided right down the middle, providing troops for each side. Thus, if a Marylander in blue fell into the hands of Marylanders in gray or vice versa, he was likely to be looked upon as a traitor, rather than merely an enemy combatant.

Many of the Marylanders in Miles's command had been recruited from the counties immediately adjacent to Harpers Ferry, which proved to be a distinct advantage. In September 1862, maps were rare and notoriously incomplete and inaccurate. The locals, on the other hand, were likely to be intimately familiar with the terrain, roads, and paths. As we shall see, this familiarity proved to be of the greatest importance.

Several of Miles's Maryland officers proved to be key players in the unfolding events. These included Major Cole, Captain Russell, and Lieutenant Colonel Downey, all of whom we shall hear more of later. Major Cole was already becoming an almost legendary cavalry leader, and was one of the few in the North to have his unit bear his name. Captain Russell was a clergyman who had been the pastor of the Presbyterian church in Williamsport, Maryland. Prior to the war, Russell's parish split down the middle between the Union and the Confederacy.

Russell chose to follow the Union and raised a cavalry company of which he became captain. (Clergymen heading combat units were not unusual in the Civil War. In fact, Confederate general William Nelson Pendleton, chief of artillery in Lee's army, was a practicing Episcopal rector; Confederate general Leonidas Polk, corps commander in the West, was a practicing Episcopal bishop. Both regularly presided over church services on Sunday and were prepared to blast their enemies' heads off on Monday.)

There was another officer in Miles's command who had excellent reasons for staying out of Confederate hands. This was Capt. Samuel C. Means, commanding officer of an independent cavalry company called the "Loudoun Rangers." Loudoun County was the county in Virginia in which both Leesburg and Harpers Ferry were located. Means and his men were thus Virginians fighting against the Confederates. If Confederate Marylanders were likely to consider fellow Union Marylanders traitors, any Confederate was likely to consider Means and his Virginia men traitors. Means had a bounty on his head and firmly believed that he would be hanged if he fell into Confederate hands.

It would be expected that from the time Miles realized that he would have to fight, his troops would be occupied day and night with axe and spade converting Harpers Ferry into Fortress Harpers Ferry. Unfortunately, this was not the case. Few defenses were constructed.

Soon after Colonel Ford took charge of Brigade Three on Maryland Heights, he examined his new domain and found the physical defenses inadequate. He attempted to requisition axes from the supply department to improve his defenses but was told that they had only ten. This apparently presented an insoluble problem, and for the lack of axes little was done. At that time, the garrison still had access to half the state of Maryland. Essentially, every homestead in western Maryland had an axe, and every general store sold axes. When the crunch finally came a few days later, what defenses existed were woefully inadequate, particularly in light of what could have been.

In conclusion, we can see that Miles, after examining all of the alternatives for defense, did little to strengthen his physical defenses and carefully arranged his forces in conformity with a strategy that could not succeed.

This was the situation at Harpers Ferry at the close of Tuesday, September 9, 1862. Miles's defense arrangements are as indicated in map 8.

Chapter 4

The Lee and McClellan Leadership Teams

Lee's Team

When Lee invaded Maryland in September 1862, his army contained nine infantry divisions divided into the corps of James Longstreet and Thomas (Stonewall) Jackson, and a cavalry division of three brigades under James Ewell Brown (Jeb) Stuart. Of the thirteen top generals, eleven were graduates of West Point, one of the Virginia Military Institute, and one, Gen. John Walker, was a graduate of neither.

The leadership of the Army of Northern Virginia had gelled earlier than that of the Army of the Potomac. By September 1862, the best had already risen to the top in Lee's army. Most changes beyond this point were the result of casualties. This gelling had not yet happened in the Army of the Potomac. One reason for the earlier maturing of the leadership of the Southern army may have related to the two presidents. President Davis, unlike President Lincoln, had wide military experience. He was a graduate of West Point, participated in the Mexican War as a colonel, and, in fact, became a war hero. After the war, he served as secretary of war in the Franklin Pierce administration. Consequently, Davis had a long-standing interaction with the officer corps and probably had a better understanding of who was competent and who was not.

In short, we may say that in September 1862, a first-rate leadership team of the South went into action against a second-rate leadership team of the North.

Thomas Jonathan Jackson was born in Clarksburg, Virginia, in 1821. Thus, at the time of the invasion, he was still only thirty-eight years old. Jackson was orphaned at an early age, handed around among relatives, and then taken in by an uncle who was modestly well off. Jackson had little formal schooling until his uncle, anxious to get him a free education, secured him an appointment to West Point. There, by sheer persistence, Jackson advanced in class standing each year, and it was generally accepted that, had the course continued another year, he would have finished on top. Jackson's classmates included none other than George B. McClellan.

Jackson found his true calling in war. In the Mexican War, he was the only member of his class to be brevetted three times and ended up as major. Jackson left the service in 1850 to accept an appointment as professor of physics at the Virginia Military Institute. It was generally agreed that he was a lousy professor. He was not only a boring lecturer, but he discouraged questions because he did not know the answers. His students referred to him as "Tom Fool." As such, he would probably have finished his life in obscurity and never entered the pages of history had not war come to his rescue again.

At the outset of the Civil War, Jackson was given a colonelcy and made commanding officer of Harpers Ferry. He subsequently participated in the battle of First Bull Run. It was here that he was given the sobriquet, "Stonewall." While Confederate general Bernard Bee was getting trounced in the valley, he noticed Jackson's brigade in line of battle on the hill and cried, "Look, men! There stands Jackson like a stone wall. Rally behind the Virginians."[1] Now there were those who insisted that what General Bee really meant when he said "There stands Jackson like a stone wall" was, "Why doesn't he do something?" However, General Bee was killed and never had a chance to explain himself. Be that as it may, Jackson was forever after known as Stonewall Jackson.

Jackson did, however, fully justify his reputation in what has become known as Jackson's Valley campaign. Jackson was assigned to conduct operations in the Shenandoah Valley so as to convince the North that invasion was threatened. This was actually a diversion intended to keep as many Union troops as possible from reinforcing McClellan in his Peninsula campaign. Jackson was eminently successful, and his campaign is looked upon as a classic that is studied worldwide in military schools to this day. If anything more was required to demonstrate Jackson's military prowess, his performance in the Second Bull Run campaign silenced all skeptics.

Jackson was—well, strange. He was a hypochondriac who had strange habits, such as sucking lemons to promote good health and holding one arm above his head to increase blood circulation. His appearance was what one might call "seedy," and he even rode a seedy looking horse. Jackson was also a religious zealot of Presbyterian persuasion. He saw the hand of the Almighty in everything and sincerely believed he was doing God's work in making war. He attributed all of his successes to the Almighty.

Jackson and Lee hit it off. Lee quickly recognized Jackson's talents, and, in temperament and judgment, Jackson was a man after Lee's own heart. Together, they could quickly agree on operations that, to an outsider, would appear to involve outrageous risks. Despite appearances, their plans were not really rash. Rather, they were carefully calculated risks premised on a realistic assessment of their opponents' stupidity.

Jackson and Lee formed a perfect team: Lee the conceiver, Jackson the implementer. Lee recognized that Jackson possessed tactical capabilities superior even to his own. Consequently, Lee never told Jackson how to do anything but always gave him the widest possible latitude. Once Lee lost Jackson, things just didn't work out so well anymore.

If there was one thing lacking in Jackson's capabilities, it was the ability to work smoothly with his subordinate generals. Jackson never took any subordinate into his confidence and demanded blind obedience. This attitude did not set well with some talented subordinates and was a source of problems.

Jackson was third in seniority, so was not Lee's top subordinate. That distinction went to James Longstreet. Longstreet was born in 1821 in South Carolina, making him forty-one years old at the time of the events herein described. He was brought up in Georgia and considered himself a Georgian. This made him something of an oddity in the hierarchy of Lee's army, which was composed mostly of Virginians. Longstreet graduated from West Point in 1842, four years before Jackson.

Among Longstreet's close friends was his classmate, Ulysses Grant, the future general in chief of the U.S. Army. Grant married Longstreet's cousin, and Longstreet served as the best man. Despite being on opposite sides, they continued their friendship after the war. Longstreet, like Jackson, participated in the Mexican War, where he was twice brevetted to major and was wounded. Unlike Jackson, he remained in the army right up to the Civil War and gained additional combat experience fighting Indians.

At the outset of the Civil War, Longstreet, who by that time had almost twenty years' experience, was offered a brigadier general's commission. Longstreet, like Jackson, participated in the battle of First Bull Run. He then moved off to the peninsula to contest McClellan's Peninsula campaign, while Jackson moved off to his Valley campaign. It was on the peninsula that Longstreet came under Lee's command.

Longstreet was imperturbable, exuded confidence and competence, and, unlike Jackson, had an impressive military bearing. Lee recognized Longstreet's abilities and, in addition, took a personal liking to him. He was to become Lee's "Old War Horse." With some breaks in late 1863 and 1864, Longstreet was to remain Lee's top subordinate until the end of the war.

Longstreet, unlike Lee and Jackson, had a decided conservative bent and always leaned toward a conventional solution that would entail minimal risks and casualties on their side. Of course, Lee, Jackson, and Longstreet were all fighting to achieve the South's independence. But Lee and Jackson were inclined to try to achieve it by winning, while Longstreet's approach was to avoid losing. In the long run, Longstreet's approach just might have been the right one. In any event, the triumvirate of Lee, Longstreet, and Jackson made a most formidable team; once one of them had dropped out, it was never again to be equaled during the war.

No matter how good the powers of decision may be, it is impossible to make good decisions without good information. Here is where the cavalry and its commander come into play. When armies were on the move, it was the function of the cavalry to conceal the movements of their own army while, at the same time, to provide good information on the opposing army. Fortunately for the Lee triumvirate, they possessed a first-rate cavalry headed by a cavalryman *par excellence*. His name was James Ewell Brown (Jeb) Stuart.

Jeb Stuart was born in Laurel Hill, Virginia, in 1832 and thus, at the time of the Maryland invasion, was not yet thirty years old. Stuart graduated from West Point in 1854, and though the Mexican War was long since over, he saw plenty of action. He was assigned to the First U.S. Cavalry at Ft. Leavenworth, Kansas. Kansas, at the time, was a hotbed of armed activity between pro- and anti-slavers, even though the Civil War had not yet begun. In addition, Stuart participated in the fighting against the Cheyenne Indians and was wounded.

Stuart's association with Robert E. Lee predated the war. Lee was superintendent of West Point while Stuart was a student, and, in 1859, while Lieutenant Stuart was in Washington on personal business, he was ordered to join Col. Robert E. Lee in putting down John Brown's insurrection at Harpers Ferry.

At the beginning of the Civil War, Stuart was made colonel of the First Virginia Cavalry. He participated in the battle of First Bull Run, and his contribution was such that he was promoted to brigadier general. He was then transferred to the peninsula in response to McClellan's Peninsula campaign. Here, he ultimately came under the command of Lee. Stuart's actions were so outstanding during the Peninsula campaign that he was promoted to major general and given command of all the cavalry of the Army of Northern Virginia.

By the time Lee entered Maryland in September 1862, he had already become accustomed to and dependent on the excellent information regularly provided by his young cavalry commander.

The Lee team in September 1862 was as indicated below:

Longstreet (Corps)	Jackson (Corps)	Stuart (Division Cavalry)
Divisions	*Divisions*	*Brigades*
McLaws	Lawton	Hampton
Anderson	A. P. Hill	Fitz Lee
D. R. Jones	J. R. Jones	Munford
Hood	D. H. Hill	
Walker		

McClellan's Team

As McClellan moved out on September 7, he took with him the First, Second, Sixth, Ninth, and Twelfth Corps, and was later to be joined by the Fifth. These were commanded by Hooker (First), Sumner (Second), Porter (Fifth), Franklin (Sixth), Reno (Ninth), and Mansfield (Twelfth). Major General Ambrose Burnside, who was normally commander of the Ninth Corps, relinquished command of his corps to Reno when he assumed the function of northern wing commander. These seven then, along with McClellan's cavalry commander, Brig. Gen. Alfred Pleasonton, constituted McClellan's principal subordinates during the Maryland campaign.

It is said that the wheels of justice grind slowly, but they grind exceedingly fine. The same can be said for the wheels of military competence in wartime, except that they can grind faster. In September 1862, in the North, the incompetents had not yet been fully separated from the competents. The Grants, Shermans, and Sheridans had not yet fully ascended, and, to many, the McClellans, Hallecks, and Burnsides still looked like the great ones.

Of McClellan's eight principal assistants, seven had graduated from West Point. The only exception was General Sumner. Five of these seven were there when McClellan was there. These were Franklin (class of '43), Pleasonton (class of '44), Porter (class of '45), Reno (class of '46, as was McClellan), and Burnside (class of '47). Burnside, Franklin, and Porter in particular, became close friends of McClellan.

Two of McClellan's eight principal subordinates had been colonels in the old army and were a generation older than McClellan and his chums. These were Joseph Mansfield (age fifty-nine) and Edmund Voss Sumner (age sixty-four). These two were not members of McClellan's circle of confidantes.

The eighth man on McClellan's team was Joseph Hooker. In age, Hooker, at forty-seven, was about midway between McClellan's youthful group and the old colonels. Hooker had attended West Point but had graduated in 1837, well before McClellan and his friends arrived. Hooker belonged neither to McClellan's inner circle of friends nor to the old colonels. Actually, Hooker was a member of a group of one, headed by Joseph Hooker, whose objective was to maximize the authority of Joseph Hooker. But to give the man his due, he wasn't without talent, and he wasn't without courage. Hooker was known as "Fighting Joe" Hooker in the press. If there was some controversy about the bestowing of the name "Stonewall" on Jackson, there was none about the bestowing of the name "Fighting Joe" on Hooker. It came about as follows: A newspaper reporter, following a battle on the peninsula, filed a report with one sentence ending in the word "fighting" and the next beginning with the words "Joe Hooker." The period was lost in the transmission, and the phrase "Fighting Joe Hooker" appeared in the newspapers. The name stuck. One last thing before we leave Hooker: Yes, he was a ladies' man; but no, the word "hooker" did not originate with him. It was around earlier.

The senior among McClellan's subordinates and second in

command was Ambrose Burnside. In a way, this was strange, inasmuch as Burnside, at age thirty-eight, was the youngest (next to McClellan), the last to graduate from West Point, the one with the least prewar active duty, and the only one who had not participated in combat in the Mexican War.

Burnside's seniority in rank can probably be attributed to the patronage of his good friend McClellan, who approved the "Burnside expedition" of early 1862. The Burnside expedition was a land-sea operation to secure lodgments on the North Carolina coast. It proved a modest success and provided Burnside with what the others did not have—that is, name recognition associated with success and independent command. As history shows, there is more fame attached to being first in a second-class operation than to being second in a first-class operation.

After graduation from West Point in 1847, Burnside served on garrison duty in Mexico and then on the Southwestern frontier against the Apache Indians. In 1853, he resigned from the army and opened a factory in his native Rhode Island to manufacture a breech-loading carbine that he had invented. When a contract failed to materialize, Burnside's factory was forced into bankruptcy, and his creditors acquired his patent. The carbine then became an immediate success. This type of thing proved to be a recurring theme for Burnside. He then turned to his friend, George McClellan, who was vice president of the Illinois Central, for work.

At the outset of the Civil War, Burnside was commissioned colonel of the First Rhode Island and led a brigade at the battle of First Bull Run. He was promoted to brigadier general of volunteers on August 6, 1861, and placed in command of training provisional brigades of the new Army of the Potomac. It was here that he came under the patronage of his friend McClellan, and it was here that the Burnside expedition was conceived.

Burnside, unlike many of the other generals, was exceptionally modest, and as subsequent events were to show, had much to be modest about. In recent times he has been compared to Gen. Jubilation T. Cornpone of Li'l Abner's Dogpatch fame. Cornpone had presided over Cornpone's Rout, Cornpone's Fiasco, and Cornpone's Disaster. Burnside was ultimately to match all three. However, as of September 1862, this was all in the future.

One thing that Burnside was justly famous for then, and still remembered for today, was his magnificent mutton chop facial hair. The style was originally known as "Burnsides," but like so much associated with him, it became a little twisted and came down to us as "sideburns."

Fitz John Porter was another intimate of McClellan's West Point days. Porter, unlike Burnside, served under McClellan throughout McClellan's Peninsula campaign and rose to become commander of the Fifth Corps. McClellan closeted himself with Porter for discussions and advice more often than with any other subordinate.

Porter was a loyal McClellan man, and when McClellan's troops (including Porter's) were taken from him and transferred to General Pope, Porter made some disparaging comments about his new commander. This indiscretion caused some to believe that Porter, in his pique, actually hoped that Pope would lose and be humiliated. This event, of course, did not endear him to Pope, and when, during the Second Bull Run campaign, Porter appeared to be slow in executing one of Pope's orders, Pope leveled charges against him. These charges were a serious matter, and Porter could have faced dismissal from the service or worse.

McClellan requested that the resolution of the charge against Porter be deferred until after the September invasion crisis, and the request was granted. During the campaign, McClellan resumed his old association with Porter and, as we shall see, took advice from him once too often, with the most dire of consequences.

In the pre-Civil War days, it was customary for the top graduates of West Point to enter the engineers, and those lower on the totem pole to enter the cavalry, infantry, or artillery. William Buel Franklin, of the class of '43, finished first in his class and thus entered the U.S. Army Corps of Topographical Engineers. The corps was not just concerned with military matters, but with all government construction, including lighthouses, office buildings, and the capitol building itself. Thus, Franklin was to spend almost his entire eighteen prewar years in nonmilitary matters and, at the outbreak of the war, was superintending the construction of the dome of the capitol building. Being academically the smartest of McClellan's subordinates, Franklin entered the war as the least experienced in troop and combat matters.

Sumner and Mansfield were both colonels from the old army.

As of September 1862, Sumner was sixty-four and Mansfield was fifty-nine. Neither was McClellan's choice for a corps command in his army.

Sumner, unlike all of the other corps commanders, was not a West Point graduate. He had entered the army way back in 1819 and, as of the outset of the war, had served forty-two years on active duty. Despite his long service, he had no experience in commanding large numbers of men in combat. He served under McClellan in the Peninsula campaign and, during the early years of the war, acquired the reputation of being an aggressive, but not necessarily a careful, commander. His commands were noted for their high casualties.

Mansfield graduated from West Point in 1822, two years before Colonel Miles. Mansfield graduated second in a class of forty-four and thus, like Franklin, entered the engineers rather than one of the three primary combat services. Like Franklin, he spent almost his entire career in either engineering or staff work. In the final eight years before the war, he served as inspector general of the army. On September 8, when McClellan marched out from Rockville, his Twelfth Corps commander, Gen. Nathaniel P. Banks, was ill and therefore left behind in Washington. This left a vacancy, and Mansfield was ordered to join the Army of the Potomac to fill it. He arrived on September 15, two days before the battle of Antietam, and was assigned command of the Twelfth Corps. Mansfield's career as a troop commander was to last two days. He was killed on September 17.

Of McClellan's eight leading subordinates in September 1862, three were to be dead within a year; two were to preside over the Army of the Potomac's biggest fiascos; one was to be charged by a joint congressional committee with being responsible for a disastrous defeat; one was to be dismissed from the service; and one was to march off into mediocrity, superseded by more talented juniors.

McClellan's team in September 1862 was as follows:

Marched Off September 7

North Wing	Center Wing	South Wing	Cavalry
Burnside	Sumner	Franklin	Pleasonton
Hooker (First Corps)	Sumner (Second Corps)	Franklin (Sixth Corps)	
Reno (Ninth Corps)	Mansfield (Twelfth Corps)		

Joined Later
Porter (Fifth Corps)

Remained Behind to Support Washington Garrison
Heintzelman (Third Corps)
Sigel (Eleventh Corps)

And last, let us say a word about those to whom McClellan and Lee reported. We have already run into Henry Halleck, McClellan's boss. To put it charitably, Halleck doubted McClellan's competence, and McClellan undoubtedly felt the same in regard to Halleck. Their relationship was at best shaky. Lincoln, McClellan's ultimate boss, was an excellent judge of men and fully recognized McClellan's great capabilities as an organizer and as one who was able to bring order out of chaos. Thus, after the Second Bull Run fiasco, Lincoln was able to swallow his pride and bring McClellan back. However, even though Lincoln recognized McClellan's capabilities as an organizer, he had developed great misgivings as to McClellan's capabilities for waging offensive war and had even begun to doubt his patriotism. Lincoln suspected that McClellan was less than totally cooperative in turning his troops over to Pope and suspected that McClellan may even have rejoiced at Pope's destruction. Any further relationship between McClellan and Lincoln was likely to be short-termed.

Lee, contrary to the belief of many, was at no point in the Civil War the senior general of the Confederate army. That distinction belonged, from the beginning to the end, to Gen. Samuel Cooper. In September 1862, Samuel Cooper was sixty-four years old. He had graduated from West Point in 1815 and served continuously until the outbreak of the war. In July 1852, Cooper was named adjutant general of the U.S. Army and remained in that post until he resigned to join the Confederacy. Throughout Jefferson Davis's tenure as secretary of war, he worked closely with Cooper, who had become his ally and confidant.

When Cooper applied for a position in the Confederate army, Davis appointed him senior general and adjutant and inspector general. Cooper held a position somewhat similar to that of Henry Halleck, the senior administrative officer of the army at the seat of government. Cooper retained his position to the end of the war. He was widely admired for his dignity and courtesy to all. President Davis described Cooper as "a man as pure in heart as he was sound in judgment." Davis stated that:

> I never, in four years of constant consultation, saw Cooper man-
> ifest prejudice, or knew him to seek favors for a friend, or to with-
> hold what was just from one to whom he bore reverse relations. This
> rare virtue—this supremacy of judgment over feelings—impressed
> me as being so exceptional, that I have often mentioned it.[78]

Lee's ultimate boss was, of course, President Jefferson Davis.
Their relationship had extended back over thirty years to the
time they were cadets at West Point. Davis graduated in 1828,
and Lee a year later in 1829. In their long relationship, Davis
had always held the higher position: first as upper class cadet,
then as senior officer, then as secretary of war, and finally as president of the Confederacy. Their relationship was harmonious
and governed by mutual respect and trust.

Thus, as of mid-September 1862, the Southern top triumvirate of Lee, Cooper, and Davis was smooth functioning, relatively friction free, and to be enduring. The Union top echelon,
however, had not yet sorted itself out. Halleck had the confidence of Lincoln, but not that of McClellan; McClellan had the
confidence of neither Halleck nor Lincoln. The relationship was
unstable, and McClellan was destined to be odd man out.

Although the functioning of the Confederate army from
corps level up was smooth and relatively friction free, this was
not true from the corps level down. There was quibbling
between division commanders and their corps commanders,
and between the division commanders. General Jackson, in particular, was notorious for placing subordinate generals under
arrest at the drop of a hat.

As the Confederate army entered Maryland in September
1862, two of its nine infantry division commanders were marching behind their troops, relieved of command, and under arrest.
These were Generals A. P. Hill and John Bell Hood, considered
two of Lee's most capable subordinates. Hill had quarreled with
Jackson when Jackson had given an order to Hill's men without
going through Hill; Hood had quarreled with a senior about the
disposition of ambulances that Hood's men had captured at
Second Bull Run. Both Hill and Hood were restored to command before serious fighting began in September 1862, and
both played key roles in the invasion. Both were also destined to
achieve higher rank and greater responsibility.

Chapter 5

Special Order 191

On September 7, the Confederate army was camped in the vicinity of Frederick, Maryland, with Stuart's three cavalry brigades deployed between the encampment and McClellan's army to the east. There was wild speculation in the Union as to what the Confederates would do next. Was the objective Washington? Baltimore? Philadelphia? Harrisburg? Or what? Unknown to the Union commanders, there was dissension in the Confederate camp as to what they would do.

Soon after the Confederate army crossed the Potomac, General Lee had proposed to Longstreet that he should organize a force, surround the garrison at Harpers Ferry, which was now in their rear, and capture it. Longstreet objected. He argued that the troops were worn with marching and were on short rations, and that it would be a bad idea to divide their forces in the enemy's country where the enemy could get information in a few hours on any movement they might make. He argued that the Federal army, though beaten at Second Bull Run, was not disorganized. It certainly would come out to look for them, and they should guard against being caught in such a condition. Longstreet considered that their army, although it consisted of a superior quality of soldiers, was in no condition to be divided in the enemy's country. He urged that they keep the army well in hand, recruit its strength, get up supplies, and then they could do anything they pleased. Lee made no reply to Longstreet's arguments, and Longstreet assumed that the Harpers Ferry scheme was abandoned.

However, a day or two later, when the army was camped at Frederick, Longstreet went up to Lee's tent, where he found Lee and Jackson discussing the move against Harpers Ferry, with both heartily approving of it. Longstreet was invited in to participate in the discussion. He quickly realized that things had progressed to the point that there was going to be an operation against Harpers Ferry and that he might as well constructively accept it. He suggested that, if it was going to take place, they use the whole army rather than divide it.

On September 8, Lee at Frederick received the final reinforcement to his army that he was going to get for the Maryland campaign. It consisted of a small division of just two brigades commanded by Brig. Gen. John Walker. Lee now had the four divisions of Longstreet (McLaws's, Anderson's, D. R. Jones's, and Hood's), the four divisions of Jackson (Lawton's, A. P. Hill's, J. R. Jones's, and D. H. Hill's), plus Walker's division and Stuart's three brigades of cavalry. His total strength was about forty-three thousand. McClellan's nearby field army was about ninety thousand.

John Walker was a professional officer from the peacetime army who had served continuously from the Mexican War until he joined the Confederacy. He was an oddity in that he had not attended West Point, VMI, or the Citadel, but was a graduate of the Jesuit University in St. Louis. He had an outstanding reputation, which was to grow with the war, and probably knew Lee from both the Mexican War and their peacetime service. In any event, when Walker reported to Lee on September 8, Lee's plans had solidified in his mind, and he outlined them to Walker. Here is Walker's recollection of Lee's words (see map 9):

> Here (tracing his finger on a map) is the line of our communications from Rapidan Station to Manassas, thence to Frederick. It is too near the Potomac, and is liable to be cut at any day by the enemy's cavalry. I have therefore given orders to move the line back into the Valley of Virginia (Shenandoah) by way of Staunton, Harrisburg and Winchester, entering Maryland at Shepherdstown.
>
> I wish you to return to the mouth of the Monocacy and effectually destroy the aqueduct of the Chesapeake and Ohio Canal. By the time that is accomplished you will receive orders to cooperate in the capture of Harpers Ferry, and you will not return here, but after the capture of Harpers Ferry, will rejoin us at Hagerstown where the army will be concentrated. My information is that there are between 10,000 and 12,000 men at Harpers Ferry and 3,000 at Martinsburg. The latter may escape toward Cumberland, but I think the chances are that they will take refuge in Harpers Ferry and be captured. Besides the men and material of war which we shall capture at Harpers Ferry, the position is necessary to us, not to garrison and hold, but because

Map 9
Lee's Plan

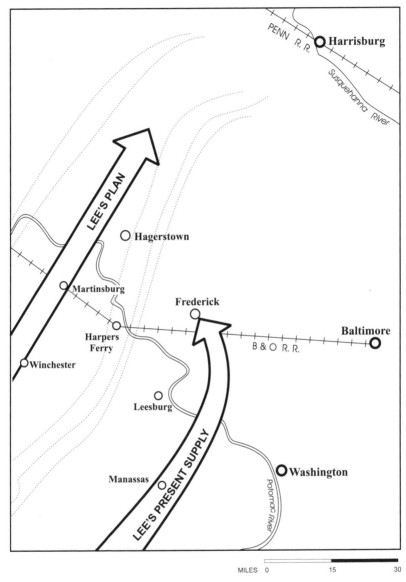

in the hands of the enemy it would be a break in our new line of communications with Richmond.

A few days rest at Hagerstown will be of great service to our men. Hundreds of them are barefoot, and nearly all of them are ragged. I hope to get shoes and clothing for the most needy. But the best of it will be that the short delay will enable us to get up our stragglers—not stragglers from a shirking disposition, but simply from inability to keep up with their commands. I believe that there are not less than from eight to ten thousand of them between here and Rapidan Station. Besides this we shall be able to get a large number of recruits who have been accumulating at Richmond for some weeks. I have now requested that they be sent forward to join us. They ought to reach us at Hagerstown. We shall then have a very good army and, he smilingly added, one that I think will be able to give a good account of itself.

In ten days from now, he continued, if the military situation is then what I confidently expect it to be after the capture of Harpers Ferry, I shall concentrate the army at Hagerstown, effectually destroy the Baltimore and Ohio Railroad, and march to this point, placing his finger at Harrisburg, Pennsylvania. That is the objective point of the campaign. You remember, no doubt, the long bridge of the Pennsylvania Railroad over the Susquehanna, a few miles west of Harrisburg. Well, I wish eventually to destroy that bridge, which will disable the Pennsylvania Railroad for a long time. With the Baltimore and Ohio in our possession, and the Pennsylvania Railroad broken up, there will remain to the enemy but one route of communications with the west, and that very circuitous, by way of the lakes. After that I can turn my attention to Philadelphia, Baltimore or Washington, as may seem to our interests.

You doubtless regard it hazardous to leave McClellan practically on my line of communication, and to march into the heart of the enemy's country? I admitted that such a thought occurred to me.

Are you acquainted with General McClellan? he inquired. I replied that we had served together in the Mexican War, under General Scott, but I had seen little of him since that time.

He is an able general but a very cautious one. His enemies among his own people think him too much so. His army is in a very demoralized and chaotic condition, and will not be prepared for offensive operations—or he will not think it so—for three or four weeks. Before that time I hope to be on the Susquehanna.[1]

Reading between the lines, it seems evident that Lee's description of McClellan is merely his charitable and gracious way of saying that McClellan is a bumbling incompetent.

On September 9, 1862, Lee, after much consultation with Jackson, came up with Special Order 191 for the capture of the

Major General Thomas "Stonewall" Jackson CSA
Victor at Harpers Ferry

garrisons at Martinsburg and Harpers Ferry. It provided for breaking up the army into four components, sweeping up the two garrisons, and reuniting the four components before

McClellan realized anything was amiss. Like other Lee-Jackson plans that resulted in resounding successes, its success was premised on the calculated stupidity of their opponents.

The principal opponents were, of course, General McClellan and Colonel Miles, who was destined to command both the Harpers Ferry and Martinsburg garrisons. Lee knew McClellan well from the Mexican War. Jackson knew him even better, having been his classmate at West Point for four years. Lee also knew Colonel Miles from the old army when both had been colonels. If we could encapsulate the reputations of each at that time in a single sentence, it would be: Lee—why is that man not higher? Miles—how did that man get that high? As an added ace to their plan, Jackson had been the commanding officer at Harpers Ferry from the outbreak of the Civil War until June 1861 and knew the terrain like the back of his hand.

Longstreet still objected to the plan as too risky. He apparently expected their opponents to react in an energetic and rational manner. Lee and Jackson knew better, and Lee overruled Longstreet. Was the plan risky? Of course it was.

The essence of Special Order 191 is as indicated in map 10. The army would withdraw behind the mountains west of Frederick. Stuart would guard the mountain passes. Three detachments would be created under Jackson, McLaws, and Walker. These would then approach the garrisons at Martinsburg and Harpers Ferry from three different directions, drive them together, surround them, and capture them. They would then reunite with the army at Boonsboro or Hagerstown as circumstances dictated. All this was to be accomplished in three to four days, before McClellan realized what was happening.

To better understand the plan with its potential risks and gains, and to understand subsequent developments, it is necessary to become familiar with the terrain and road layout beyond Frederick (see map 11).

The National Road (currently Alt. US 40) ran from Frederick through the mountains to Hagerstown twenty miles to the west. Hagerstown was the largest city of the Cumberland Valley and at the intersection of the National Road with a main north-south road (currently US 11) running up and down the valley. Hagerstown would thus be the logical starting point for Lee's visualized Valley campaign to Harrisburg and the valley road (US 11) his main supply line.

Map 10
Special Order 191

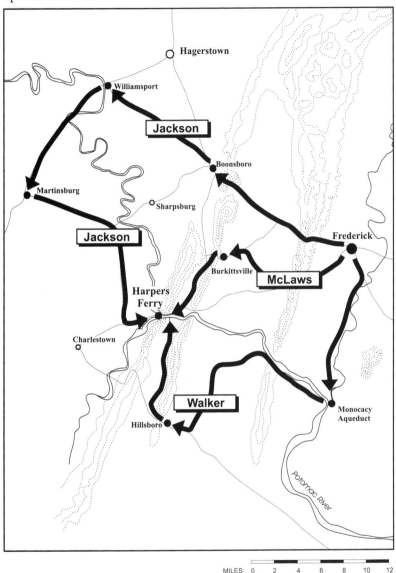

The north-south mountain ridge just west of Frederick was called South Mountain. However, just to the northwest of Frederick, South Mountain split into two ridges that separated to about six miles and then ran parallel all the way down to the Potomac. The ridge closest to Frederick was called Catoctin

Map 11
Attacking Harpers Ferry from the North

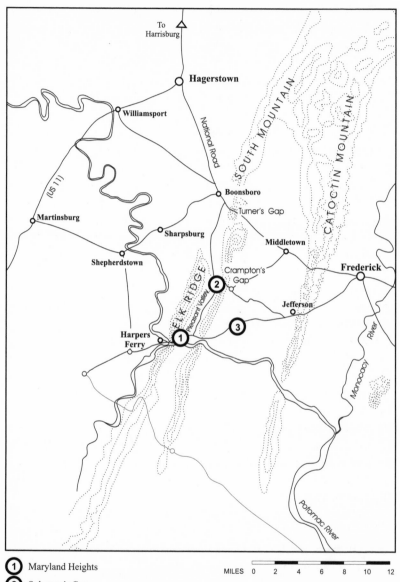

① Maryland Heights

② Solomon's Gap

③ Direct Road (Currently US 15/340)

MILES 0 2 4 6 8 10 12

Mountain, while the western ridge retained the name of its parent, South Mountain. The valley between the ridges was called Catoctin Valley. In the middle of Catoctin Valley, there was a small town on the National Road, appropriately called Middletown.

The valley between South Mountain and Elk Ridge was called Pleasant Valley. In order to attack Harpers Ferry from the north, it would be necessary to occupy Maryland Heights (indicated by 1 on map 11). To get to 1, it would be necessary to ascend Elk Ridge at Solomon's Gap (indicated by 2 on map 11). To get to 2, an army could follow the National Road to Boonsboro and turn left on the Boonsboro-Harpers Ferry road (currently US 67). Alternatively, an army could turn left at Middletown on the Burkittsville road (currently US 17), pass through South Mountain at Crampton's Gap (or Brownsville Gap, just one mile south) and hit the Boonsboro-Harpers Ferry road just below Solomon's Gap.

To attack Harpers Ferry via the direct road from Frederick (currently US 15, indicated by 3 on map 11), it would be necessary to pass through an easily defended choke point between South Mountain and the river.

To attack the garrison at Martinsburg, an army could follow the National Road to Boonsboro, turn left on the Sharpsburg road (currently US 34), and cross the river at Boteler's Ford. Alternatively, the army could continue on the National Road to the Williamsport road (currently US 68) and cross the Potomac at Williamsport. If the army elected the first option, it would approach Martinsburg from the east and merely drive the garrison to the west. If it wanted to force the garrison into the bag at Harpers Ferry, there was no alternative to the Williamsport Road.

Special Order 191 called for Lee's army to begin its march on September 10. Jackson was the first of the generals to be tasked. Like all Lee-Jackson assignments, it provided Jackson a maximum of discretion. It read as follows:

> General Jackson's command will form the advance, and, after passing Middletown, with such portion as he may select, take the route toward Sharpsburg, cross the Potomac at the most convenient point, and by Friday morning (September 12) take possession of the Baltimore and Ohio Railroad, capture such of

them as may be at Martinsburg, and intercept such as may .
attempt to escape from Harpers Ferry.[2]

Jackson elected to take all three of his divisions that were not
assigned elsewhere in the special order (Lawton's, A P. Hill's,
and J. R. Jones's). This represented a total force of about twelve
thousand. Jackson's orders said nothing about capturing
Harpers Ferry. They merely tasked him with intercepting "such
as may attempt to escape from Harpers Ferry."

The next of the generals to be tasked in the special order was
Longstreet. He was directed to take the part of his command not
assigned elsewhere (D. R. Jones's and Hood's divisions) to pursue the same road (the National Road) as far as Boonsboro,
where he would remain with the reserve artillery, supply, and
baggage trains of the army. This command consisted of approximately eight thousand men.

The third assignment went to McLaws. The plan stated,

> General McLaws with his own division and that of General R.
> H. Anderson will follow General Longstreet. On reaching
> Middletown it will take the route to Harpers Ferry, and by Friday
> morning (Sept 12) possess himself of Maryland Heights and
> endeavor to capture the enemy at Harpers Ferry and vicinity.[3]

General McLaws's command consisted entirely of troops from
Longstreet's corps and contained about eight thousand men.

The fourth assignment went to General Walker. Unlike the
others, who all began their assignments from Frederick, Walker
had been sent back to the Potomac on September 9 to destroy
the aqueduct over the mouth of the Monocacy River, and his
assignment began at that point. He was directed to recross the
Potomac into Virginia, proceed to and take possession of
Loudoun Heights (overlooking Harpers Ferry on the south), if
practicable, by Friday morning, September 12, and then cooperate with Generals Jackson and McLaws in intercepting the
retreat of the enemy. Walker's forces consisted of about three
thousand.

General D. H. Hill of Jackson's corps received the next
assignment. He was to form the rear guard of the army as it
marched westward on the National Road from Frederick. He was
to follow the reserve artillery, ordnance, and supply trains to
Boonsboro, where he, the trains, and Longstreet would remain.

The last assignment in the special order went to Jeb Stuart and the cavalry. Stuart was directed to detach a squadron of cavalry for each of the columns of Jackson, McLaws, and Walker, and to cover the route of the army. Independently, Stuart was directed to screen the movements of the army through Friday, September 12.

After Jackson, McLaws, and Walker completed their assignments, they were to reunite with the army at Boonsboro (or Hagerstown as circumstances dictated). The selection of Boonsboro for the wagon park and the reuniting point was logical, as it was a road junction on the National Road with routes radiating out to Harpers Ferry, Boteler's Ford between Shepherdstown and Sharpsburg, and the ford at Williamsport.

The distances in miles to be covered by each column from its departure point to Harpers Ferry were as follows:

Jackson	60
McLaws	20
Walker	22

The plan called for each of the three columns to reach its objective on the morning of September 12, and for Stuart to screen the movements of the army through that day. Considering that the start of the plan was the morning of September 10, it would have been a physical impossibility for Jackson to reach Harpers Ferry on the morning of the twelfth if he had to go to Martinsburg first. Consequently, Lee must have visualized the surrender or flight of the garrison upon the approach of McLaws and Walker. This is all the more astounding when we consider that Lee had a realistic assessment of the size of the garrisons at Martinsburg and Harpers Ferry, and that the combined garrisons exceeded the combined forces of McLaws and Walker.

The plan contained in Special Order 191 violated just about every maxim of warfare. First, it divided an already inferior force in the face of the enemy—and that not into two, but into four parts. Second, it depended upon the coordination of three widely separated forces attacking a distant objective while there were no communications between the forces. Third, the two objective forces (Harpers Ferry and Martinsburg) were only seventeen miles apart; were connected by road, railroad, and telegraph; and could unite more quickly than any of the approaching forces could unite—and once united, were numerically superior to any of the three. Fourth, each of the three approaching forces was separated from the other two by a major river, and the enemy controlled the only bridges. Fifth, the defending forces could be expected to have better intelligence, inasmuch as two of the three approaching forces were moving through unfriendly territory, where it would be expected that their movements would be made known; in any event, the defenders had greater cavalry resources and hence, a greater potential for reconnaissance. And last, but not least, the defenders were already at the scene of the potential conflict, were rested, and had time to prepare physical defenses.

All in all, Lee must have considered that his opponents were incredibly stupid or that one Confederate was worth two Union soldiers, or a combination of the two. He probably believed the latter.

As late as September 12, the garrisons of Harpers Ferry and Martinsburg had a number of viable options:

• They could unite at Harpers Ferry (which they did).
• They could move the entire force to Maryland Heights, take a nearly impregnable position, and wait for relief.
• They could retreat eastward on the road north of the Potomac and join McClellan (after the tenth, there were no Confederate infantry between them and McClellan in this direction).
• They could retreat eastward south of the Potomac on the reverse of Walker's approach. In this case, the thirteen to four teen thousand of the garrisons would have met Walker's three thousand.
• They could have retreated westward, in which case, Miles might have met Jackson's twelve thousand.
• They could have improved their defenses at Harpers Ferry with axe and spade in preparation for an attack.

The garrisons did none of the above, other than to unite at Harpers Ferry.

Special Order 191 was an unusually sensitive document. It fully revealed the Confederate plan with all its vulnerabilities.

General Walker stated,

On receiving my copy of the order I was so impressed with the disastrous consequences which might result from its loss that I pinned it securely in an inside pocket. In speaking with General Longstreet afterward, he remarked that the same thought occurred to him, and that as an absolutely sure precaution, he memorized it and then chewed it up.[4]

Jackson was unusually secretive and cautious by nature. When he read his copy, he noticed that D. H. Hill, who was one of his subordinates, was tasked. The document itself did not indicate who had copies. Jackson, fearing that Hill did not, recopied the document in his own hand and sent the copy to Hill. Thus, the following copies existed:

Drafter	*Recipient*
Col. Robert H. Chilton (Lee's chief of staff)	Longstreet
	Jackson
	McLaws
	Walker
	D. H. Hill
	Stuart
	File
Jackson	D. H. Hill

Chapter 6

Wednesday, September 10

Wednesday, September 10, was D day for the commencement of the implementation of Special Order 191. All of the participating units were in the Frederick area except for Walker's division. Walker had been told to proceed back to the junction of the Potomac and Monocacy Rivers on the ninth and to destroy the aqueduct carrying the C & O canal over the Monocacy and, while there on the tenth, he would receive his assignment for Special Order 191.

The C & O canal was a vital freight artery for the Union. It ran along the north bank of the Potomac its entire length. However, the Monocacy River entered the Potomac from the north, southeast of Frederick, and when the construction of the canal reached the Monocacy, it was necessary to construct an aqueduct to carry the canal over the river. The aqueduct was a major engineering undertaking, and its destruction would put the canal out of operation for the Union indefinitely.

Walker's assignment was a dangerous one. Unlike the other Confederate forces, which would be marching west, away from McClellan's slowly advancing army, he would be marching toward it. Specifically, he would be marching toward Franklin's wing, which was advancing along the north bank of the Potomac, and Pleasonton's cavalry, which was operating in front of Franklin.

When Walker arrived at the aqueduct after dark on the ninth, he found it already occupied by enemy cavalry. He engaged in a shoot-out and drove them off with the loss of one of his men, severely wounded. He then undertook to destroy the aqueduct, but found it far sturdier than he had anticipated and finally decided that, with the tools on hand, he could not succeed. He then moved his division two miles upriver, away from the advancing Union forces, and toward dawn went into camp to rest his men.

During the early hours of the tenth, a courier arrived from

Lee with Walker's assignment for Special Order 191. Walker was to cross the Potomac into Virginia at Cheek's Ford, proceed to Harpers Ferry, and occupy Loudoun Heights by the twelfth if practicable.

Cheek's Ford was immediately adjacent to the aqueduct that Walker had just vacated during the night. He sent a reconnaissance party back downriver to the aqueduct and ford, and found that both of them had been strongly occupied by the Union in the short time since he had left. He then moved his division five miles farther upriver, away from the advancing Union forces, to Point of Rocks. Although Point of Rocks was not normally considered a ford, he found that the river was sufficiently low to permit his crossing, and he crossed his division over into Virginia during the night of September 10-11. (See map 12 for Walker's movements.)

The pickets that Walker encountered at the aqueduct on the night of the ninth reported the incident to headquarters, but they overestimated the number of Confederates by a factor of two and erroneously reported that the Confederates had crossed into Virginia while, in fact, they had not at that time.

On the morning of the tenth, the Union cavalry detected Walker's force still camped on the Maryland side of the river and reported it, again greatly overestimating the number of men. Inasmuch as Walker's force had already been erroneously reported as crossing into Virginia, this was presumed to be another force. The Washington defense forces, probably including Halleck, were now convinced that a large number of Confederates were crossing back into Virginia for an attack on Washington from the south. This was Halleck's consistent, preconceived notion of what would happen, and the Washington defense forces were put on the alert for the approach of a Confederate force down the south side of the Potomac.

In fact, the only Confederates that had crossed the Potomac from Maryland to Virginia consisted of Walker's small division of three thousand, and these were headed upriver to Harpers Ferry, not downriver to Washington.

Back at Frederick, Jackson, with his three divisions, set out on the Frederick-Hagerstown National Road first on the morning of the tenth as he had the greatest distance to travel. His first task was either to capture General White's Martinsburg garrison directly or to drive it into the bag at Harpers Ferry where the lot

Map 12
Walker's Route of September 9-10

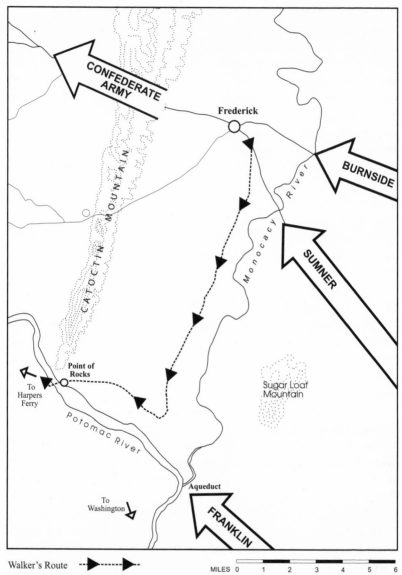

would be captured. As usual, the taciturn Jackson kept his plans
secret, even from members of his staff. In addition, he created
false leads that he anticipated would reach the enemy. The day
previous, he sent for maps of the road to the north leading to
Chambersburg, Pennsylvania. He also made various inquiries as
to the condition of the roads in that direction. Jackson sent a

cavalry detachment to proceed him on the National Road and to prevent anyone from passing through in his direction of march. Consequently, as his column arrived in each town, there was no prior warning of its approach.

As the column passed through Middletown, Jackson personally received evidence that they were not in friendly territory. Two pretty girls with red, white, and blue ribbons in their hair and carrying American flags, ran up to him with gales of laughter and defiantly waved the flags in his face. Jackson tipped his hat to the girls, and smiling to his accompanying staff, said, "We evidently have no friends in this town."[1]

Jackson passed through Turner's Gap into the Cumberland Valley and camped just east of Boonsboro, having covered fifteen miles since leaving Frederick.

Jackson had a reason for terminating his march before Boonsboro. Just ahead, two roads radiated off the National Road to the left. The first went to the nearer ford on the Potomac, Boteler's Ford at Shepherdstown; the second led to the more distant Light's Ford at Williamsport. If General White had already vacated Martinsburg and proceeded to Harpers Ferry, Jackson could take the nearer road. But if General White was still at Martinsburg, Jackson would have to take the more distant road (see map 11). Jackson intended to find out before he resumed his march on the morrow.

Colonel Henry Kyd Douglas of Jackson's staff, accompanied by a cavalryman, rode into Boonsboro to make some inquiries. In the meantime, General White, back at Martinsburg, had heard rumors of some Confederates in the vicinity of Boonsboro and ordered Lieutenant Colonel Downey to investigate. Downey was commander of the Third Maryland Regiment of the Potomac Home Brigade, based at Kearneysville. Kearneysville was on the B & O Railroad, about halfway between White's force at Martinsburg and Miles's at Harpers Ferry, and had telegraphic communications with both. Downey took twenty horsemen and headed for Boonsboro. At Boonsboro, he encountered a small group of Confederate cavalrymen and, while pursuing them, encountered Colonel Douglas and his cavalryman escort. For what happened next, we will turn to Colonel Douglas's own words:

> We ran into a squadron of cavalry that proceeded to make war on us. We retraced our steps and although we did not stand upon the order of our going, a squad of them escorted us out of town

Colonel Henry Kyd Douglas CSA
A Member of "Stonewall" Jackson's Staff

with great rapidity. When I tried a couple of Parthian shots at
them with my revolver, they returned them with interest, and shot
a hole in my new hat, which with the beautiful plume that a lady
in Frederick had placed there, rolled in the dust. This was of little moment, but at the end of the town, reaching the top of the
hill, we discovered, just over it, General Jackson, walking slowly
toward us, leading his horse. There was but one thing to do.
Fortunately, the chase had become less vigorous, and with a cry

of command to unseen troops, we turned and charged the enemy. They, suspecting trouble, turned and fled, while the general quickly galloped to the rear. I recovered my hat and plume, and as I returned to camp, I picked up the gloves which the general had dropped in mounting and took them to him . . . The only allusion he made to the incident was to express the opinion that I had a very fast horse.[2]

Lieutenant Colonel Downey didn't know it, of course, but he had come within an ace of capturing or killing General Jackson. Downey got back to Kearneysville toward evening and telegraphed both Colonel Miles and General White about the encounter and of the presence of Confederate troops in Boonsboro.

In addition to sending Lieutenant Colonel Downey to Boonsboro, General White also sent, independently, a favorite civilian scout of his, Thomas Noakes, to find out what was going on. Noakes returned after Downey and advised White that not less than fifteen thousand Confederates were passing through Boonsboro with a probable destination of Hagerstown.

During the night, Jackson learned that General White had not evacuated Martinsburg. This meant that in the morning Jackson would have to take the Williamsport road. His total march to Harpers Ferry would have to be via Martinsburg. The distance to be covered was sixty miles. He could not arrive at Harpers Ferry before the thirteenth.

The third and final group of the encircling force to hit the National Road was McLaws's force, consisting of his own division and Anderson's, in all about eight thousand men. McLaws followed the National Road to Middletown and then turned left to Burkittsville. At Burkittsville, he could pass through South Mountain into Pleasant Valley either via Crampton's Gap or Brownsville Gap, one mile to the south. He chose Brownsville Gap (see map 11).

McLaws had covered fourteen miles during the day and was now within three miles of the vital Solomon's Gap, gateway to Maryland Heights, and within ten miles of Harpers Ferry itself.

Stuart's cavalry effectively screened the movements of the Confederates on the tenth. The only points where Union forces observed and reported Confederate infantry movements this date were in the vicinity of the aqueduct, where Pleasonton's cavalry observed and reported Walker's movements, and at Boonsboro, where Lieutenant Colonel Downey and the civilian Noakes observed and reported Jackson's movements.

The cost to Jackson's, McLaws's, and Walker's forces on the tenth was modest. It consisted of one man of Walker's force wounded and one man of Jackson's force suffering a holed hat.

Now that all the encircling Confederate forces were on the National Road, the remaining Confederates took to the road. First came Longstreet's two divisions, then the wagon train, and finally, D. H. Hill with his division as rear guard.

Special Order 191 called for Longstreet, the wagon train, and Hill to stop at Boonsboro where they would wait for the reuniting of the army. However, about this time, Lee heard that large numbers of Pennsylvania militia were gathering at Hagerstown and, consequently, ordered Longstreet and his two divisions to continue to Hagerstown. This vital change did not appear in any of the draft copies of Special Order 191 and was to have important ramifications.

As the Confederates at Frederick withdrew through the mountains to the west, and as Walker's minidivision moved to its crossing of the Potomac at Point of Rocks, the only Confederates between McClellan's army and the mountains consisted of Stuart's cavalry screen: Munford to the south, Hampton in the middle, and Fitz Lee to the north. McClellan, of course, did not know this and continued his snail's pace advance to the west at the rate of about six miles per day.

At 10:15 a.m., Lincoln sent McClellan a message that simply said, "How does it look now?"[3] McClellan responded with a long message at noon that, among other things, said,

> General Pleasonton, at Barnesville reports that movement of the enemy last night is said to have been made across the Potomac from this side to the other side . . .
>
> He [Pleasonton] has sent out this morning to occupy Sugar Loaf Mountain, from which a large extent of the country can be seen in all directions . . .
>
> The statements I get regarding the enemy's forces that have crossed to this side range from 80,000 to 150,000 . . .
>
> I was informed last night by General Pleasonton that his information rendered it probable that Jackson's force had advanced to New Market.[4]

Note that every statement McClellan made was carefully qualified to give *him* credit if it was right but blame someone else if it was wrong. The information that McClellan provided to the president ranged from the horse's mouth aft—mostly aft. The Confederates that were reported to have crossed into Virginia during the night (Walker's force) were actually still on the Maryland side. The enemy force in Maryland was actually little more than 40,000, rather than from 80,000 to 150,000, and Jackson had not marched eastward from Frederick to New Market but was, in fact, marching westward from Frederick toward Boonsboro.

Reports did come in to McClellan during the day relating to the westward movement of the Confederates. The first good report was from Gov. Andrew G. Curtin of Pennsylvania to General Halleck and read as follows:

Harrisburg, Pa
September 10, 1862—3:30 P.M.

Major General Halleck
General-in-Chief

A paroled Union man just arrived at Hagerstown from Frederick, fully credited by operator. He reports he passed General Jackson, with a large force, on the National Road, between Middletown and Boonsboro, at 9 this morning. General Jackson commanded in person. Body-guard of cavalry in front, followed by infantry, and cavalry in rear . . . The sheriff of Hagerstown, a reliable Union man, has informed the operator that he met rebel scout, a personal friend, to-day, who advised him to leave Hagerstown immediately.[5]

The information in this message came from Governor Curtin's intrepid telegrapher in Hagerstown. The information on Jackson's force was exactly right, but, unfortunately, the additional information about the sheriff being warned to leave Hagerstown erroneously implied that Jackson was heading for Hagerstown.

Late on the tenth, McClellan received two messages from General White at Martinsburg, the first reporting Lieutenant Colonel Downey's encounter at Boonsboro, and the second reporting his scout, Noakes, reconnoitering at Boonsboro. The first message, released at 9 p.m., read,

> Lieutenant-Colonel Downey, commanding at Kearneysville, reports that he, with an escort of 20 men, encountered the enemy at Boonsboro, advancing to-day. He does not say whether in this direction or toward Hagerstown; probably cannot tell. The enemy in considerable force. Colonel Downey and Captain Shamburg, commanding the escort, charged upon the enemy, who retreated in confusion, till they ascertained how small a force attacked them, and then turned upon our men, who were obliged, of course, to recede. Colonel Downey was wounded, though not severely.[6]

White's second message was released at 11 p.m. and read as follows:

> A reliable spy (who I have had in Maryland for two days past) has just arrived, and reports the forces of the enemy passing through Boonsboro, northwestward, to-day, at not less than 15,000 of all arms—at least twelve regiments of infantry. Probable destination Hagerstown.[7]

Back at Martinsburg and Harpers Ferry, General White and Colonel Miles were becoming increasingly uneasy. First, the Confederate army had passed to their east, cutting them off from McClellan. Now, there were reports that large Confederate forces were to their north, heading west, thus cutting them off from the north. There was no succor to the south, as that was all Confederate territory. General White was convinced that even if McClellan defeated the Confederate forces to their north and east, the garrisons were doomed to be swept up in the Confederate retreat.

As of the tenth, the route west was still open to the garrisons but was about to be closed by fiat. Although it was no longer possible take a train from Harpers Ferry to the east, the railroad west to Martinsburg and points beyond was still open. On the afternoon of the tenth, Gov. Francis Harrison Pierpont, the Union governor of the liberated parts of Virginia, sent a message to Halleck and Wool, requesting that the garrisons of Martinsburg and Harpers Ferry be immediately sent to western Maryland, as the situation there urgently required their help. Wool answered (undoubtedly after consulting with Halleck) that "under the present uncertain state of affairs he did not feel justified in removing either garrison at this time."[8] In a day or two, this would be academic as Jackson was already en route to block escape to the west.

The Harpers Ferry garrison maintained an observation tower on top of Maryland Heights that was locally referred to as the "lookout." From the lookout, it was possible to see up Pleasant Valley as far as Crampton's Gap and Solomon's Gap. During the day of the tenth, members of Miles's staff made several trips to the lookout and peered anxiously up Pleasant Valley, but could see nothing. They still did not know of the approach of McLaws, who was close—very close. He was to debouch into Pleasant Valley via Brownsville Gap on the morn.

Late on the tenth, reports of Lieutenant Colonel Downey's exploits at Boonsboro earlier in the day began to filter into Harpers Ferry. Here is the version that was recorded by Miles's aide, Lt. Henry M. Binney:

> Colonel Downey, Third Maryland, scouts with a squad of Capt. Shanburg's cavalry into Maryland; meets the enemy near Boonsboro Maryland, 1500 strong. Downey has but 19 cavalry, and boldly dashes into the enemy who are composed of infantry, artillery and cavalry. So suddenly does he come upon them that they are thrown into utter confusion, but soon rally on ascertaining Downey's small party, and charge on him with their cavalry. Col Downey's horse is killed and himself wounded in the head; thinks he killed 9 or 10 of the enemy, and he lost himself but one killed and 3 wounded.[9]

So in a couple of hours, Downey's feat had grown from shooting a hole in a man's hat to attacking fifteen hundred infantry and cavalry equipped with artillery. Had the Union let it go a couple of more hours, they might have had the Confederates suing for peace.

To summarize the situation at the close of September 10, as of noon, McClellan still believed that not only were the Confederates congregating at Frederick, but that they were moving east. Now he had these disturbing reports that they were actually moving west. Most thought that they were heading for Hagerstown, which was on the main north-south road in the valley. To the north, the road went up into Pennsylvania to

Map 13
Situation at the End of September 10

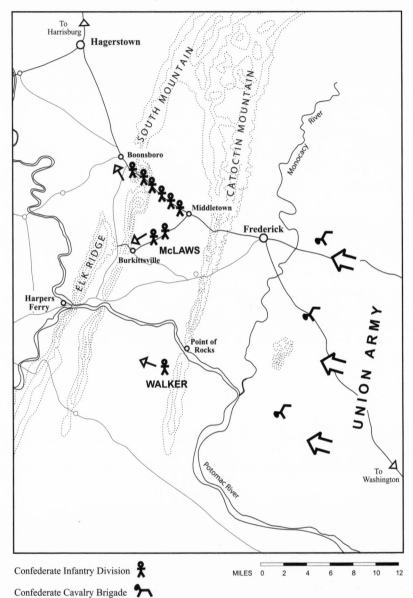

Confederate Infantry Division
Confederate Cavalry Brigade

MILES 0 2 4 6 8 10 12

Harrisburg. To the south, it went down the Shenandoah Valley to Martinsburg, Winchester, and Staunton. Most thought Lee would turn north and head for Pennsylvania. In fact, this was his original plan before he decided to divide his army and surround and capture Harpers Ferry and Martinsburg in his rear. Nobody in the Union camp put two and two together as of the end of September 10 and realized that the ultimate objective of the Confederate moves in progress was Harpers Ferry. As of the end of the tenth, Union headquarters was still not aware of McLaws's force moving on Harpers Ferry from the north.

Then there was the puzzling news of the Confederate force at the aqueduct crossing back into Virginia from Maryland. This movement fit in only with Halleck's assessment of the situation. Halleck, in his heart of hearts, probably believed that McClellan was an incompetent who was being duped by the Confederates. He was obsessed with the idea that the Confederates were purposely luring McClellan to the west, away from Washington, with the intention of giving him the slip, crossing back over the Potomac into Virginia, making a forced march eastward down the south bank of the Potomac, and seizing Washington from the south. Consequently, Halleck, supported by Lincoln, always tried to keep all the troops he could get his hands on in the defense of Washington.

The situation at the close of September 10 is as indicated in map 13.

Chapter 7

Thursday, September 11

In retrospect, it is probable that this was the day on which decisions were made that saved Lee's army. When McClellan left Washington for Rockville on September 7 to take command of his new field army, the situation was still chaotic. No one knew or understood the Confederates' intentions, and it appeared that Washington was still in imminent danger. Consequently, McClellan left three of his corps behind (those of Heintzelman, Porter, and Sigel) to bolster the garrison of Washington.

Since that time, the situation had been clarifying in his mind, and by September 11 his thinking had crystallized. He reasoned that if the whole of the Confederate army was in front of him, Washington could not be in danger behind him unless he was defeated. Consequently, it was imperative that the strength of his field army be maximized.

At 9:45 a.m., McClellan sent the following message to Halleck:

> Colonel Miles is at or near Harpers Ferry, as I understand with 9,000 troops. He can do nothing where he is, but could be of great service if ordered to join me. I suggest that he be ordered to join me by the most practicable route.[1]

Halleck answered as follows:

> There is no way for Colonel Miles to join you at present. His only chance is to defend his works till you can open communications with him. When you do he will be subject to your orders.[2]

Was Halleck right? Probably not. As we now know, all the Confederate infantry had vacated Frederick by the eleventh and was moving westward or southward behind the mountains. The only Confederate infantry force east of the mountains was Walker's, and by that time it was across the Potomac in Virginia. The road north of the Potomac to the east was open except for a thin cavalry screen. Miles's troops almost surely could have joined Franklin's, who were then only twelve air miles away (see map 14).

Miles then, too, could still have taken the reverse of Walker's route south of the Potomac. In this case, Miles's ten thousand would have encountered Walker's three thousand with unknown results.

At 3:45 p.m., McClellan sent a bombshell to Halleck. He requested that the corps of Porter, Heintzelman, and Sigel join him as soon as possible. In the aggregate, these totaled 46,800 and would leave 26,500 garrison troops to defend Washington. McClellan followed his requests for the corps with a couriered letter of justification. It read as follows:

> At the time that this army moved from Washington, it was not known what the intentions of the rebels were in placing their forces on this side of the Potomac. It might have been a feint to draw away our troops from Washington, for the purpose of throwing their main army into the city as soon as we were out of the way, or it might have been supposed to be precisely what they are now doing. In view of this uncertain condition of things, I left what I conceived to be a sufficient force to defend the city against any army they could bring against it from the Virginia side of the Potomac. This uncertainty, in my judgment exists no longer. All the evidence that has been accumulated from various sources since we left Washington goes to prove conclusively that almost the entire rebel army in Virginia, amounting to not less than 120,000 men, is in the vicinity of Frederick City. These troops, for the most part, consist of their oldest regiments, and are commanded by their best generals. Several brigades joined them yesterday, direct from Richmond, two deserters from which say that they saw no other troops between Richmond and Leesburg. Everything seems to indicate that they intend to hazard all upon the issue of the coming battle. They are probably aware that their forces are numerically superior to ours by at least 25 percent. This with the prestige of their recent successes, will, without doubt, inspire them with a confidence which will cause them to fight well. The momentous consequences involved in the struggle of the next few days impels me, at the risk of being considered slow and overcautious, to most earnestly recommend that every available man be at once added to this army.

I believe this army fully appreciates the importance of a victory at this time, and will fight well; but the result of a general battle, with such odds as the enemy appears to have against us, might, to say the least, be doubtful; and if we should be defeated the consequences to the country would be disastrous in the extreme. Under these circumstances, I would recommend that one or two of the three army corps now on the Potomac, oppo-site Washington, be at once withdrawn and sent to re-inforce this army. I would also advise that the force of Col. Miles, at Harpers Ferry, where it can be of but little use, and is continually exposed to be cut off by the enemy, be immediately ordered here. This would add about 25,000 old troops to our present force, and would greatly strengthen us.

If there are any rebel forces remaining on the other side of the Potomac, they must be so few that the troops left in the forts, after the two corps shall have been withdrawn, will be sufficient to check them; or, with the large cavalry force now on that side kept well out in front to give warning of the distant approach of any very large army, a part of this army might be sent back within the intrench-ments to assist in repelling an attack. But even if Washington should be taken while their armies are confronting each other, this would not, in my judgment, bear comparison with the ruin and disaster which would follow a signal defeat of this army. If we should be suc-cessful in conquering the gigantic rebel army before us, we would have no difficulty in recovering it. On the other hand, should their force prove sufficiently powerful to defeat us, would all the forces now around Washington be sufficient to prevent such a victorious army from carrying the works on this side of the Potomac, after they are uncovered by our army? I think not.

From the moment the rebels commenced the policy of concen-trating their forces, and with their large masses of troops operating against our scattered forces, they have been successful. They are undoubtedly pursuing the same now, and are prepared to take advantage of any division of our troops in future. I therefore, most respectfully, but strenuously, urge upon you the absolute necessity, at this critical juncture, of uniting all our disposable forces. Every other consideration should yield to this, and if we defeat the army now arranged before us, the rebellion is crushed, for I do not believe they can organize another army. But if we should be so unfortunate to meet with defeat, our country is at their mercy.[3]

Lincoln himself responded to McClellan. He stated that

Porter's corps would be sent immediately and then made a vague promise that others would follow when and if they could be spared. In the event, no others followed, and two corps remained behind and contributed nothing to the unfolding events. Had all three corps been sent to McClellan, there is a strong possibility that it all would have worked out differently.

Jackson crossed the Potomac at Light's Ford at Williamsport during the day of the eleventh. He had General Hill continue straight down the turnpike (US 11) toward Martinsburg, while the other two divisions swung around to the west to cut off escape in that direction. Jackson's troops bivouacked outside Martinsburg for the night. By then, the road and railroad to the west were blocked, and all telegraphic communications with the outside world were cut. However, telegraphic communications between Martinsburg and Harpers Ferry, seventeen miles to the east, were still open, and the railroad was still in operation between these points.

General White was aware of the approach of Jackson and had authority of sorts to evacuate if he considered it necessary. General Wool sent White the following instructions on September 6:

> Defend yourself to the last extremity. No running before the enemy is coming. Reconnoiter.[4]

However, on the seventh, White was attacked by a large cavalry force and requested guidance from Wool. Wool responded as follows on September 8:

> If 20,000 men should attack you, you will of course, fall back. Harpers Ferry would be the best position I could recommend, but be sure you have such a force against you, or any other that would overwhelm you. Any surplus property will be ready for instant removal should you find it absolutely necessary to abandon Martinsburg. No property will be destroyed if by any means it can be saved.[5]

General White believed that this message gave him the discretion to evacuate if he considered it necessary. The force confronting White was not exactly twenty thousand men. In fact, it was little more than half that number. White, however, thought it was twenty thousand, and, in any event, Wool's instructions did include the words "or any other [force] that would overwhelm you."

During the day, White managed to send off the Confederate prisoners he was holding to the west via rail before the railroad was closed off in that direction. We now turn to General White's own words for his actions on the eleventh:

On the 11th instant reports reached me, through scouts and others, that the enemy were crossing the Potomac into Virginia at or about Williamsport and Cherry Run in force; also that they were passing to the west of Martinsburg, between it and North Mountain, thus cutting off our retreat in that direction.

It being ordered by Major General Wool that the place should be held to the last extremity, at noon on the 11th instant I sent out one section of Captain Phillip's battery and four companies of the Sixty-fifth Illinois, together with half a company of cavalry and two teams, with axes etc., the whole under command of Col. Cameron, of the Sixty-fifth Illinois, with orders to proceed out upon the Williamsport road [US 11], as far as practicable, and to obstruct the roads, tear up the bridges, and in every way possible, retard the advance of the enemy.

At night-fall, it having been well ascertained that the enemy were between us and North Mountain, and were in very large force near Falling Waters, on the Williamsport road, some 7 miles from Martinsburg, and were still crossing, it became evident that with the small force at my disposal the position could not longer be held.

Colonel Cameron's party was accordingly recalled, and every exertion made to convey the public property to Harpers Ferry, that being the only line of retreat left open.

The railroad agent had, the previous day, sent off some 11 empty cars, in defiance of my orders for them to be retained, but I had detained the train up from Harpers Ferry that day, consisting of but 6 cars, and I caused all the surplus arms, clothing, ammunition, and camp equipage to be conveyed to the railroad depot, to be sent thence by rail to Harpers Ferry, as but one of the regiments of my command was provided with transportation (being divided as equally as possible between the several regiments) being wholly insufficient for the purpose.

The railroad train was loaded to the extent of its capacity and sent to Harpers Ferry, where it arrived safely. The transportation was then employed to have the most valuable property remaining, and the troops and wagons took up their line of march at 2 o'clock on the morning of the 12th.

But little public property was abandoned, consisting mostly of tents and camp equipage, which could not be conveyed with the means at disposal.[6]

Meanwhile, back at Harpers Ferry, members of Miles's staff returned to the lookout early in the morning and, peering north up Pleasant Valley, saw what they had hoped they would not see. Long columns of Confederate troops were pouring through Brownsville Gap into Pleasant Valley. McLaws's force had at last been sighted.

Miles knew that he was in trouble and telegraphed Halleck. This was not only to be the last message to get through, but it was to be the last message of Miles's life. It read as follows:

> My eastern front is threatened. The ball will open tomorrow morning. Force opposing me is estimated at ten regiments of infantry with proportionate artillery, before dusk; others have come into camp since. General White will abandon Martinsburg some time tonight, and I expect this will be the last you will hear from me until this affair is over. All are cheerful and hopeful.
>
> Goodbye.[7]

Things looked bad for Miles, but they were to get worse. By this time he knew of a Confederate force (Jackson's) following White's retreat from the west. He also knew of McLaws's force to the north. He still did not know of the approach of Walker's force from the south side of the Potomac. Throughout the day, Miles's pickets engaged in desultory exchanges with McLaws's advancing troops. There was no major engagement on the eleventh.

Walker, having crossed the Potomac during the night of September 10-11 at Point of Rocks, went into camp on the Virginia side and rested his men during the day of the eleventh. He did not resume his march until daylight on the twelfth.

Longstreet's two divisions arrived in Hagerstown during the day, and the wagon train, followed by the rear guard under D. H. Hill, arrived in Boonsboro. Stuart's cavalry continued to fall back and, by the end of the day, the Union occupied Sugar Loaf

Mountain approximating the line of the Monocacy. Union troops were then within five miles of Frederick.

For the next twenty-four hours, reports on the rebels' movements flowed into McClellan's headquarters. Following are excerpts:

Sent: 11 a.m.
Received: ?
Operator at state line reports body of rebel cavalry entered Hagerstown at 9 o'clock this morning . . . It is believed that Jackson will move down Cumberland Valley with at least part of his column and may attack White at Martinsburg with balance.[8]

Sent: Noon
Received: ?
Person of utmost confidence says rebels broke encampment in Frederick yesterday at 1:30 A.M. and moved in direction of Hagerstown. Jackson leading.[9]

Sent: 1:50 p.m.
Received: ?
Report that Jackson and Lee encamped at Boonsboro last night with 40-60000 men and that enemy is leaving Frederick.[10]

Sent: 3:30 p.m.
Received: 6:30 p.m.
At 9 o'clock this morning the rebel cavalry occupied Hagerstown . . . gentleman who saw Jackson and was in his camp on Monday between Boonsborough [sic] and Middletown . . . had about 15000 troops convened with him—men who expected to enter Pennsylvania.[11]

Sent: ?
Received: 8:00 p.m.
Have advices that enemy broke up whole encampment at Frederick yesterday morning at 3 o'clock and marched in direction of Hagerstown . . . Jackson is now in Hagerstown . . . men all believed they were going to Pennsylvania . . .[12]

Sent: ?
Received: 8:30 p.m.

Info believed entirely reliable, that whole of rebel army has been moved from Frederick, and their destination is Harrisburg and Philadelphia.[13]

Sent: 8:00 p.m.
Received: Sept 12, 1:55 a.m.
Irishman named Kingsly reports that as of 11 A.M. Frederick evacuated except for pickets. Took Hagerstown road and consisted of divisions of Jackson and Longstreet.[14]

Sent: 10:30 a.m.
Received: ?
John Doll, proprietor of Eutah House reports main force of enemy left Frederick yesterday for Harrisburg.[15]

By the end of the eleventh, it was fairly clear at Union headquarters that most, if not all, of the Confederates had vacated Frederick and moved west. It was also fairly clear that the Confederates had occupied Hagerstown. Communications with both Harpers Ferry and Martinsburg had been cut. Miles's message told them that Harpers Ferry was being approached by Confederate troops from the north, and that General White intended to evacuate Martinsburg for Harpers Ferry that night.

Unknown to McClellan, the Confederate moves had opened a temporary escape route for the Harpers Ferry garrison to the east, but this was to close in twenty-four hours.

There were no reports on the movements or intentions of the Confederate force (Walker's) that had been reported crossing from Maryland back into Virginia on the tenth.

The general belief at Union headquarters was still that Lee intended to move north from Hagerstown into Pennsylvania. Although bit by bit the Confederate moves to encircle and capture the garrisons at Martinsburg and Harpers Ferry were coming into focus, Lee's plan and intentions were still not understood at Union headquarters.

From the Confederate point of view, their plan seemed to be falling behind schedule. It appeared increasingly unlikely that Harpers Ferry would fall on the twelfth as planned. For this to happen, Miles would either have to flee or surrender at the approach of McLaws's force, and McLaws's force was numerically inferior to his own. As of the end of the eleventh, McLaws had

Map 14
Situation at the End of September 11

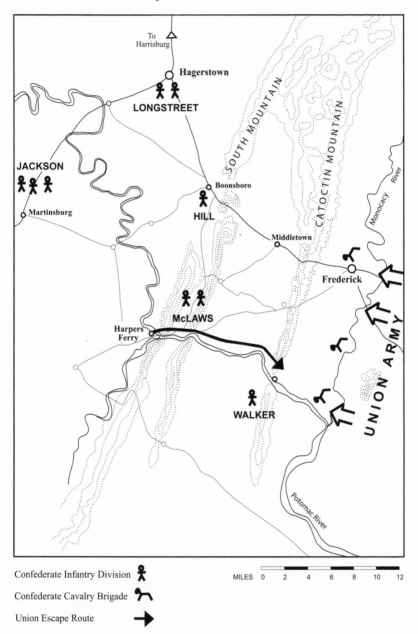

Confederate Infantry Division

Confederate Cavalry Brigade

Union Escape Route

MILES 0 2 4 6 8 10 12

not even reached Miles's main line of defense, and it was becoming increasingly evident that neither Jackson nor Walker would be in the vicinity of Harpers Ferry before the thirteenth.

The situation at the end of September 11 is as indicated in map 14.

Chapter 8

Friday, September 12

Walker, who was camped on the Virginia side of the Potomac near Point of Rocks, resumed his march on the morning of the twelfth. He covered only thirteen miles and then went into bivouac at Hillsboro (see map 15). Most of the march to Hillsboro was to the south, and his intentions could be ambiguously interpreted by an observer. However, once at Hillsboro, he was on the main east-west highway and turned west. From there, it was obvious that he could only be going to one of two places. One was Charlestown, five miles southwest of Harpers Ferry. The other was Loudoun Heights. The base of Loudoun Heights was just nine miles from Hillsboro. For a man whose orders required him to be in Loudoun Heights Friday morning if practicable, Walker did not seem to be in any hurry. He had covered just nineteen miles since leaving the aqueduct the night of Tuesday-Wednesday, September 9-10, when he went into camp at Hillsboro the night of Friday, September 12. He was already behind schedule.

The Federals had heard nothing of Walker since he was reported crossing the Potomac from north to south. Halleck still feared that he might be moving in the direction of Washington and had Heintzelman out looking for him.

On the early morning of Friday, September 12, Jackson entered Martinsburg, just three hours after General White's last men had departed. At Martinsburg, Jackson was definitely back in friendly territory. Less than forty-eight hours after leaving the mean girls of Middletown, Jackson was greeted by an adoring crowd of women. A member of his staff, Col. Henry Kyd Douglas, described the scene:

> Here the general was welcomed with great enthusiasm, and a great crowd hastened to the hotel to greet him. At first he shut himself up in a room to write dispatches, but the demonstration became so persistent that he ordered the door to be opened. The crowd, chiefly ladies, rushed in and embarrassed the general with

Map 15
Walker's Movements on September 12

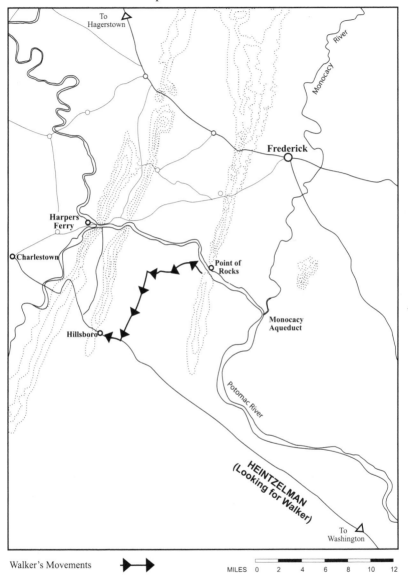

To Hagerstown

Monocacy River

Frederick

Harpers Ferry

Charlestown

Point of Rocks

Monocacy Aqueduct

Hillsboro

Potomac River

HEINTZELMAN
(Looking for Walker)

To Washington

Walker's Movements

MILES   0   2   4   6   8   10   12

every possible outburst of affection, to which he could only reply, "Thank you, you're very kind." He gave them his autographs in books and on scraps of paper, cut a button from his coat for a little girl, and then submitted patiently to an attack by the others, who soon stripped the coat of nearly all the remaining buttons. But when they looked beseechingly at his hair, which was thin, he drew the line there, and managed to close the interview. These blandishments did not delay his movements, however, for in the afternoon he was off again.[1]

Jackson had nineteen more miles to go to reach Harpers Ferry.

In the meantime, McLaws, who was in Pleasant Valley, had been in contact with Union pickets since dawn, and there was intermittent gunfire throughout the day. McLaws directed two of his brigades (those of Kershaw and Barksdale) to ascend Elk Ridge at Solomon's Gap and proceed south to attack Maryland Heights. He ordered one brigade to ascend South Mountain and proceed south to the river. He left two brigades to guard the passes in his rear and, with the remaining force, proceeded down the valley toward the river at Sandy Hook, keeping abreast of the forces on the ridges to his left and right (see map 16).

The going on Elk Ridge was slow. There were no roads. The terrain was far more rugged and the vegetation far thicker than anticipated, and, even without the harassment of the Union pickets, the advance would have progressed at a snail's pace.

Near the end of daylight, the brigades on Elk Ridge finally reached the main Union defense line at Maryland Heights in front of the lookout. Both sides slept on their arms that night, and it was evident that the fate of Maryland Heights would be decided on the morrow, Saturday, September 13.

General White showed up on Colonel Miles's doorstep for the second time, a little after noon on the twelfth. It had been just nine days since Miles got rid of him the first time. Again, being senior in rank to Colonel Miles, White was eligible and entitled to assume command. However, after his earlier experience, it was perfectly clear to White that General Wool preferred Miles in command. This preference for Miles to remain in command was further fortified in White's mind by the message Miles had received from Halleck on September 7 stating that the government had the utmost confidence in Miles and was ready to give him full credit for the defense of Harpers Ferry.

Map 16
McLaws's Brigade Deployments, September 12

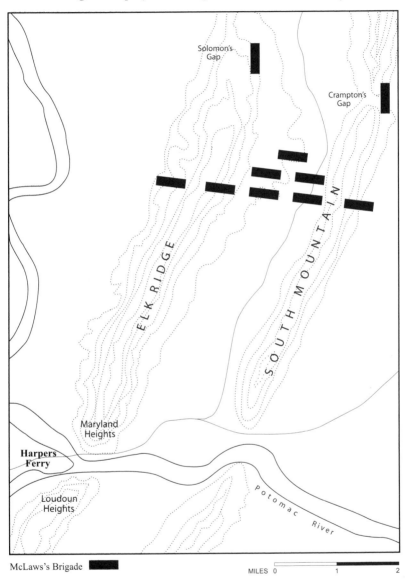

McLaws's Brigade   MILES 0   1   2

Another consideration was that the garrison of Harpers Ferry was already in action on Elk Ridge when White arrived, and White knew nothing of Miles's deployments. It was not unknown for a senior arriving on the scene during an action to temporarily defer to a junior who was already there. In fact, Gen. Joseph Johnston had done just that to Gen. P. G. T. Beauregard at First Bull Run.

White verbally conceded command to Miles and then followed it up the next day with a written concession that read as follows:

> Colonel: I have the honor to state that I arrived at this post last evening with my command consisting of the following named troops: Twelfth Illinois Cavalry; Sixty Fifth Illinois Infantry; One Hundred and Twenty-Fifth New York Infantry; Phillip's battery (four guns), Second Illinois Artillery.
>
> On an occasion prior to this, I was ordered by Maj. Gen. J. E. Wool, commanding, to repair to Martinsburg and take command of that post, thus leaving you in command here, which I consider an indication that the general desires you to retain this command.
>
> Your familiarity with the topography of the vicinity, the fact that the troops and the guns have been placed under your direction, coupled with the additional important fact that the enemy is in heavy force in the immediate vicinity, and skirmishing with their advance already commenced, rend it improper, at least for the present, to deprive you of the command for the sole reason of superior rank, believing that the interests of the service would not be subserved thereby.
>
> Meanwhile, I respectfully tender my services and those of the officers of my staff to render any aid in our power in the defense of the position.[2]

Miles responded by issuing the following order to the garrison:

> Brigadier-General White with a magnanimity equal to his valor, proffers to the undersigned commanding officer of the post, his services and those of the troops brought with him, for its defense in its present necessity. This act of high-toned chivalric generosity, of which there are but few precedents in our army, overwhelms me with the deepest gratitude.
>
> I cheerfully accept the invaluable assistance of the gallant general, and will assign his troops to important positions.
>
> It is hereby ordered that, whenever present during the siege of this post, the troops will obey implicitly and with alacrity all orders given by General White.[3]

Now that the pleasantries were over and it was agreed that

Colonel Dixon Miles USA
Commanding Officer at Harpers Ferry

Miles was in command, Miles proceeded to pooh-pooh White's suggestions. Among other things, White suggested that the entire garrison be moved to Maryland Heights, as this was the most defensible position and was in the direction from which relief could be expected. Miles countered that he was ordered to defend Harpers Ferry, and that Maryland Heights was not Harpers Ferry; and furthermore, he continued, there were no natural sources of water on Maryland Heights. This argument that the lack of natural sources of water on Maryland Heights was an impediment to keeping a large number of troops there had been raised more than once before. Considering that Maryland Heights plunged directly into the Potomac River, and that a road ran from the river to the top, it is surprising that some enterprising individual had not come up with some ingenious solution, such as carrying water from the bottom to the top. In any event, White's suggestions were rejected, and Miles assigned White to take charge of the refused flank on Bolivar Heights.

Friday, September 12, was to be a key day for Confederate cavalry commander Jeb Stuart and his three subordinate brigades. All three brigades were led by first-rate commanders. The northernmost brigade was commanded by twenty-six-year-old Brig. Gen. Fitzhugh Lee. The young Lee was Robert E. Lee's nephew and was to become the second most prominent member of the Lee clan in the war, eclipsing Lee's sons. Fitz's father, Lee's brother, had been a senior naval officer. He was the commanding officer of Commodore Matthew Perry's flagship during Perry's historic visit to Japan in 1853 and was the superintendent of the Naval Academy at Annapolis while Fitzhugh was a cadet at West Point.

Fitzhugh graduated from West Point in 1856 and quickly established a reputation for gallantry and daring in the Indian Wars. Like his uncle, he threw in his lot with the Confederacy, and by September 1862 was considered a seasoned and competent cavalry commander.

Stuart's central brigade was commanded by Brig. Gen. Wade Hampton, the old man of the group. In September 1862, Hampton was forty-four compared to Stuart's twenty-nine, Fitzhugh Lee's twenty-six, and Munford's thirty-one. Hampton, unlike the others, attended no military school and had no military background. He was, however, one of the wealthiest plantation owners in South Carolina, if not the entire South. He was active in South Carolina politics and, at the outbreak of the war, outfitted a military unit at his own expense that was known as Hampton's Legion. Hampton was given the rank of colonel and quickly acquired a reputation of leading from the front. He was personally in the thick of any conflict in which his men were involved. By September 1862, Hampton was highly regarded by friend and foe alike and was second in command to Stuart.

The third brigade commander, the one farthest to the south and anchored on the Potomac, was thirty-one-year-old Col. Thomas Munford. Munford graduated from the Virginia Military Institute in 1852 but was not active in the army before the war. At the outset, he was given a commission of lieutenant colonel and became closely associated with Gen. Stonewall Jackson. He participated in First Bull Run, Jackson's Valley campaign, the Peninsula campaign, and the Second Bull Run campaign. He was a favorite of Jackson and, by September 1862, a seasoned and highly respected commander.

Under Special Order 191, Stuart had been tasked with concealing from the Union the movements of the dividing Confederate army by keeping the Union forces east of Frederick. Now that it was Friday the twelfth, Stuart assumed that Harpers Ferry had fallen as the plan called for and that he was free to retire westward to the passes in Catoctin Mountain.

The intelligence available to Stuart on the Union army was as bad as, or even worse than, the intelligence available to the Union command on the Confederates. This was in part because the Union army was operating in friendly territory, and the Confederate army, in large part, was not. Stuart did not know if the forces facing him consisted merely of a cavalry screen supported by some infantry, with the main army back in Washington, or if the army was directly in back of the cavalry screen. In short, he did not know whether he was confronting a reconnaissance in force or an aggressive move by the entire Union army. Consequently, he wanted to get around the Union flank and to the rear of the Union army to find out.

The southern flank of the Union army rested on the Potomac, so he could not get around on that end. The only possibility was to get around the northern flank, which rested on no natural barrier. This was Fitzhugh Lee's sector, so he was given the assignment while the other two brigades retired toward Catoctin Mountain.

Fitzhugh Lee proceeded ever farther north until reaching Westminster, Maryland, twenty-five miles northeast of Frederick (see map 1), the northernmost point of the Southern invasion. Fitz

Lee never did succeed in turning the Union flank and gaining the rear but merely succeeded in causing panic in northern Maryland and southern Pennsylvania.

By the end of the twelfth, Stuart had conceded all territory east of Catoctin Mountain, including the city of Frederick, to the Union. Hampton occupied the pass in the mountain on the National Road just west of Frederick, and Munford occupied the pass at Jefferson, six miles to the south. Stuart set up his new headquarters at Middletown in the Catoctin Valley. The Confederate force nearest to Stuart was D. H. Hill's division at Boonsboro, guarding the wagon park just six miles from Middletown (see map 17). As of the end of the twelfth, Stuart still did not know whether he was being followed by the main Union army or just a reconnaissance force.

There was much talk in the Union camp on the twelfth about reestablishing communications with Harpers Ferry, but it was mostly just that—talk. Halleck telegraphed to McClellan: "Is it not possible to open communications with Harpers Ferry so that Miles can cooperate with you?"[4] Halleck followed up with a message to Miles. However, inasmuch as the telegraph wires were now cut and he had no way of reaching Miles, he sent it to McClellan for delivery if and when possible. The message was as follows:

> You will obey such orders as General McClellan may give you. You will endeavor to open communications with him and unite your forces to his at the earliest possible moment. His army is near the line of the Monocacy.[5]

Miles never got the message.

McClellan responded to Halleck by acknowledging that he had received the message for Miles and that he had tasked his cavalry with opening communications with Miles. The cavalry never did so.

The signal corps made a more determined effort to open communications with Harpers Ferry on this date. Prior to the Confederate invasion of September, the Union had two visual signal stations that could communicate with the signal station at the lookout on Maryland Heights. These were the station on Sugar Loaf Mountain, which was at extreme range, and the station at Point of Rocks, which was at easy range. By the night of the twelfth, both were in Union hands again and both attempted to reestablish contact with the station on Maryland Heights. They employed red lights and rockets to gain attention, followed by torch signals. However, unknown to the Union signalmen, Lieutenant Fortesque had abandoned his post on Maryland Heights the previous week when he found that he had no one to communicate with. It was probably too late anyway. By the night of the twelfth, the Confederates were already on Elk Ridge, sleeping on their arms, just in front of the Union lines on Maryland Heights. If anyone had waved torches on Maryland Heights that night, he probably would have been shot.

Reports began to come into Union headquarters during the day about Jackson's crossing the Potomac at Williamsport. As usual, they were embellished with misleading information and false conclusions. Many of the reports flowed through Governor Curtin's intrepid telegrapher on the railroad handcar just north of Hagerstown. These reports were often passed from Governor Curtin to President Lincoln, who in turn passed the information to McClellan.

At 5:45 p.m., Lincoln passed the following to McClellan:

> Governor Curtin telegraphs me: "I have advices that Jackson is crossing the Potomac at Williamsport, and probably the whole rebel army will be drawn from Maryland." Receiving nothing from Harpers Ferry or Martinsburg to-day, and positive information from Wheeling that the line is cut, corroborates the idea that the enemy is recrossing the Potomac. Please do not let him get off without being hurt.[6]

At 10:00 p.m., Governor Curtin sent the following message to Lincoln:

> A reliable gentleman came from Hanover to give me the following information:
> "I left the rebel encampment at Liberty Md. last night at 12 o'clock. I spent twenty four hours among their men and officers, from whom I learned the following general programme, after satisfying them that I was a citizen of Maryland and favorable to their cause: They intend to cross about 70,000 men, forming their reserve at Williamsport, and occupy the Virginia shore as a general depot for all supplies they can gather. Part of this reserve to attach and capture Martinsburg and Harpers Ferry. The main

rebel army to occupy Maryland between Williamsport and Hagerstown, from which they will move on the Cumberland Valley and other points in Pennsylvania. Their force in Maryland was about 190,000 men. That they have in Virginia about 250,000 men, all of whom are being concentrated to menace Washington and keep the union armies employed there, while their forces in Maryland devastate and destroy Pennsylvania."

The gentleman who gives me this information is vouched for as reliable and truthful by the best citizens of the place where he lives. I give to you for consideration.[7]

At 4:00 a.m., Lincoln had sent a message to McClellan that read, "How does it look now?"[8] McClellan responded at 9:00 p.m. as follows:

> Headquarters Army of the Potomac,
> Camp near Urbana,
> September 12, 1862 9 P.M.

His Excellency the President

You will have learned by my telegram to General Halleck that we hold Frederick and the line of the Monocacy. I have taken all possible means to communicate with Harpers Ferry, also that I may send to its relief if necessary. Cavalry are in pursuit of the Westminster party, with orders to catch them at all hazards. The main body of my cavalry and horse artillery are ordered after the enemy's main column, with orders to check its march as much as possible, that I may overtake it. If Harpers Ferry is still in our possession, I think I can save the garrison if they fight at all. If the rebels are marching into Pennsylvania I shall soon be up with them. My apprehension is that they may make for Williamsport, and get across the river before I can catch them.

Geo. B. McClellan
Major General[9]

A careful reading of McClellan's message reveals that it conveys the appearance of dynamic action without actually saying anything. If one thing is clear, it is that McClellan did not understand the situation. His statement that "The main body of my cavalry and horse artillery are ordered after the enemy's main column" reveals that he still did not understand that, at this time, there was no enemy main column. The enemy had broken up into four widely separated components in accordance with Special Order 191.

As of the close of September 12, 1862, McClellan occupied Frederick, and Porter's corps had taken the road from Washington to join McClellan in the Frederick area. The Confederate plan to surround and capture Harpers Ferry with its garrison was falling behind schedule. Two of the three surrounding columns, Walker's and Jackson's, were not yet in place, and McLaws's column, which was in contact with the garrison, had not yet opened the battle for Maryland Heights. The garrison of Martinsburg had united with the garrison at Harpers Ferry, bringing the total to more than fourteen thousand. Communications between the garrison and higher authority had been lost, and McClellan had failed to reopen them. The Confederate cavalry had withdrawn to the passes of Catoctin Mountain and still did not realize that the whole Union army was before them. And last, but not least, McClellan still did not understand the situation before him.

At the close of September 12, McClellan was confronted with a new problem. Up to this point, he had been advancing slowly, at the rate of about six miles per day, on a broad front. The Confederates were withdrawing slowly before him, and the only contact he had with them was an occasional clash of cavalry. The country had been open with low, rolling hills, and there had been no physical obstacles other than the easily fordable Monocacy River that he was already across. Now, however, the Confederates had disappeared through a pass in Catoctin Mountain on the National Road, and McClellan was confronted with a mountain barrier across his entire front. To proceed, he had to pass through mountain passes, and these constituted narrow stricture points that could be easily defended. Advance on a broad front was no longer possible.

McClellan was by nature a very cautious man. A favorite phrase of his in his orders to subordinates was "if it can be accomplished without too much risk."

McClellan now wanted to proceed through the pass in Catoctin Mountain on the National Road. His nearest troops were Burnside's two corps. Let us now see the wording of the written order he gave to Burnside:

Headquarters Army of the Potomac
Near Urbana, Sept 12, 1862—11 P.M.

Major General Burnside
    Frederick, Md.

General: The general commanding directs you to ascertain if
the enemy moved from Frederick by way of the National Road. In
case he took that direction, you will move your command at daylight in the morning along the National road cautiously, and
obtain possession, if possible, of the pass by which the National
road passes through the Catoctin range of mountains, so as to
allow General Pleasonton's cavalry to debouch into the Catoctin
Valley beyond. Should you gain this pass, you will hold it for the
purpose specified and report for further orders. Should you find
the pass occupied by so strong a force of the enemy as to render
the taking it by your command a matter of too much risk, you will
report the fact at once to the commanding general at Frederick,
who will foreward [sic] a sufficiency of troops to your assistance.
The general desires you to learn, if possible, the condition of affairs
in the direction of Harpers Ferry and to communicate the same to
him. Governor Curtin telegraphs that he has advices that Jackson
is crossing the Potomac at Williamsport to return into Virginia.
Ascertain if this movement is being made by Jackson, and communicate with these headquarters the result of your investigations.
Communicate the contents of this dispatch to Brigadier-General
Pleasonton, who will cooperate with you as far as may be necessary.
The staff officer who carries this will accompany you to-morrow
and bring back a report of the result of your operations. Two orderlies are sent with him. Please communicate to these headquarters,
by means of these orderlies, such information as you may deem
important. The commanding general desires to impress upon you
that he does not wish you to run too great a risk with your own
command in taking the pass referred to. If the enemy has marched
by the National road the pass must be taken, but the attack upon it
must be made only with a sufficiency of troops.

    I am, general, very respectfully,
    Your obedient servant,
        R.B. Marcy
        Chief of Staff[10]

Map 17
Situation at the End of September 12

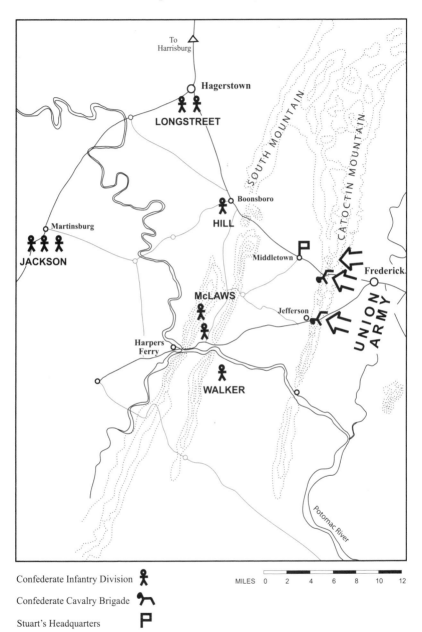

To Harrisburg

Hagerstown

LONGSTREET

SOUTH MOUNTAIN

CATOCTIN MOUNTAIN

Boonsboro

HILL

Martinsburg

JACKSON

Middletown

Frederick

McLAWS

Jefferson

UNION ARMY

Harpers Ferry

WALKER

Potomac River

Confederate Infantry Division

Confederate Cavalry Brigade

Stuart's Headquarters

MILES   0   2   4   6   8   10   12

Note the words "cautiously," "if possible," "of too much risk," "if possible," "he does not wish you to run too great a risk." As we shall see later, this type of order sent to a general such as Franklin, who was at least as cautious as McClellan, was unlikely to achieve the desired objective.

The situation at the close of Friday, September 12, 1862, is as indicated in map 17.

Chapter 9

Saturday, September 13

Walker resumed his march from Hillsboro at daylight on Saturday the thirteenth and reached the foot of Loudoun Heights at about 10 a.m. Here he was joined by a detachment of signalmen and a company of Maryland cavalry. He detached two regiments under the command of Col. J. R. Cooke and directed him to ascend Loudoun Mountain and take possession of the Heights but, in case they found no enemy, not to reveal their presence to the garrison at Harpers Ferry. He also sent the signalmen up with orders to open communications, if possible, with Jackson, whose force was expected to be in the vicinity, approaching from the west. Walker then disposed the remainder of the division between the point of the mountain and the Potomac to block any egress of the garrison.

About 2 p.m., Walker received a report from Colonel Cooke that he had taken possession of Loudoun Heights without opposition, that Jackson was not in sight, but that the activity of the Federals on Bolivar Heights indicated that he was near.

From the time Walker had received his orders under Special Order 191 on the afternoon of Wednesday, September 10, until he set foot on Loudoun Heights on the afternoon of Saturday, September 13, seventy-two hours had elapsed. During this period, he had covered only twenty-seven miles and was only thirteen air miles from his starting point. As of the close of the thirteenth, he still had not succeeded in getting any cannons up to the crest, still had not fired upon the garrison, and still had not contacted either Jackson or McLaws. His only casualties since leaving Frederick on the ninth consisted of the single man wounded at the aqueduct on the night of the ninth. Walker's position on the Heights was noted by the garrison during the afternoon and was subjected to a few ineffective artillery rounds.

The head of Jackson's column began arriving at Halltown, about two miles from Bolivar Heights on the Charlestown road, at about 11 a.m. Jackson gradually extended his lines in front of Bolivar Heights to the Potomac, completing the encirclement of the garrison. He placed J. R. Jones's division on his left abutting the river, then Alexander R. Lawton's division, and lastly, A. P. Hill's on the other side of the Charlestown road. The action between Jackson's force and the garrison on the thirteenth was limited to an artillery exchange that died down at sunset. It produced few, if any, casualties.

Jackson spent the afternoon unsuccessfully attempting to establish visual communications with Walker and McLaws. Near dark, he gave up and sent couriers to both to ascertain their readiness. Even though Maryland Heights was only about two miles from Bolivar Heights, it is probable that Jackson's courier had to cover twenty or more miles to reach McLaws, inasmuch as the Potomac River intervened and he had to ride back to Boteler's Ford to cross. By far, the main action of the day took place on Maryland Heights.

The climactic part of the battle for Maryland Heights took place on Saturday, September 13, 1862. The battle was of crucial importance. Its outcome had a strong impact on all that followed in the Maryland campaign of September 1862, up to and including the battle of Antietam.

The holding of Maryland Heights was critical for two reasons. First, it held a dominating position overhanging Harpers Ferry. Second, and probably even more important, it controlled the most likely junction point for the meeting with a relief force.

The potential relief routes are indicated in map 18. Since McClellan's army was north of the Potomac, the relief would have to come from north of the Potomac. The first possible relief road (indicated by the circled 1 in the map) was via the Boonsboro-Harpers Ferry road that passed through Pleasant Valley. The second (indicated by the circled 2) was to break through Crampton's Gap at Burkittsville in South Mountain into Pleasant Valley and intersect with the same Boonsboro-Harpers Ferry road. Crampton's Gap could be reached either via Jefferson or Middletown. The third (indicated by the circled 3) was to follow the Frederick-Harpers Ferry road around the southern tip of South Mountain. The first and second possibilities were the most likely and, in either event, the junction would be in Pleasant Valley. If Maryland Heights was lost, Miles's entire position north of the Potomac would be lost, and no junction in

Map 18
Relief Routes for Harpers Ferry

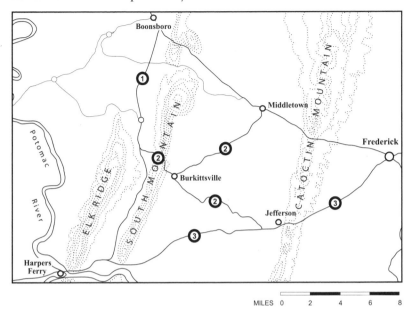

Pleasant Valley would be possible. In this event, the prospects for an early relief would be drastically reduced.

When McLaws entered Pleasant Valley on September 12, he ordered two of his ten brigades to ascend Elk Ridge at Solomon's Gap and seize Maryland Heights. The two assigned were a South Carolina brigade commanded by Brigadier General Kershaw and a Mississippi brigade commanded by Brigadier General Barksdale. Kershaw's brigade contained 1,041 men and Barksdale's contained 960. Thus, at no point did the Confederate force contending for Maryland Heights exceed 2,001 men.

The senior of the two Confederate brigadier generals was forty-year-old Joseph Brevard Kershaw, a native of South Carolina. Kershaw did not attend West Point or, for that matter, any other military school. His profession was the law, and he was in fact another politician in general's uniform. Prior to the Civil War, his only military experience had been a brief stint in the Mexican War when he volunteered and served as a first lieutenant in the Palmetto Regiment. Kershaw served in the South Carolina legislature and was a delegate to the Secession Convention of 1860. At the outset of the war, he was appointed

colonel of the Second South Carolina Infantry, participated in
First Bull Run, was promoted to brigadier general in February
1862, and served throughout the Peninsula campaign with distinction. From the beginning of the war until the time he
showed up on Elk Ridge (and long afterward), he served under
Maj. Gen. Lafayette McLaws.

Brigadier General William Barksdale, like Kershaw, was a
politician in uniform. His only pre-Civil War military experience
had been during the Mexican War when he served as a captain
of the Second Mississippi Volunteers. After the Mexican War,
Barksdale entered the newspaper business and became editor of
the Columbus, Mississippi, *Democrat*. Barksdale, an ardent seces-
sionist, had represented Mississippi as a delegate to the U.S.
House of Representatives until he volunteered his services to the
Confederacy. He was appointed colonel of the Thirteenth
Mississippi, participated in First Bull Run, the Peninsula campaign with distinction, and was promoted to brigadier general
on August 12, 1862, just one month before the battle of
Maryland Heights.

The two Confederate political generals were faced off against
a Union political colonel. The Union brigade commander
entrusted with defending Maryland Heights was forty-seven-year-
old Col. Thomas Ford. Ford, like Kershaw, was a lawyer-politician
and had risen to the position of lieutenant governor of Ohio.
His only prior military experience was during the Mexican War,
where he volunteered, served as a captain, saw action, and was
wounded. It is just possible that he knew Colonel Miles from this
time, which would account for their apparent familiarity. At the
outset of the Civil War, Ford helped organize the Thirty-second
Ohio, and was appointed its colonel. Ford's regiment operated
in the Shenandoah Valley during Jackson's Valley campaign,
from whence he ended up in Winchester with General White,
and then Harpers Ferry. Miles had appointed Ford to his position as brigade commander on Maryland Heights less than a
week before Kershaw and Barksdale showed up.

Ford did, however, have a problem. He had just recently
returned from a medical leave wherein he had an operation.
The nature of his malady is unclear, but if it was not actually
hemorrhoids, it was something akin to it and savaged the same
organ. He was still convalescent, in pain, could barely ride a
horse, and in fact walked kind of funny. In reality, he was not fit

to return to duty, much less to be thrust into the middle of a hot spot as the central figure. There is an old saying that for the lack of a horseshoe nail the battle was lost. Ford's problem was not exactly a horseshoe nail, but in retrospect, his problem just might have been the reason the battle was lost.

When Ford first took command of his brigade on September 5, it consisted of the Thirty-second Ohio Volunteers, three companies of the First Maryland Potomac Home Brigade, squadrons of Maryland and Rhode Island cavalry, and McGrath's battery. Ford estimated the total to be 1,150, and Lieutenant Binney of Colonel Miles's staff estimated it to be 1,500. Whatever the total, on September 12, after Miles learned that Kershaw and Barksdale were advancing on Elk Ridge, he reinforced Ford with the following: six companies of the 39th New York, three companies of the 111th New York, and the entire 126th New York. The total of these reinforcements was 1,800. At a minimum, by the afternoon of September 12, Ford had 2,950 men to contest Kershaw and Barksdale's 2,001.

Of the 1,800 reinforcements sent to Ford on the twelfth, 1,031 were from the 126th New York. Sending the 126th New York proved to be a mistake. It was a completely green, short-term unit that had been mustered in just twenty-one days earlier. None of the members had fired a weapon in battle, and most, if not all, had probably not even fired one in practice. They were being called upon to face Kershaw's and Barksdale's veterans, who had not only been at First Bull Run, but had distinguished themselves in the desperate fighting on the peninsula.

Elk Ridge ran north and south and formed the western boundary of Pleasant Valley. Its crest was heavily wooded and strewn with boulders. The level area on top was barely wide enough to accommodate two regiments deployed in line of battle side by side. Contrary to information to General Kershaw, there was no Union artillery on top and no road. There were only footpaths. The sides of the ridge, particularly the east side facing Pleasant Valley, were steep, and in places there was a nearly vertical stone facing for twenty feet or more near the crest, preventing direct ascent to the top.

The road leading to the top that the Union troops took was carved into the face of the ridge and was just a short walk up the Potomac from the bridge. About halfway up was a plateau on the western slope of the mountain that served as an artillery position and brigade headquarters (see map 19). The artillery there originally consisted of three large-caliber guns called the naval battery. (A "naval gun" is merely a euphemism for a large-caliber gun that is not road mobile and occupies a fixed position.) The naval battery was later augmented by a battery of four brass twelve-pounders commanded by Capt. Eugene McGrath, and the whole complex began to be referred to as McGrath's Battery. The artillery position had been selected for the defense of Harpers Ferry below and not for the defense of Maryland Heights above. In fact, the fighting above could not be observed from the gun position, and the battery contributed little, if anything, to the battle of Maryland Heights. This plateau was relatively safe from the fighting on top, and no casualties were experienced there during the battle.

The man-made defenses on top of Elk Ridge were few and meager (see map 20). At the highest point of Maryland Heights, there was a tower referred to as the lookout. From the lookout, it was possible to see Crampton's Gap and beyond. Had the Union retained Maryland Heights one more day than it did, an observer at the lookout would have been able to see the Federal relief force debouching into Pleasant Valley through Crampton's Gap.

Just north of the lookout, there was a log barricade extending across the width of the ridge. This was not a formidable, shoulder-high, bulletproof breastwork constructed under the direction of engineers. Rather, it was a thrown-together affair put up two days before the battle by a single company that had been there on picket duty with nothing to do. The exact nature of the barricade is not known, but at best it was flimsy and afforded minimal protection. In front of the barricade, facing north, was an abatis, which is nothing more than a group of felled trees with the branches pointing toward the enemy. An abatis cannot stop an enemy advance, but it can slow it down, and it can break up its formation as individuals attempt to climb up, over, under, and around branches, sometimes having to put down their rifles to do so.

About four hundred yards north of the abatis in front of the barricade, there was another abatis that extended fully across the ridge and was flanked on each side by a ledge of precipitous rocks. It was this abatis that Kershaw's force reached just before dark on the twelfth and that separated Kershaw from the Union defenders.

Map 19
Maryland Heights

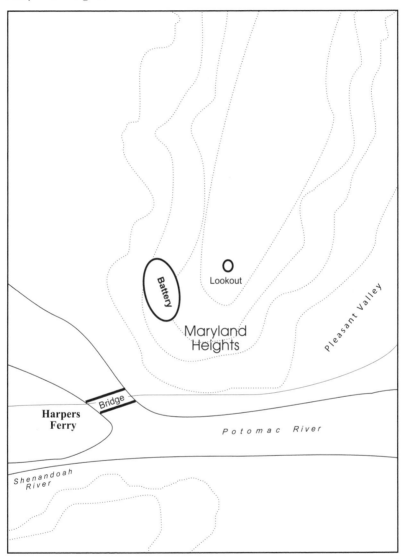

It was evident to all that the deciding battle for Maryland Heights would begin at dawn on the thirteenth. Major Sylvester M. Hewitt of the 32nd Ohio, Colonel Ford's senior officer on the scene, went down to brigade headquarters after dark on the twelfth and reported the situation to Ford, who sent two messages to Colonel Miles at Harpers Ferry requesting reinforcements. He then sent Hewitt back to see if he could get a good

Map 20
The Battle of Maryland Heights

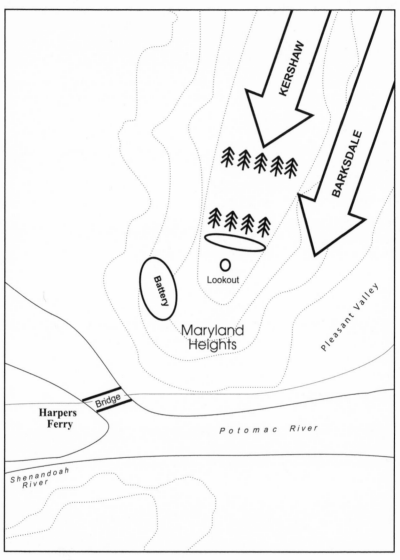

Abatis

Breastwork

estimate of the size of the enemy on the other side of the abatis. Hewitt came back with an estimate that the enemy outnumbered the Union troops ten to one. In actuality, Ford's total force outnumbered Kershaw's ten to seven. Upon receiving Hewitt's report, Ford sent him in person down to Harpers Ferry to plead with Colonel Miles for those reinforcements.

When Hewitt arrived at Miles's quarters, it was already after 11 p.m. Miles was asleep, and Hewitt had him awakened. When Miles came out of his bedroom, Hewitt advised him that Union forces were outnumbered ten to one and that, unless they got three more regiments before dawn, all was lost on Maryland Heights. After hearing Hewitt out, Miles promised that they would have their reinforcements. Two regiments would come up on the road from the river, and the third would come up on a path on the western side of the mountain and hit the Confederates on the right flank. Hewitt delivered the message to Ford and then returned to his position at the abatis to await the morn.

After Hewitt left, Miles realized that he did not have three regiments to spare, but ordered Lieutenant Colonel Downey with eight companies of his Third Maryland Regiment of the Potomac Home Brigade to reinforce Ford at dawn. In the morning, he ordered Colonel Simeon Sammon to reinforce Ford with an additional seven companies of Sammon's 115th New York. Neither Downey nor Sammon was to arrive before action opened at daylight on the thirteenth.

Kershaw realized that he could not pass the abatis on either side because of the drop-off, and there was only room enough on the ridge to deploy two regiments abreast. Kershaw's own brigade had four regiments. He formed them into two lines (a line always has two ranks). He placed the Eighth South Carolina on his right and the Seventh on his left in the first line, and he placed the Third on his right and the Second on his left in the second line. Barksdale's brigade remained behind in column. In the case of two lines, only the first line will fight, unless it is stopped, in which case the second line will pass through to press the attack.

The attack commenced at about 6:30 a.m., Saturday, September 13, 1862, with the advance of Kershaw's first line. Early in the advance, the Eighth South Carolina on the right encountered a formation of rocks that cut them off from further participation in the attack. The fight was left to Kershaw's 466-man Seventh South Carolina. After just about twenty minutes,

Brigadier General Joseph Kershaw CSA
Victor at Maryland Heights

the Union line gave way and retired through the second abatis,
four hundred yards in their rear, and took up position behind
the log barrier.

When Kershaw continued his advance toward the second abatis, he placed Barksdale's division on the slope of the mountain toward Pleasant Valley on his left as an extension of the first line. Barksdale was ordered to continue after Kershaw's first line met resistance and to gain the enemy's rear.

On reaching the second abatis, Kershaw reported that he had encountered a most obstinate resistance and that a fierce fire was kept up at about a hundred yards' distance. Kershaw stated that his loss was heavy and that he was required to advance the Third South Carolina from the second line to the front.

On the Union side, Lieutenant Colonel Downey's reinforcements began to arrive in driblets up a footpath and were placed in line behind the barricade. Up to this time, the 126th New York was adequately contesting the Confederate advance with its colonel, Eliakim Sherrill, conspicuously exposing himself to danger in encouraging his inexperienced troops. At about 10 a.m., Colonel Sherrill was shot in the face in full view of many of his troops and carried from the field seriously wounded. At this point, the 126th New York began to disperse to the rear, and the men could not be rallied.

The remaining Union troops behind the barricade continued the resistance for about a half hour, but then someone (it was never established who) gave the order to retreat, and the barricade was abandoned to the Confederates.

Disorganized Union resistance continued on top of the mountain near the lookout until about 2 p.m. At this point, Major Hewitt, the senior officer of the Thirty-second Ohio on the scene, but not the senior officer present, was informed that a large Confederate force (Barksdale's) was advancing along the eastern slope of the mountain and flanking the Union position. Hewitt ordered a retreat from the top of the mountain.

About 3 p.m., Colonel Ford ordered the entire position on the mountain to be abandoned, the guns spiked, and the troops to conduct an orderly retreat across the bridge into Harpers Ferry.

When Colonel Miles learned of the evacuation, he was with his aide, Lieutenant Binney, on Bolivar Heights. Binney described Miles's reaction:

> I was standing on Bolivar Heights. Colonel Miles rode up there and halted his horse, perhaps 30 feet from me, and with his glass took a survey of the heights. In his apparent astonishment, as he saw the first movement of the retreat from Maryland Heights, he

exclaimed "God Almighty; what does that mean? They are coming down! Hell and damnation."[1]

Miles then accepted a fait accompli and ordered Colonel Maulsby, who was in command of the troops on the north side of the Potomac at the base of Elk Ridge, to cover Ford's retreat and then to cross the bridge into Harpers Ferry after Ford. Thus, Miles's entire position north of the Potomac was lost, and any hope of a union of his forces with relief forces in Pleasant Valley was gone with the wind.

Following is an approximate chronology of the battle:

6:30 a.m.
  • Confederates attack first abatis.
7:00 a.m.
  • Union troops begin retreat.
8:30 a.m.
  • Union troops occupy breastwork behind second abatis.
  • Kershaw's division attacks breastwork.
  • Barksdale's division is ordered to advance along east side of Elk Ridge and flank Union defenders.
9:30 a.m.
  • Lieutenant Colonel Downey arrives with Union reinforcements.
10:00 a.m.
  • Colonel Sherrill, commanding officer of the 126th New York and senior officer present, is seriously wounded in view of his green troops.
  • The 126th begins to disperse and retreat without authorization.
10:30 a.m.
  • Unknown party orders Union troops behind breastwork to retreat.
  • Confederates capture breastwork.
12:00 p.m.
  • Colonel Sammon arrives at brigade headquarters with Union reinforcements. Most are retained at brigade headquarters.
2:00 p.m.
  • Disorganized Union resistance continues on top of mountain near lookout.
  • Major Hewitt of the Thirty-second Ohio receives report that

large Confederate force is advancing along east side of Elk Ridge and is flanking Union troops on top. He orders retreat from summit.

3:00 p.m.

• Colonel Ford orders cannons spiked and entire Elk Ridge position abandoned.

Total Union casualties for the battle of Maryland Heights were estimated at 140 to 160, with 28 to 32 of them killed.

Colonel Ford estimated that the total Confederate casualties were 600 to 700. The actual number was 230, of which 37 were killed. The preponderance of the Confederate casualties was in Kershaw's brigade. He suffered 35 killed and 178 wounded, while Barksdale's brigade suffered only 2 killed and 15 wounded.

One question is how effectively did the Union artillery support the troops fighting on the summit? The Union gunners at Camp Hill and McGrath's Battery on the slope of Elk Ridge threw large numbers of shells at targets above them that they could not see. In Colonel Ford's official report of the battle, he described McGrath's performance as follows:

> Captain McGrath, throughout the entire engagement, proved himself every inch a soldier, and it is unnecessary for me to say that as an artillerist he has few equals and no superiors. Under his well directed fire, shot and shell spread dismay and death on every side of the enemy.[2]

The Confederate reports of the battle on the summit make no mention of artillery fire at all. Troops of Kershaw that were not in his first line of attack, such as the Second South Carolina, and hence did not confront any Union infantry, reported no casualties at all. So it is entirely possible that the Union artillery barrage killed no one and injured no one.

The question becomes, why did the Union lose the battle of Maryland Heights when it had both the favored position of defender and a superiority of numbers? The answer is a lack of leadership. Confusion reigned in the command structure of the Union forces on the summit from the outset of the battle until the final abandonment of the position. This confusion became even more acute after the wounding of Colonel Sherrill, the senior officer on the scene. Each officer commanded only his own unit. No one was in overall charge. To this date, no one knows who gave the order to abandon the barricade. Major Hewitt gave the order to abandon the summit, even though he was not the senior officer present as Lieutenant Colonel Downey was on the scene, and he did not consult Downey. The commanding officer of the brigade, Colonel Ford, who should have been in charge, never rode up to the summit from his headquarters on the slope during the action. Here we come to his malady. It appears that the battle was lost not for a horseshoe nail, but for the lack of a tube of Preparation H.

By the end of the thirteenth, McLaws's men were on the Potomac and occupied both Sandy Hook, the small village at the base of Pleasant Valley, and the pass between South Mountain and the river.

At the close of the day, the garrison still held the bridges. It could cross the Potomac on the pontoon bridge to the Maryland side, but if it turned right (to the east), it would quickly run into Confederates. However, if it turned left (to the west), it could march without impediment along the near vertical base of Maryland Heights to the steep road carved into the stone that the Union troops had used for access and egress. The Confederates were on top, fourteen hundred feet above, but the road itself was in no-man's-land. At this point, it was unclear as to how much farther the garrison could go west on the river road without running into Confederates. The road itself climbed over a shoulder of Elk Ridge and then continued to Sharpsburg, twelve miles to the west. It was later learned that the garrison could have gone all the way to Sharpsburg without encountering Confederates.

As darkness fell on the thirteenth, a sense of hopelessness settled on Harpers Ferry. All telegraphic communications with the outside world had been cut since the eleventh. The Union troops were seemingly hemmed in on all sides by what they believed to be overwhelmingly superior forces. General White estimated a minimum of forty thousand. Although McClellan had ordered Pleasonton on the twelfth to open communications with Harpers Ferry, no couriers had arrived. At the close of light on the thirteenth, not only did the Harpers Ferry defenders face a large force in front at Bolivar Heights, they also had Confederates looking down at them from Maryland and Loudoun Heights. They did not know where McClellan was or whether he was advancing or being pushed back.

Miles decided that it was time to try to get a message to the outside world and sent for Capt. Charles H. Russell of the First Maryland Cavalry. Russell was a native of the area, knew the roads, and had been one of the most intrepid defenders of Maryland Heights. Miles asked him if he thought he could get through with a message to McClellan. Russell said that he was willing to give it a try. Miles gave Russell the following instructions: Get to any general of the United States Army or to any telegraph station or, if possible, to General McClellan (whom he supposed was at Frederick) to report that he (Miles) could hold out forty-eight hours (until Monday night, September 15), but if he was not relieved by that time he would have to surrender. Russell selected nine men to accompany him and set out about 9 p.m. along the Virginia bank of the Potomac toward Boteler's Ford at Shepherdstown.

About three hours later, Miles sent for Maj. Henry Cole of the First Maryland Home Brigade. Cole, like Russell, was also a native of the area and knew the roads intimately. Cole was given the same offer and the same instructions. He accepted and set out about midnight. Cole, unlike Russell, traveled alone. He crossed the bridge and set out on the Maryland side of the river toward Sharpsburg.

How bad were things really at Harpers Ferry the night of Saturday, September 13, 1862? Not good, but not nearly as bad as Miles and White thought. The besieging forces were far smaller than estimated. Jackson, McLaws, and Walker together had fewer than twenty-five thousand men. This number provided them with a ratio of only five to three over the defenders. Many a successful defense has been conducted with a far less favorable ratio.

As of the end of daylight, the three besieging forces had not succeeded in establishing communications with each other. Neither Walker nor McLaws had as yet succeeded in getting cannons up to their heights, and McLaws was not even close. Worse yet, the siege was behind schedule. The plan called for Harpers Ferry to be taken on the twelfth. It was already the end of the thirteenth, and Lee was becoming increasingly nervous and already contemplating calling off the attack.

The situation of prospective relief forces was also much better than Miles contemplated. As far as Miles knew, both South

Mountain and Catoctin Mountain stood between him and McClellan. During the day of the thirteenth, the Union army had succeeded in pushing through both the Frederick and Jefferson passes into the Catoctin Valley, and now only South Mountain stood between McClellan and Harpers Ferry.

Most important of all, McClellan had already ordered Franklin to proceed through Crampton's Gap in South Mountain to relieve Harpers Ferry. Once Franklin broke through the gap, McLaws the besieger would become the besieged—and this movement was to take place in less than twenty-four hours. Unfortunately, Miles had none of this information.

In the Frederick area, Pleasonton, with the help of infantry of Cox's division of the Ninth Corps, pushed Hampton's brigade (with Stuart present) west along the National Road during the day—first through the pass in Catoctin Mountain, then across the Catoctin Valley to Middletown. As they approached Turner's Gap in South Mountain at the far side of the valley, Stuart sent to D. H. Hill in Boonsboro for help. Hill, who was guarding the wagon park on the far side of South Mountain, had only five brigades. However, he dispatched two to Turner's Gap. When Stuart reached Turner's Gap and encountered the infantry brigades, he considered the pass secure and dispatched Hampton to proceed to Crampton's Gap, six miles to the south, to join Munford in defense of the gap. He himself stayed at Boonsboro to meet with Hill and Lee.

At the close of the day, the only Confederate forces in the vicinity of Turner's Gap on the National Road or Fox's Gap (one mile to the south) consisted of Hill's two brigades at the gaps and his remaining three brigades near the western base of the mountain at Boonsboro. This combined force constituted a total of fewer than five thousand men. The nearest possible support was from Longstreet, seventeen miles to the west at Hagerstown.

On the Union side of the gap, Cox's division was already bivouacked at Middletown. The remaining three divisions of the Ninth Corps were already on the road conducting a night march to join him, and the remaining corps at Frederick were already under orders to proceed at dawn to join up. Thus, more than sixty thousand Union troops would shortly be available to confront the five thousand Confederates in the contest for Turner's and Fox's Gaps.

Six miles to the south, Colonel Munford's cavalry brigade had retired from Jefferson to Crampton's Gap. There he met the two brigades McLaws had left behind to protect his rear. These were Brig. Gen. Paul J. Semmes's brigade and a minibrigade commanded by Col. William A. Parham. Semmes took up position at Brownsville Gap, one mile to the south of Crampton's Gap. Hampton's brigade, which had been ordered down from Middletown, joined Munford late in the afternoon. The total Confederate force thus available to defend the two southern gaps consisted of about three thousand, half of it cavalry. As things turned out, this force was to be reduced before the crunch came.

Confronting the Confederates at Brownsville and Crampton's Gaps was Franklin's Sixth Corps. The corps comprised three divisions, for a total of about twenty thousand men. As of nightfall, two of the divisions were camped at Jefferson, about nine road miles from Burkittsville at the base of the gaps, and the third division was a half-day's march behind. At nightfall on the thirteenth, the corps was already under orders to proceed at daylight to Burkittsville, seize the gaps, destroy McLaws, and relieve Harpers Ferry.

Special Order 191 anticipated the fall of Harpers Ferry on the twelfth; it was already the thirteenth, and the fall did not appear imminent. Lee grew increasingly concerned during the day and became convinced that the Union army was going to relieve the garrison.

Lee sent two dispatches to McLaws during the day warning him and expressing increasing concern. The first was sent during the morning and was as follows:

> General: General Lee desires me to say that he has not heard from you since you left the main body of the army. He hopes that you have been able to reach your destined position. He is anxious that the object of your expedition be speedily accomplished. The enemy have doubtless occupied Frederick since our troops have abandoned it, and are following our rear. The enemy have abandoned Martinsburg and retreated to Harpers Ferry, about 2,500 or 3,000 strong. General Jackson will be at Harpers Ferry by noon today to cooperate with you. General Stuart with his cavalry occupies the Middletown Valley. General D. H. Hill is a mile or two west of Boonsboro, at the junction of the Sharpsburg and

Hagerstown roads, and General Longstreet is at Hagerstown. You are particularly desired to watch well the main road from Frederick to Harpers Ferry, so as to prevent the enemy from turning your position. The commanding general hopes that the enemy about Harpers Ferry will be speedily disposed of, and the various detachments returned to the main body of the army. You are also desired to communicate as frequently as you can with headquarters.[3]

At 10 p.m., Lee sent a more urgent dispatch to McLaws. By this time, Lee had become sufficiently concerned to order Longstreet back from Hagerstown to assist Hill in defending the passes and preventing the Union army from breaking through McLaws's rear. The dispatch was as follows:

General: General Lee directs me to say that, from reports reaching him, he believes the enemy is moving toward Harpers Ferry to relieve the forces they have there. You will see, therefore, the necessity of expediting your operations as much as possible. As soon as they are completed, he desires you, unless you receive orders from General Jackson, to move your force as rapidly as possible to Sharpsburg. General Longstreet will move down tomorrow and take a position on Beaver Creek, this side of Boonsboro. General Stuart has been requested to keep you informed of the movements of the enemy.[4]

To summarize, by the end of Saturday, September 13, 1862, Harpers Ferry was surrounded, and Maryland Heights had fallen—but the garrison still held out. The Confederate cavalry continued to withdraw to the west to the passes in South Mountain and conceded Catoctin Valley to the Union. Lee now suspected that he was confronted by the entire Union army and that it had aggressive intentions. He ordered Longstreet to start back in the morning to South Mountain to support Hill. He also directed McLaws to hurry up the capture of Harpers Ferry.

McClellan's day had started out badly on the thirteenth when he was handed a message from Halleck in reply to two of his. The message responded to both McClellan's request that eight additional regiments of infantry be sent from Washington to join Gen. Darius Nash Couch's division, and it responded to McClellan's long letter justifying his requirement for the corps

Map 21
Situation at the End of September 13

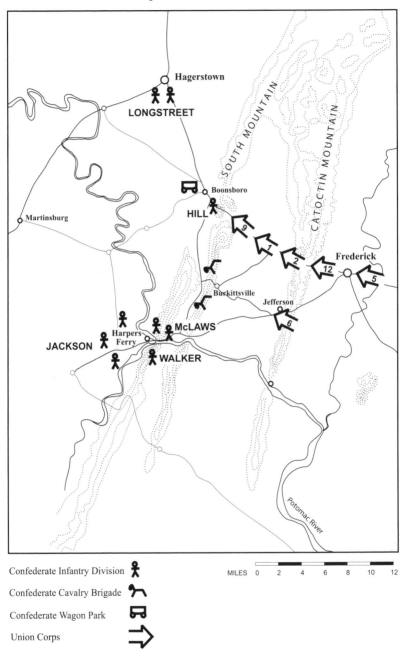

Confederate Infantry Division

Confederate Cavalry Brigade

Confederate Wagon Park

Union Corps

MILES 0   2   4   6   8   10   12

that he had left behind in Washington. Halleck's message was as
constructive as tossing a block of concrete to a drowning man. It
read as follows:

> Yours of 5:30 P.M. yesterday is just received. General Banks
> cannot safely spare eight new regiments from here. You must
> remember that very few troops are now received from the north,
> nearly all being stopped to guard the railroad. Four regiments
> were ordered to General Dix to replace Peck's division. Porter
> yesterday took away over 20,000. Until you know more certainly
> the enemy's force south of the Potomac, you are wrong in thus
> uncovering the capitol. I am of opinion that the enemy will send
> a small column toward Pennsylvania, so as to draw your forces in
> that direction; then suddenly move on Washington with the
> forces south of the Potomac and those he may cross over. In your
> letter of the 11th you attach too little importance to the capitol.
> I assure you that you are wrong. The capture of this place will
> throw us back six months, if it should not destroy us. Beware the
> evils I now point out to you. You saw them when here, but you
> seem to forget them in the distance. No more troops can be sent
> from here till we have fresh arrivals from the north.[5]

Just as McClellan was about to send for his pacifier of choice,
the next paper handed to him completely transformed his
mood. It was a copy of Lee's secret Special Order 191.

The situation at the close of September 13 is as depicted in
map 21.

Chapter 10

Finding Special Order 191

One version of the finding of the lost dispatch Special Order 191 and its reaching General McClellan is that of Col. Silas Colgrove. His version is as follows:

> The Twelfth Army Corps arrived at Frederick Maryland, about noon on the 13th of September 1862. The 27th Indiana Volunteers, of which I was colonel at that date, belonged to the Third Brigade, First Division, of that corps.
>
> We stacked arms on the same ground that had been occupied by General D. H. Hill's division the evening before.
>
> Within a very few minutes after halting, the order was brought to me by First Sargeant [*sic*] John M. Bloss and Private B. W. Mitchell, of Company F, 27th Indiana Volunteers, who stated that it was found by Private Mitchell near where they had stacked arms. When I received the order it was wrapped around three cigars, and Private Mitchell stated that it was in that condition when found by him.
>
> General A. S. Williams was in command of our division. I immediately took the order to his headquarters, and delivered it to Colonel S. E. Pittman, General William's Adjutant-General, and the signature was at once recognized by Colonel Pittman, who had served with Colonel Chilton at Detroit, Michigan before the war, and was acquainted with his handwriting. It was at once taken to General McClellan's headquarters by Colonel Pittman.[1]

The handling of the document from the time of its discovery until its delivery to McClellan was amazingly efficient. This was, in large part, thanks to Sergeant Bloss, who immediately recognized the document's importance and the necessity of getting it to McClellan as soon as possible. Bloss was hardly the typical top sergeant of his day but was, in fact, the only college graduate in his regiment. Bloss was an unusually erudite man, as his postwar career will show.

145

Colonel Colgrove's description of the handling of the document provided a good overview but contained one major error. Captain Pittman (not Colonel Pittman as Colgrove said) did not recognize Colonel Chilton's signature because he had served with Colonel Chilton before the war. In fact, Captain Pittman was not even in the army before the war, and probably never even met Colonel Chilton. Pittman was a bank teller in Detroit, and Colonel Chilton was army paymaster for the area. Many of the checks that passed through Pittman's window bore Chilton's signature—and it was Pittman's business to recognize signatures.

The document, as presented to McClellan, is as follows:

Special Orders, No. 191
Headquarters Army of Northern Virginia
September 9, 1862

1. The citizens of Fredericktown being unwilling while overrun by members of this army, to open their stores, in order to give them confidence, and to secure to officers and purchasing supplies for benefit of this command, all officers and men of this army are strictly prohibited from visiting Fredericktown except on business, in which cases they will bear evidence of this in writing from division commanders. The provost marshal in Fredericktown will see that this guard rigidly enforces this order.

2. Major Taylor will proceed to Leesburg, Va., and arrange for transportation of the sick and those unable to walk to Winchester, securing the transportation of the country for this purpose. The route between this and Culpepper Court-House east of the mountains being unsafe, will no longer be traveled. Those on the way to this army already across the river will move up promptly; all others will proceed to Winchester collectively and under the command of officers, at which point, being the general depot of this army, its movements will be known and instructions given by commanding officer regulating further movements.

3. The army will resume its march tomorrow, taking the Hagerstown road. General Jackson's command will form the advance, and, after passing Middletown, with such portion as he may select, take the route toward Sharpsburg, cross the Potomac at the most convenient point, and by Friday morning take possession of the Baltimore and Ohio Railroad, capture such of them as may be at Martinsburg, and intercept such as may attempt to escape from Harpers Ferry.

4. General Longstreet's command will pursue the same roads as far as Boonsborough [*sic*], where it will halt, with reserve, supply and baggage trains of the army.

5. General McLaws, with his own division and that of General R. H. Anderson, will follow General Longstreet. On reaching Middletown [he] will take the route to Harpers Ferry, and by Friday morning possess himself of the Maryland Heights and endeavor to capture the enemy at Harpers Ferry and vicinity.

6. General Walker, with his division, after accomplishing the object in which he is now engaged, will cross the Potomac at Cheek's Ford, ascend its right bank to Lovettsville, take possession of Loudoun Heights, if practicable, by Friday morning, Key's Ford on his left, and the road between the end of the mountain and the Potomac on his right. He will, as far as practicable, cooperate with General McLaws and Jackson, and intercept retreat of the enemy.

7. General D. H. Hill's Division will form the rear of the army, pursuing the road taken by the main body. The reserve artillery, ordnance, and supply trains, and c., will precede General Hill.

8. General Stuart will detach a squadron of cavalry to accompany the command of Generals Longstreet, Jackson and McLaws, and, with the main body of the cavalry, will cover the route of the army, bringing up all stragglers that may have been left behind.

9. The commands of Generals Jackson, McLaws and Walker after accomplishing the objects for which they have been detached, will join the main body of the army at Boonsborough [*sic*] or Hagerstown.

10. Each regiment on the march will habitually carry its axes in the regimental ordnance-wagons, for use of the men at their encampments, to procure wood and c.[2]

When McClellan read Special Order 191 he declared, "Here is a paper with which if I cannot whip Bobbie Lee, I will be willing to go home."[3] He couldn't, and he didn't.

From the moment Special Order 191 was handed to McClellan, the clock started running. The information was perishable. If he was to destroy Lee's army, he had to destroy each piece before the pieces reunited. Most disturbing of all, the plan called for Harpers Ferry to fall on the twelfth, and it was already the thirteenth. Time was of the essence. There are those who thought it was as simple as reading the document and shouting "charge" with all forces rushing forward. Life isn't that simple; neither is military strategy.

The first thing McClellan had to decide was, is it a trick? How did it compare to the intelligence available to him? Once he had decided it was authentic, he had to consider the possibility that there could have been later changes or amendments to the order that he did not know about and which changed the situation. In fact, as things turned out, there was a significant amendment that he did not know about. Then he had to consider that if all was as portrayed by Special Order 191, what courses of action were open to him? He then had to select from the options.

Once McClellan concluded that it was not a trick, that the situation was still as portrayed in the document, and he had selected his option of action, he was faced with the mechanics of implementation. These were formidable and time consuming. First he had to write up his orders for his corps. Then he had to deliver them. There was no radio in those days, so he had to rely on either telegraph or courier. If he chose telegraph, he was limited in how quickly the message could be sent to all of his commanders and how quickly they would actually receive it and act on it. At that time, only one message could be sent on one wire at one time. The speed of transmission depended on the skills of the operators at both ends of the wire. A speed of twenty words per minute was typical. McClellan's order to Franklin late that afternoon was more than six hundred words and would have required more than thirty minutes of transmission time.

Then too, the intended recipient of a telegraph message was unlikely to be sitting at the telegraph terminal when the message came in. If he was a corps commander, he could be doing anything from sleeping in his tent to inspecting his troops by horseback. It was the practice at that time to write on the message the time of origin when the message was given to the telegrapher and the time of receipt when the message was delivered to the recipient. In the case of McClellan's message to Lincoln that night, the time of origin was 12:00 midnight, and the time of receipt was 2:35 a.m. on the thirteenth. This time differential was typical.

If the message were sent by courier, the obstacles would be even more formidable. McClellan at Frederick was twelve miles from Franklin at Jefferson, and by the time McClellan was ready with his orders, it was already getting dark. The incandescent light had not yet been invented, and a courier would have had to traverse twelve miles of unmarked country roads in the dark.

At times it could become so dark that one could literally not see one's hand in front of one's face. A courier might become lost. He might, albeit unlikely, be intercepted by Confederate cavalry. As he approached Franklin's command, he would likely be challenged one or more times to identify himself. When he finally reached Franklin's encampment, he would see a vast expanse of campfires, tents, tethered horses, and men sleeping on the ground, amongst which was somewhere located the headquarters tent. Once he delivered his message, the courier had to obtain a receipt and return to McClellan's headquarters. It was only then that McClellan could be sure that Franklin had his message. It was unlikely that a courier would be back before dawn the following day.

To cite some examples: Just two weeks earlier, on the evening of August 29, General Pope handed a message to a courier before 9 p.m. to deliver to General Porter. Porter's headquarters were just three miles from Pope's. It took the courier more than six hours to reach Porter. In our own narrative, we have General McClellan at Frederick giving a message to Captain Russell to deliver to General Franklin at Burkittsville. Burkittsville was twelve miles away and it was broad daylight. Russell delivered the message to Franklin five hours after he received it from McClellan.

Finally, when the recipient received the message, he had to read it, digest it, and act upon it. If he was a corps commander, he had to pass down his orders to his division commanders, the division commanders to the brigade commanders, and the brigade commanders to the regimental commanders. It all took time.

How did the tasking in the Special Order fit with what McClellan had observed? Fairly well, but not completely. There had been reports that a Confederate force estimated at five thousand had crossed the Potomac into Virginia near Point of Rocks on September 10. These reports would correspond to Walker's assignment in Special Order 191. It was also reported that Jackson had crossed the Potomac into Virginia at Williamsport on September 12. This report would correspond to Jackson's assignment in the Special Order. And last, there had been reports of Confederate forces in Pleasant Valley. These reports would correspond to McLaws's assignment. In addition, heavy cannon fire had been heard in the direction of Harpers Ferry on September 13, and all communications wires to Martinsburg and Harpers Ferry had been cut since the eleventh.

All these pieces of information tended to validate the Special Order as genuine.

There was one piece of intelligence, however, that did not conform to the plan as presented to McClellan. There had been a number of seemingly accurate reports that the Confederates had occupied Hagerstown in force. Hagerstown was mentioned only as one of two possible reuniting points *after* the fall of Harpers Ferry (the other being Boonsboro).

Unknown to McClellan, Special Order 191 had been modified after the drafting of the copy before him. Longstreet's two divisions had been directed to proceed to Hagerstown, seventeen miles beyond Boonsboro, rather than stopping at Boonsboro as indicated in his copy of the plan. Hence, the situation confronting McClellan was actually more favorable to him than indicated in his copy. Instead of three divisions guarding the wagon park at Boonsboro, just on the other side of the mountain from him, there was only one—that of D. H. Hill. Longstreet's two divisions were a full day's march farther to the west.

McClellan, after due consideration, accepted the plan as gospel, just as it lay before him, and began to consider his options.

Now we come to the matter of numbers. In understanding McClellan's subsequent actions, we must consider his perception of the number of Confederates facing him. Special Order 191 directed the movements of units by name and made no mention of the numbers of men involved. In McClellan's report of the finding of the document, he estimated the number of Confederates involved as 120,000. This was approximately three times the actual number.

Lee's army consisted de facto of two corps (although corps had not yet been officially established), with four divisions in each corps. In addition, there were Walker's division and Stuart's cavalry division. Thus, McClellan had to believe one of two things: either that Lee had thirty divisions instead of the actual ten, or that each of the ten contained three times as many men as it actually did. At this period, the organization of Lee's army was well understood by the Union commanders, so McClellan probably believed the latter—that each corps and division of the Confederate army contained three times as many men as it actually did. So, when McClellan read Special Order 191, he probably believed that each of the separately tasked components was three times its actual size.

Now that we have reached the point where McClellan considered the document authentic, what were the options available to him? What should he do?

If McClellan broke through Turner's Gap on the National Road and Fox's Gap one mile to the south, and seized the road junction at Boonsboro, the Confederates could not reunite at Boonsboro, and their only recourse would be to reunite via Boteler's Ford between Sharpsburg and Shepherdstown, or via the more distant ford at Williamsport. Furthermore, depending on the speed of his movements, the wagon park at Boonsboro could be in jeopardy.

If McClellan seized Boonsboro, and Harpers Ferry had not surrendered, McLaws's only way out would be to march back up Pleasant Valley to Rohrersville where the road from Sharpsburg intersected the Harpers Ferry-Boonsboro road, and head for Sharpsburg (see map 22).

It was clear that much depended on the Harpers Ferry garrison, and it was late—very late. The Confederate plan had called for Harpers Ferry to fall on the twelfth, and it was already late on the thirteenth as McClellan digested the plan. If Harpers Ferry held, Walker could reunite with Lee only via a very circuitous route that involved an extra full day's march. The direct route from Walker to Boteler's Ford went right through Harpers Ferry.

And most important, if Harpers Ferry held, and General Franklin, who was nearest Harpers Ferry, broke through Crampton's Gap into Pleasant Valley behind McLaws, Franklin would be between McLaws and his only escape route at Rohrersville. McLaws would be trapped between Franklin and the Harpers Ferry garrison. It was thus McLaws's force that was the most vulnerable of all Lee's components.

If Harpers Ferry were not relieved quickly, or at least contacted, it is clear that it could not, or rather, would not, hold out much longer. If Miles had no contact with the outside world, knew nothing of any pending relief force or his part in a strategic plan, and visualized nothing but more casualties in a hopeless contest for no gain, it could be expected that he would soon surrender. On the other hand, if he understood the larger situation, that his holding out would be instrumental to a great Union victory and that a potential relief force was within a couple hours' march, he might be inclined to view more casualties as a sacrifice rather than a waste, and hold on.

Map 22
McClellan's Options

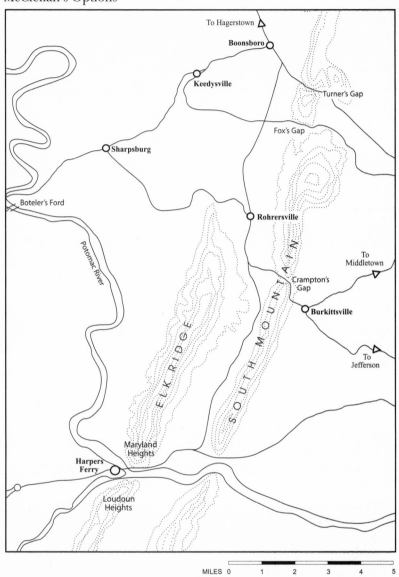

The man of the hour was General Franklin, commander of the Sixth Corps. It was his corps that was nearest to Harpers Ferry, nearest to Crampton's Gap. If McLaws was to be trapped and the Harpers Ferry garrison relieved, or at least contacted, Franklin would be the one who would have to do it.

William Buel Franklin was born in 1823 and graduated first in his class at West Point in 1843. He spent almost his entire career up to the war in the U.S. Army Corps of Topographical Engineers, overseeing various building projects, including the construction of the dome of the U.S. capitol building. He demonstrated both before and after the war that he had many talents, but unfortunately, they did not include generalship. At the outset of the war, he had practically no experience in commanding troops. He was a close friend of McClellan's, and, probably because of their relationship, he had by 1862 risen to corps commander. He was now at the level of his incompetence, but this was not yet evident in September 1862. It became increasingly evident as the war progressed. He shared one characteristic with his mentor, George B. McClellan. He could always see the limitations of his own troops, but not those of the enemy's.

About 6 p.m. McClellan made his decisions. He already had one division of his Ninth Corps in the Catoctin Valley at Middletown in position to attack Fox's and Turner's Gaps. He ordered the remaining three divisions of the Ninth Corps to make a night march from Frederick to the base of South Mountain and to join the first division in preparation for an attack on the morrow. He ordered the remaining corps in the Frederick area (First, Second, Fifth, and Twelfth) to follow at daylight. Most important, at 6:20 p.m. he sent the following order to Franklin at Jefferson:

General: I have now full information as to the movements and intentions of the enemy. Jackson has crossed the upper Potomac to capture the garrison at Martinsburg and cut off Miles's retreat toward the west. A division on the south side of the Potomac was to carry Loudoun Heights and cut off his retreat in that direction. McLaws, with his own division and that of R. H. Anderson, was to move by Boonsboro and Rohrersville and carry the Maryland Heights. The signal officers inform me that he is now in Pleasant Valley. The firing shows that Miles still holds out. Longstreet was to move to Boonsboro and there halt with the reserve corps, D. H. Hill to form the rear guard, Stuart's cavalry to bring up stragglers etc. We have cleared out all cavalry this side of the mountains and north of us.

The last I heard from Pleasonton he occupied Middletown, after several sharp skirmishes. A division of Burnside's command started several hours ago to support him. The whole of Burnside's command, including Hooker's Corps, march this evening and early tomorrow morning, followed by the Corps of Sumner and Banks (Mansfield's) and Sykes division (Porter), upon Boonsboro to carry that position. Couch has been ordered to concentrate his division and join you as rapidly as possible. Without waiting for the whole of that division to join, you will move at daybreak in the morning, by Jefferson and Burkettsville, upon the road to Rohrersville. I have reliable information that the mountain pass by this road is practicable for artillery and wagons. If this pass is not occupied by the enemy in force, seize it as soon as practicable, and debouch upon Rohrersville in order to cut off the retreat of or destroy McLaws' command. If you find this pass held by the enemy in large force, make all your dispositions for the attack, and commence it about an half an hour after you hear severe firing at the pass on the Hagerstown Pike, where the main body will attack. Having gained the pass, your duty will be first to cut off, destroy or capture McLaws command and relieve Colonel Miles. If you effect this, you will order him to join you at once with all his disposable troops, first destroying the bridges over the Potomac, if not already done, and leaving a sufficient garrison to prevent the enemy from passing the Ford, you will then return by Rohrersville on the direct road to Boonsboro if the main column has not succeeded in its attack. If it has succeeded, take the road by Rohrersville to Sharpsburg and Williamsport, in order to cut off the retreat of Hill and Longstreet toward the Potomac, or to prevent the repassage of Jackson. My general idea is to cut the enemy in two and beat him in detail. I believe I have sufficiently explained my intentions. I ask of you, at this important moment, all your intellect and the utmost activity that a general can exercise.[4]

All in all, it was a reasonable plan. When we consider time again, it is likely that the order was not handed to Franklin before 8:30 p.m. We can readily see that it is not the sort of thing that could be digested in five, or even fifteen, minutes. We can picture Franklin reading the plan by lantern light, ordering maps, consulting with his staff, and finally issuing orders to his divisions. Time! Time! Time!

Could McClellan have ordered Cox's division, which was already at Middletown, to attack Turner's Gap on the eve of the thirteenth and Franklin to conduct a night march to the base of Crampton's Gap on the night of the thirteenth? He could have.

However, when we consider that he believed that he was contending not just with Hill at the northern passes, but with Hill
and Longstreet, and that he further believed that each enemy
division was three times its actual strength, his decision to defer
the attack to the morning of the fourteenth, when additional
troops were up, was logical.

There was one flagrant omission, however, to both McClellan's
and Franklin's activities on the night of the thirteenth. Neither
took any action, as far as we can ascertain, to send couriers to
Colonel Miles at Harpers Ferry to advise him of the situation. As
we now know, the encirclement of Harpers Ferry was porous.
Subsequent events show that anyone who wanted to get out was
able to get out, and presumably anyone who wanted to get in
could have gotten in.

After General McClellan issued orders to all his corps commanders, he advised General Halleck of the finding of Special
Order 191. The message to Halleck was released at 11 p.m. and
read as follows:

> An order from General R. E. Lee to General D. H. Hill,
> which has accidentally come into my hands this evening—the
> authenticity of which is unquestionable—discloses some of the
> plans of the enemy, and shows most conclusively that the main
> rebel army is now before us, including Longstreet's, Jackson's,
> the two Hill's, McLaws', Walker's, R. H. Anderson's and Hood's
> commands. That army was ordered to march on the 10th, and
> to attack and capture our forces at Harpers Ferry and
> Martinsburg yesterday, by surrounding them with such a heavy
> force that they conceived it impossible they could escape. They
> were also ordered to take possession of the Baltimore and Ohio
> Railroad; afterward to concentrate again at Boonsboro or
> Hagerstown. That this was the plan of the campaign on the 9th
> is confirmed by the fact that heavy firing has been heard in the
> direction of Harpers Ferry this afternoon, and the columns took
> the roads specified in the order. It may therefore, in my judgment,
> be regarded as certain that this rebel army, which I have good
> reasons for believing amounts to 120,000 men or more, and known
> to be commanded by Lee in person, intended to attempt penetrat-
> ing Pennsylvania. The officers told their friends here that they were
> going to Harrisburg and Philadelphia. My advance has pushed
> forward today, and overtaken the enemy on the Middletown

and Harpers Ferry roads, and several slight engagements have taken place, in which our troops have driven the enemy from their position. A train of wagons, about three-quarters of a mile long, was destroyed today by the rebels in their flight. We took over 50 prisoners. The army marches forward early to-morrow morning, and will make forced marches, to endeavor to relieve Colonel Miles, but I fear, unless he makes a stout resistance, we may be too late. A report came in just this moment that Miles was attacked today and repulsed the enemy, but I do not know what credit to attach to the statement. I shall do everything in my power to save Miles if he still holds out. Portions of Burnside's and Franklin's Corps moved forward this evening. I have received your dispatch of 10 A.M. You will perceive, from what I have stated, that there is but little probability of the enemy being in much force south of the Potomac. I do not, by any means, wish to be understood, as undervaluing the importance of holding Washington. It is of great consequence, but upon the success of this army the fate of the nation depends. It was for this reason that I said everything else should be made subordinate to placing this army in proper condition to meet the large rebel force in our front. Unless General Lee has changed his plans, I expect a severe general engagement to-morrow. I feel confident that there is now no rebel force immediately threatening Washington or Baltimore, but that I have the mass of their troops to contend with, and that they outnumber me when united.[5]

McClellan's message contained an excellent summary of Special Order 191, but it contained two shadings of the truth and one outright falsity. First, the Special Order had not been given to McClellan "this evening" but about noon; and, second, Franklin's corps had not been pushed forward "this evening," but would be upon daylight on the fourteenth. The out-and-out falsity was the estimate of the Confederate forces before McClellan. It was not 120,000 but 40,000.

McClellan's last message of the day relating to the finding of the plan was to Lincoln. It was released at midnight and read as follows:

I have the whole rebel force in front of me, but am confident, and no time shall be lost. I have a difficult task to perform, but with God's blessing will accomplish it. I think Lee has made a gross mistake, and that he will be severely punished for it. The army is in motion as rapidly as possible. I hope for a great success if the plans of the rebels remain unchanged. We have possession of Catoctin. I have all the plans of the rebels, and will catch them in their own trap if my men are equal to the emergency. I now feel that I can count on them as of old. All forces of Pennsylvania should be placed to co-operate at Chambersburg. My respects to Mrs. Lincoln. Received most enthusiastically by the ladies. Will send you trophies. All well, and with God's blessing will accomplish it.[6]

Was then McClellan dilatory in responding to the finding of Special Order 191 in the remaining hours of September 13? It doesn't seem so. Rather, it appears that he was actually a dynamo of activity. If he could be faulted for anything, it would be for not ordering Franklin to make a night march to the base of Crampton's Gap and for not ordering Franklin and Pleasonton to make every effort to contact Miles at the earliest moment and advise him of McClellan's plans.

Now that we have conceded that McClellan, in general, was not derelict in his actions after reading Special Order 191, but rather, devised a reasonable plan in a reasonable amount of time, we come to the question, could he have selected a better plan? Indeed, he could have, and that plan was the very one that Gen. D. H. Hill was later to say he was thankful that McClellan did not select.

McClellan was to make his main attack along the National Road against Turner's and Fox's Gaps. On the basis of the copy of Special Order 191 before him, he believed that D. H. Hill's division and Longstreet's two divisions were defending the gaps and that the Confederate wagon and artillery park was at Boonsboro, just on the other side of the gaps. If he succeeded in forcing the gaps, which he did, he would merely push the Confederate force back, as there was no impediment to its retreat.

On the other hand, if he had made his main effort against Crampton's Gap, six miles to the south, rather than the limited attack he was to make there with Franklin's Sixth Corps alone, he could have achieved multiple objectives. First, he would have had sufficient force on the scene not only to quickly seize the gap but also to destroy McLaws's force, which would have been trapped between Harpers Ferry and the breakthrough force. Second, he would have relieved the Harpers Ferry garrison, which then would have been free to join him. And third, he would have had sufficient force on the scene to continue down the Rohrersville-Sharpsburg road (see map 22) and thus place himself between Jackson's force and the Longstreet-Hill force and prevent their reuniting via Boteler's Ford.

Considering the conditions that existed on the night of the thirteenth, was it practicable for McClellan to shift his main effort from the northern gaps to Crampton's Gap? Not only could he, but the road layout was ideal for just such an action (see map 18). As of the night of the thirteenth, one division of the Ninth Corps was already at Middletown, and the remaining three divisions were under orders to make a night march to join it. The Sixth Corps was at Jefferson, and most of the remainder of the army was camped in the Frederick area. Thus, at daylight on the fourteenth, the Sixth Corps at Jefferson and the Ninth Corps at Middletown each would have its own road to Burkittsville, at the base of Crampton's Gap. The roads were roughly equidistant, each less than ten miles. Thus, the two corps could have united at Burkittsville by 10 a.m. on the fourteenth. This action would have provided overwhelming, on-the-scene force to quickly seize Crampton's Gap, destroy McLaws's force, relieve Harpers Ferry, and take the Rohrersville-Sharpsburg road. In the meantime, McClellan's remaining corps (most of which, incidentally, were to play no part in the pending battle of South Mountain) could have easily marched to Turner's and Fox's Gaps and gotten there before Longstreet arrived to reinforce Hill.

Had McClellan removed McLaws's force from Lee's army and joined the Harpers Ferry garrison to his army, Lee's army would no longer have been strong enough to contest him in Maryland. But alas, this was not the plan McClellan selected.

The plan selected was to make the main attack against the northern gaps and to leave Crampton's Gap in the south to General Franklin's Sixth Corps. As we shall see, the force allocated for Crampton's Gap was insufficient, or at least it appeared so to its timid commander, to achieve its objectives of (1) destroying McLaws, (2) relieving Harpers Ferry, and (3) driving a wedge between Lee and Jackson.

One last nagging question that has never been answered satisfactorily is this: who lost the lost order? The lost order was the copy from Lee to D. H. Hill. It was found on Hill's vacated campsite so, presumably, it had been delivered. There is a tradition in Frederick that General Hill was seen to drop a paper in the street, which was supposed to be the order in question. The Comte de Paris, who was an observer with Lee's army, says it was found in a house in Frederick that had been occupied by Hill. One thing is fact, however—three cigars were wrapped in the order when it was found, and it is hardly likely that a courier or anyone else wrapped their cigars with the document before it was delivered to Hill. Logic would indicate that the order was used as a cigar wrapper after it had been delivered and read. This leads us to conclude that the order was actually lost by Hill himself or perhaps his chief of staff.

Before leaving this day, let us look at the probabilities of what actually happened happening. What was the likelihood of a top-secret document, the revealing of which could jeopardize an army, being lost? What was the likelihood of its being picked up within a few hours by an enemy who immediately realized its significance? And last, what was the likelihood of its being handed to an individual who immediately recognized the signature of its drafter and could attest to its authenticity? Not very likely. But it did happen.

See map 21 for the situation at the close of September 13.

Chapter 11

Sunday, September 14

September 14, 1862, was to be a day of decision. Up to this time, McClellan had been cautiously creeping forward at the rate of six miles per day into the vacuum created by the retiring Confederates. His objective thus far had been defensive—to maintain a position between the Confederates and Baltimore and Washington. Now that he had read Special Order 191, he felt confident that he had the advantage, and he was going to attack.

Five of McClellan's six corps were situated along the National Road between Frederick and the east base of South Mountain, a stretch of just thirteen miles. The only Confederate force near the other side of the mountain was the division of Maj. Gen. D. H. Hill. It consisted of five brigades with a total of fewer than five thousand men. Hill's headquarters were at Boonsboro, and Lee had given him two tasks. One was to protect the army wagon park at Boonsboro, and the other was to intercept any Union troops that might be fleeing from the siege at Harpers Ferry.

Daniel Harvey Hill was the senior division commander in Jackson's corps and was no relation to the other Hill, Gen. A. P. Hill. Hill was forty-one and had graduated from West Point in 1842, four years before Jackson, and was in the same class as Longstreet and one year ahead of Grant. Hill participated in the Mexican War and then resigned from the army to pursue a career in education. His subject was mathematics, and he first taught at Washington College (now Washington and Lee) and later at Davidson. Unlike Professor Jackson, Professor Hill appeared to know his subject, published a book on mathematics, and later rose to be superintendent of the North Carolina Military Institute. Hill, like Jackson, was an ardent Presbyterian, and, like Jackson, had married a daughter of Presbyterian minister Morrison, thus becoming Jackson's brother-in-law.

At the outset of the Civil War, Hill reentered the military as a colonel in the Confederate army. By the time of the battle of South Mountain, he had risen in rank to major general.

Although Hill was highly regarded for his military capabilities, he had a reputation for criticizing decisions of his superiors. Lee, who was slow to criticize, referred to him as a "croaker."

As Stuart and his cavalry were pushed westward on the thirteenth, first through Catoctin Mountain and then across Catoctin Valley, Stuart sent to Hill for help. In response, Hill dispatched two of his five brigades to secure the passes in South Mountain. There were two passes in the area. The one on the National Road was known as Turner's Gap, and another, one mile to the south on a secondary road, was known as Fox's Gap.

By the evening of the thirteenth, for unknown reasons, Lee became suspicious of McClellan's intentions. During the night, he ordered Longstreet, with his two divisions, to proceed at daybreak on the fourteenth back from Hagerstown to South Mountain to support Hill. He also sent a note to Hill stating that he (Lee) was not satisfied with the state of affairs on the National Road and ordered Hill to go in person at daybreak on the fourteenth to the gaps and take charge of their defense.

As morning broke on the fourteenth, the only Confederates at the gaps consisted of Hill's two brigades, totaling fewer than twenty-five hundred men. At the same time, the entire Union Ninth Corps, totaling about fifteen thousand, was gathering at the eastern base of the gap and deploying for attack, and the other corps were approaching. By all odds and logic, if the Union attack had been properly pressed, it should have swept Hill's two brigades off the mountain by noon.

As the morning progressed, Hill sent for his other three brigades, thus giving a total of five thousand Confederates defending the passes. However, even before Hill's last brigade was in place, about 1 p.m., Hooker's First Corps began arriving on the scene, providing another sixteen thousand Union troops, again lengthening the odds to more than thirty thousand Union troops against five thousand Confederates.

The view from the Washington monument north of the National Road at the crest of Turner's Gap provides a breathtaking panorama of the Catoctin Valley. If there was any doubt in Hill's mind as to what he was facing, it was dispelled when he gazed down into the valley below from the monument. In his words:

> I saw from the lookout station near the mountain house the vast army of McClellan spread out before me. The marching

columns extended back as far as the eye could see in the distance; but many of the troops had already arrived and were in double lines of battle, and those advancing were taking up positions as fast as they arrived. It was a grand and glorious spectacle, and it was impossible to look at it without admiration. I had never seen so tremendous an army before, and I did not see one like it afterward. For though we confronted greater forces at Yorktown, Sharpsburg and Frederick, and about Richmond under Grant, these were only partly seen, at most a corps at a time. But here four corps were in full view, one of which was on the mountain and almost within rifle range. The sight inspired more satisfaction than discomfort; for though I knew my little force could be brushed away as well as a strong man can brush to one side the wasp or the hornet, I felt that General McClellan had made a mistake, and I hoped to be able to delay him until General Longstreet could come up and our trains [wagons] could be extricated from their perilous position.[1]

The final Federal push was not organized until about 5 p.m. By that time, Longstreet's troops were arriving to plug the gaps. The Confederates managed to hold until after dark, which gave the wagon park time to move off; they then withdrew in an orderly retreat. However, they left behind their dead and wounded and prisoners, who largely consisted of individuals simply too exhausted to continue.

What did Hill mean when he said that the sight of the whole Union army arrayed before him in the valley "inspired more satisfaction than discomfort" and that he felt that General McClellan had made a mistake? What he meant was that McClellan could have transferred some of his corps to General Franklin six miles to the south and made his main attack through Crampton's Gap rather than along the National Road. In this event, the attacking force could have continued through Rohrersville to Sharpsburg and cut Hill, Longstreet, and the wagon park off from the Potomac. In this event, the Confederates would have been facing a disaster rather than merely a setback.

Why did the Union troops, with their overwhelming superiority, not storm Hill's slim Confederate force during the morning and seize the gaps? Hill himself admitted that they could have done so. The reason is that the Union high command thought that they were facing thirty thousand Confederates rather than twenty-five hundred. McClellan took Special Order 191 at face value and believed that Longstreet, with his two divisions, was still with Hill, and failed to recognize that Longstreet had been ordered on to Hagerstown after the copy of the plan he had seen had been drafted. Furthermore, he believed that Hill's and Longstreet's divisions were much larger than they actually were. Thus, irony of ironies, McClellan's recovery of the Confederate secret plan may have saved the Confederate army.

Before we turn to see how General Franklin made out on his attack on Crampton's Gap to the south, let us see how Captain Russell and Major Cole, who left Harpers Ferry the previous night in an attempt to get through Confederate lines, made out.

Russell left first, right after dark. Let us read in his own words what happened:

> I went from Colonel Miles quarters down to my quarters and selected 9 men. I went through our line of pickets on the Virginia side. I kept upon that side of the river, passed the enemy's line of pickets, and moved down the river through the fields until I came to Shepherdstown. I crossed the Potomac near the mouth of the Antietam. I met the enemy's pickets there again. We put spurs to our horses and dashed by that picket, and passed on through by by-roads until we came to South Mountain. There we met a picket of 71 infantry of the enemy. We got around them by taking a road through the woods, and then we went directly over the center of South Mountain until I reached Middletown.[2]

The first general Russell met was Jesse L. Reno, the commander of the Ninth Corps. Reno was already involved in his assault on Turner's and Fox's Gaps. Neither Russell nor Reno knew that Reno was in the last hours of his life. Reno listened to the message but had no telegraph. He gave Russell a fresh horse and told him to report directly to McClellan at Frederick.

Russell arrived at McClellan's headquarters at Frederick between 8 and 9 a.m. and found him at breakfast. (McClellan always seemed to be at breakfast at crucial junctures.) McClellan invited Russell to join him. Here is Russell's account of their meeting:

> I reported to him the information Col. Miles directed me to give about his situation; that he could hold out forty eight hours; that he had subsistance [*sic*] for forty eight hours; and then told him that Maryland Heights had been evacuated. He asked me if

Colonel Miles held Loudoun Heights. I told him that there was
no force there we knew of, of either army. [Wrong.] He replied
that General Franklin was then on his way to relieve the garrison;
and he immediately sent off a messenger to General Franklin to
urge him forward. He then asked me if I thought I could get back
to Col. Miles. I told him I did not think I could. He afterward
sent me with a note to General Franklin, as I told him I was
acquainted with the country there, and knew the position of the
enemy, and perhaps could be of assistance to him. I got upon my
horse and went to General Franklin. It was about 10 o-clock
Sunday morning (when I left General McClellan).[3]

We will pick up Captain Russell's narrative when he reaches
General Franklin.

Major Cole had departed Harpers Ferry three hours after
Russell the night of the thirteenth. Unlike Russell, he traveled
alone. Cole chose to cross the bridge at Harpers Ferry into
Maryland and follow the north bank of the Potomac. Cole also
successfully negotiated the Confederate lines and rode into
McClellan's headquarters about noon. Cole delivered the same
message as Russell—that Miles could hold out only forty-eight
hours, beginning the night of the thirteenth. McClellan asked
Cole if he could get back to Harpers Ferry. Cole said that he would
try. McClellan gave Cole a message to deliver to Miles. The message was that help was on the way, Miles was to hold out to the last
extremity, and he was to reoccupy Maryland Heights if he could.

After Cole left, McClellan was to claim that he gave the same
message to three different couriers to deliver to Miles.

Now let us return to General Franklin. As of the night of
September 13, Franklin, with two of his divisions, those of
Generals Henry W. Slocum and William F. Smith and comprising
12,800 men, were camped near Jefferson. His third division, that
of General Couch with an additional 7,000 men, was a half day's
march behind to the east. Jefferson was at a road junction on the
Frederick-Harpers Ferry road eight miles southwest of
Frederick. There a road led off to the west to Burkittsville, eight
miles distant. Burkittsville lay at the foot of Crampton's Gap in
South Mountain. On the other side of the gap was Pleasant
Valley, in McLaws's rear (see map 23).

During the night of September 13-14, McClellan had ordered
Franklin to proceed at dawn to Burkittsville, force Crampton's
Gap, destroy McLaws, and relieve Harpers Ferry. McClellan's

Map 23
McLaws's Dilemma

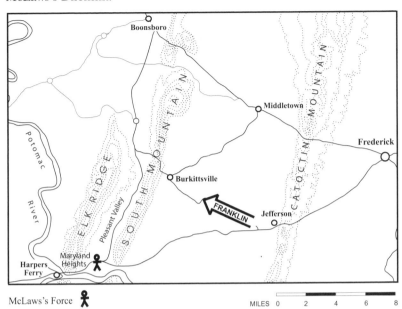

McLaws's Force 👤   MILES 0   2   4   6   8

order explained that Harpers Ferry was under siege and in dire
straits. Furthermore, during the morning of the fourteenth, after
McClellan had heard from Captain Russell about the pending
surrender of Harpers Ferry within the next forty-eight hours,
McClellan dispatched a courier to Franklin to hurry him along.

In essence then, Franklin's mission was to rescue a drowning
man. Time was everything. How fast did Franklin react? Sunup
was at 5:39 a.m. on September 14. After Franklin started, he
ordered a halt of two hours or more to permit Couch's division
to close up on him. His two divisions finally began arriving at
Burkittsville about noon. To put things in perspective, had an
old lady pushing a baby carriage left Jefferson at sunup, she
could easily have reached Burkittsville by 10 a.m.

But things didn't actually work out that bad for him. In a
way, Franklin actually lucked out. Early in the morning of the
fourteenth, Hampton's cavalry brigade, as well as Munford's
cavalry brigade and Parham's infantry brigade, were available to
defend Crampton's Gap. General Stuart then arrived on the
scene. He recognized that the Union troops at Jefferson had two
possible courses of action to relieve Harpers Ferry. They could
proceed to Burkittsville and attempt to force their way into
Pleasant Valley via Crampton's Gap, or they could continue down

the Frederick-Harpers Ferry road around the southern tip of South Mountain where it abutted the Potomac. Stuart considered the latter a possibility and ordered Hampton to proceed south to defend the pass between the mountain and the river. Thus, when Franklin arrived, he encountered only Parham and Munford at Crampton's Gap and Semmes at Brownsville Gap, one mile to the south.

Munford and Parham between them had only 850 men. More than half of these were cavalry, not equipped or expected to fight infantry in a stand-up battle. Munford, being senior, was in command.

Franklin spent the hours between noon and 3 p.m. reconnoitering the Confederate position and arraying his troops. Two of his divisions were up. Couch's was still coming on behind and was not to arrive until after dark. Franklin had 12,800 on the scene, the Confederates 850—a ratio of fifteen to one. It is true that another 700 Confederates under General Semmes were guarding Brownsville Gap about a mile to the south, but these played no part in the ensuing action other than providing artillery support.

Franklin finally began his attack at about 3 p.m. Just as it began, Captain Russell rode up. Russell had finished his account of his meeting with McClellan, stating that he rode up to Franklin at Burkittsville at 3 p.m. Burkittsville was about twelve miles from McClellan's headquarters at Frederick, and this action was taking place five hours later. One wonders what Russell needed the horse for; he could have walked that distance in five hours. Russell bore a threefold message. Harpers Ferry was in its death throes, Maryland Heights on Elk Ridge had fallen, and he, knowing the ground, offered his services.

The message that Maryland Heights on Elk Ridge was no longer in Union possession was particularly bad news. It would have been the closest point of junction between Franklin and the garrison. As recently as the previous day, pickets from the garrison stationed on Elk Ridge would have been in plain sight of Franklin's force once he broke through the gap to the Boonsboro-Harpers Ferry road in Pleasant Valley. Breaking through the gap yesterday would have been tantamount to the relief of Harpers Ferry. Today it wasn't. Now, to contact the garrison, Franklin would have to proceed six miles down Pleasant Valley to the river and bridge, and McLaws was in between. As Franklin finally moved to the attack, Munford's dismounted cavalry, plus Parham's infantry, were deployed behind a stone wall at the foot of the mountain.

Major General Lafayette McLaws CSA
Besieger and Besieged

After Stuart's visit to Crampton's Gap during the morning, he had called on McLaws, who was his senior, to report what he had done and to offer his services. Stuart had previously been at Harpers Ferry and was more familiar with the terrain than McLaws. Stuart advised McLaws that he had ordered Hampton's brigade from Crampton's Gap to the pass between South Mountain and the river, and then warned McLaws that the road leading west below Maryland Heights continued all the way to Sharpsburg and was a potential escape route and should be guarded. For whatever reason, the road was not guarded—and with serious consequences.

About noon, before Stuart left McLaws, alarming reports began to come to McLaws that a large Union force was gathering at the base of Crampton's Gap. McLaws ordered Gen. Thomas Cobb to proceed back up Pleasant Valley to be within supporting distance of Colonel Munford in case Munford required help. As additional ominous reports reached McLaws, he sent an order to Cobb that he must hold the gap, even if it cost him every man. Cobb's brigade consisted of 1,341 officers and men. With this small force, even combined with Munford's 850, the Confederates would be outnumbered almost six to one.

As Cobb approached the gap, he received increasingly desperate calls from Munford for help. By the time Cobb in person and his first troops arrived, Munford's men, who had held for three hours, were already running out of ammunition and were being flanked on both sides. Before Cobb could get all his men in action, the Confederate force was routed. The infantry fled south down Pleasant Valley toward McLaws's main force at Sandy Hook, and the cavalry fled north up Pleasant Valley to recover their horses. By dark, Franklin had secured the gap, and McLaws the besieger had now become McLaws the besieged, sandwiched between the Harpers Ferry garrison to the south and Franklin to the north.

Back at Harpers Ferry, the garrison was completely surrounded, and Confederates were looking down at them from both Maryland Heights and Loudoun Heights. Things were, however, surprisingly quiet during the morning. The three Confederate commanders were still wasting time trying to communicate with each other to coordinate their actions. Neither McLaws nor Walker had yet succeeded in getting cannons in position on Maryland or Loudoun Heights. McLaws's task in getting cannons up to Maryland Heights was particularly difficult. It took two hundred men to pull each cannon up Solomon's Gap and, once on top, the foliage was so thick that McLaws spent all morning and early afternoon cutting a road the six miles to Maryland Heights.

During the morning, Col. Frederick D'Utassy asked Colonel Miles to give him permission to cross the river, ascend Elk Ridge as far as McGrath's Battery, and recover the four twenty-pounder brass cannons that were left behind during the Union abandonment of Maryland Heights the day before. Miles equivocated, stating, "Damn it; they have spiked the guns; it is of no use."[4] Colonel D'Utassy, on his own initiative, took four companies, crossed the bridge, ascended Elk Ridge to McGrath's Battery, and recovered all four cannons plus a substantial supply of ammunition. To the surprise of all, they met no Confederates. Two of the cannons proved to have been properly spiked so as to be unusable, but the other two were fully serviceable.

By 1 p.m., Walker succeeded in getting five long-range parrot guns atop Loudoun Heights and was ready for action. It took McLaws another hour to get a battery of four guns in place on Maryland Heights. When all was ready, Jackson gave the signal to commence firing. Artillery fire rained into Harpers Ferry from three directions. Miles's aide, Lieutenant Binney, described it as follows:

> Two oclock P.M., the enemy open fire at five different points—two full batteries on Loudoun Heights, a battery on Maryland Heights, a battery of two pieces of long range on Shepherdstown Road and on the Charlestown Turnpike. The cannonade is now terrific: the enemy's shell and shot fall in every direction; houses are demolished and detonation among the hills terrible. It is kept up until dark; our long range ammunition is expended; only 36 rounds left . . .[5]

Now it is true that during the Civil War long-range cannon fire did not kill large numbers of people—not even a tenth of those killed by rifle fire. However, it could be very demoralizing, particularly to raw troops (many of whom were at Harpers Ferry) if it came from multiple directions. It is especially not conducive to morale to know that while bending over to duck a whizzing cannon ball from the front, there is a distinct possibility that another may be bounding up from behind.

Toward evening, Jackson ordered Gen. A. P. Hill, who was on his far right operating against the refused Union flank, "to move along the left bank of the Shenandoah, and thus turn the enemy's left flank and enter Harpers Ferry."[6] As Hill moved toward the Shenandoah, he came upon a hill that was on a line with the Union position along Bolivar Heights. It was the perfect position to set up an artillery battery to enfilade the entire Union line. This Hill proceeded to do as he continued his advance toward the river.

As daylight came to a close on the fourteenth, Jackson was so pleased with developments so far that he sent the following message to Lee:

Through God's blessing, the advance which commenced this evening, has been successful thus far, and I look to him for complete success tomorrow. The advance has been directed to be resumed at dawn tomorrow morning. I am thankful that our loss has been small . . .[7]

This proved to be a key dispatch of the whole campaign. By the end of daylight on the fourteenth, the fall of Harpers Ferry, in accordance with Special Order 191, was already two days overdue, and the Union army was pushing Lee's troops back from the passes in South Mountain. Lee was already contemplating calling off the siege and withdrawing his army. This dispatch was instrumental in his decision to try to reunite the army at Sharpsburg and make a stand in Maryland.

Miles had a substantial force of cavalry in his surrounded garrison. This force included the Eighth New York, Twelfth Illinois, First Maryland, Cole's Cavalry, and a battalion of Rhode Island cavalry, about sixteen hundred in all. By the fourteenth, it was evident to most in Harpers Ferry that surrender was probable. The cavalry leaders, particularly Lt. Col. Hasbrouch Davis of the Twelfth Illinois, Col. B. F. Davis of the Eighth New York, and Capt. Samuel C. Means of the Loudoun Rangers began to hound Miles with the recommendation that the cavalry be permitted to cut its way out. The arguments were as follows: The Confederate general, Nathan Bedford Forrest, had done so under similar circumstances during the Union siege of Fort Donelson; the cavalry was of little value in the defense of Harpers Ferry; and, last but not least, the sixteen hundred horses would constitute a great prize for the Confederates if the cavalry surrendered.

Captain Means had an even more cogent reason for leaving. He was convinced that if the Confederates captured him he would be hanged. Means was a thirty-three-year old miller from Waterford in Loudoun County, Virginia, who had recruited two companies from the county to fight for the Union. Means was considered a traitor in the South, and there was a bounty on his head. Means and his men had made the logical decision to leave, with or without Colonel Miles's permission.

Miles was against the cavalry's leaving in sight of the infantry for

Map 24
Situation at End of Daylight, September 14

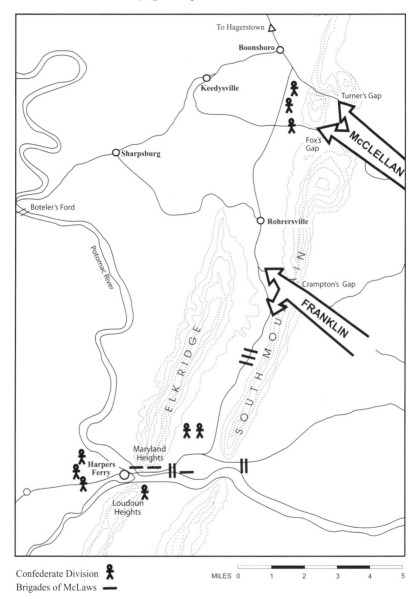

Confederate Division 👤
Brigades of McLaws ▬

MILES 0   1   2   3   4   5

fear it would demoralize them, but he finally agreed to a meeting
of the cavalry leaders, with General White present, in his office
after dark on the fourteenth. At the meeting, Miles reluctantly
acquiesced to the cavalry's request. He rejected proposed routes
along the south bank of the Potomac to Boteler's Ford or to the

east across the Shenandoah. Rather, he directed that they cross
the bridge, turn west, and follow the road to Sharpsburg. This was
the very road that Stuart had warned McLaws to guard, but, for
unknown reasons, McLaws did not do so.

Miles issued his order in writing, which was as follows:

Harpers Ferry Va.
Sept 14, 1862

Special Order #120

    The cavalry force at this post, except detached orderlies, will
make preparations to leave here at eight o'clock tonight, without
baggage wagons, ambulances, or led horses, crossing the
Potomac over the Sharpsburg road. The senior officer, Colonel
Voss, will assume command of the whole, which will form the
right at the quartermaster's officer, the left up Shenandoah
Street, without noise or loud command, in the following order:
Cole's Cavalry, 12th Illinois Cavalry, 8th New York Cavalry, 7th
squadron of Rhode Island Cavalry, and 1st Maryland Cavalry. No
other instructions can be given to the commander than to cut his
way through the enemy's line and join our army.

By order of Col. Miles
Lt. H. C. Reynolds, A. A. G.[8]

Captain Means's Loudoun Rangers were to be at the front of
the column with Cole's Cavalry. The guide was General White's
favorite scout, the civilian Thomas Noakes.

At the close of daylight on the fourteenth, the artillery died
down, but the movement of the surrounding Confederate forces
continued. The garrison artillery had wasted its ammunition the
last two days, ineffectively firing at targets above it that the gunners could not see, and its supply was nearly exhausted. No
couriers arrived at Harpers Ferry during the day, and Miles knew
nothing of McClellan's success at Turner's and Fox's Gaps. He
did not know that Franklin's relief force was just six miles to the
north in Pleasant Valley.

At the close of daylight, McLaws was no longer concerned
with capturing Harpers Ferry, but with his very survival. The situation at the close of daylight on Saturday, September 14, 1862,
is as depicted in map 24.

Chapter 12

Sunday Night, September 14

By the night of Sunday, September 14, 1862, the initiative had passed from Robert E. Lee into the hands of George B. McClellan. Lee was no longer acting in accordance with his plans but was reacting to McClellan's movements. The capture of Harpers Ferry was now already two days overdue, and McLaws's force north of the Potomac was now in mortal danger. Lee's main concern now was not to capture Harpers Ferry but to save his army. It was only Jackson's message of that evening, predicting the fall of Harpers Ferry the next day, that prevented Lee from calling off Jackson that night.

The night of the fourteenth was moonlit, permitting movement—and there was movement aplenty. By dark, Lee at Boonsboro realized that, with the forces available, he could no longer hold Turner's and Fox's Gaps, and so decided to withdraw. The original plan under Special Order 191 was for the Confederate army to reunite at Boonsboro or Hagerstown. These were no longer viable options. In fact, Boonsboro was to fall to the Union army within hours. Lee chose Sharpsburg as the new uniting point. Sharpsburg had much to offer. It was about nine miles southwest of Turner's Gap and presented a strong defensive position. It lay behind Antietam Creek, and, even more important, it was in front of Boteler's Ford on the Potomac. Boteler's Ford was the nearest point at which Lee's and Jackson's forces could reunite.

By dark, the Confederate wagon park and artillery reserve were already on the road to Sharpsburg, and by 10 p.m. the infantry began to withdraw from the gaps and follow. Fitz Lee's cavalry brigade, which had rejoined Lee after the Westminster episode, brought up the rear and covered the retreat.

The Confederates had two roads available for their retreat. One route followed the National Road from Turner's Gap to Boonsboro. At Boonsboro, a road angled off to the left that went to Sharpsburg and then on to Boteler's Ford and to

Shepherdstown on the Virginia side of the Potomac. The other road led from Fox's Gap to Keedysville on the Boonsboro-Sharpsburg road, about halfway between Boonsboro and Sharpsburg.

The Union had access to a third road to Sharpsburg that was no longer available to the Confederates. This road led from Rohrersville on the Boonsboro-Harpers Ferry road to Sharpsburg. When Franklin broke through Crampton's Gap to the Boonsboro-Harpers Ferry road to the south of Rohrersville, and McClellan broke through Turner's and Fox's Gaps to the Boonsboro-Harpers Ferry road north of Rohrersville, the six-mile stretch of the Boonsboro-Harpers Ferry road between the breakthroughs, including Rohrersville and its intersection, was entirely in Union hands (see map 24).

When Lee ordered the retreat from Turner's and Fox's Gaps, his troops were already exhausted. Longstreet's two divisions had left Hagerstown that morning at daylight, marched seventeen miles in the blazing sun to the gaps, and then went directly into action. Now, in the middle of the night, they were being tasked with making an additional nine-mile, forced night march to Sharpsburg. Some of the Confederates slipped off into the woods to sleep and could not be aroused when the orders came to fall back. Colonel Parker of the Thirtieth North Carolina stated that he could hardly keep his men awake, even when deadly missiles were flying among them; General Hood, in charge of the rear guard, said that he found it difficult to arouse and push on the tired men, who had fallen out by the wayside to get a few minutes' sleep.

While the exhausted Confederates retreated, the Union army did nothing. Despite the fact that McClellan had fresh troops available at the gaps who had not participated in the day's action and had cavalry on the scene, there was no Federal hot pursuit of the Confederates that night. In fact, none started before morning, when the Confederate infantry had already arrived behind Antietam Creek and was arranging its defense line. Furthermore, there was no rush by Union troops that night down the Rohrersville-Sharpsburg road to cut off the Confederates from Sharpsburg. Had Napoleon or Stonewall Jackson been in command of the Union army instead of McClellan, it might have been the end of Lee's army that night. The Union that night was like a boxer who had landed a telling blow, and then, instead of finishing off his opponent, stood back to admire his work while his opponent recovered.

If McClellan's failure to follow up his success at the northern gaps was bad, Franklin's at Crampton's Gap was worse. McClellan had driven the Confederates back from the northern gaps, but they had retreated in an orderly fashion. Six miles to the south, Franklin had driven the Confederates from Crampton's Gap and routed them. The Confederate infantry fled south on the Boonsboro-Harpers Ferry road toward McLaws's main force on the river, while the cavalry fled north to retrieve their horses. Franklin's objective was to the south. It was just six miles to the river and to the bridge to relieve Harpers Ferry. It was a moonlit night, and the infantry could have covered the distance in less than two hours, and the cavalry in less than an hour. Even if Franklin were stopped short of the river, he might have gotten close enough to make the garrison aware of his presence. However, Franklin did not pursue; instead, he bedded down his troops for the night.

McLaws, who had been facing to the south, now realized that the threat to his survival was from the north, from Franklin, and that the conquest of Harpers Ferry was now a secondary issue that would have to wait. First, McLaws rallied the remnants of his fleeing brigades (those of Semmes, Parham, and Cobb at Brownsville, four miles north of the river). Then he called on the bloodied brigades of Kershaw and Barksdale, who had captured Maryland Heights the day before, and Wilcox at Sandy Hook to proceed to Brownsville.

This action left only four brigades at the river. Two were near the bridge, blocking the access of the garrison to the east, and two were near the tip of South Mountain, blocking relief from the Frederick-Harpers Ferry road.

When Kershaw and Barksdale were called back from Maryland Heights, they left one regiment, from Barksdale's brigade, behind. This was the Thirteenth Mississippi, which had a total of only 202 individuals present. McLaws also withdrew two of the four cannons from Maryland Heights that he had so laboriously placed there earlier in the day. Thus, as the night progressed, Maryland Heights, captured only the day before, was ripe for the retaking by the Union garrison.

By 10 p.m. that night, Franklin's third division, under Couch, joined him at the gap. Franklin now had more than twenty thousand men. The defense line that McLaws was to organize that night, two miles to the south at Brownsville, had fewer than five thousand men. Franklin had access to unlimited reinforcements from the north via the Boonsboro-Harpers Ferry road. McLaws had access to none as long as Harpers Ferry held out.

Come morning, there was every reason to believe that Franklin would push McLaws's six brigades aside, and Harpers Ferry would be relieved. As for McLaws, it appeared that the only options then available to him would be to abandon his wagons and artillery and attempt to flee across Elk Ridge to join Lee, or to retreat to the east along the north bank of the Potomac, away from Lee. This was possibly the bleakest night for the Confederacy in the East since the beginning of the war.

Much now depended on Lafayette McLaws. McLaws was a short, chubby man who was forty-two years old in September 1862. He was a Georgian and a boyhood friend of Longstreet's. Both had attended West Point and graduated in the class of 1842 with Ulysses Grant and D. H. Hill. McLaws remained in the army until the outset of the Civil War nineteen years later, but never rose higher in rank than captain. He entered the Confederate army as a major, and, in May 1862, reached the rank of major general. McLaws proved a solid and competent division commander, but was never considered to be a "comer" or an inspired leader like A. P. Hill, John Bell Hood, Dorsey Pender, or other more youthful Confederate generals. Ultimately, McLaws's long-standing friendship with Longstreet soured and then deteriorated into outright animosity.

Back at Harpers Ferry, gloom and defeatism prevailed. Neither Major Cole nor any courier arrived from the outside on the fourteenth. Miles knew nothing about McClellan's breakthrough at Turner's and Fox's Gaps to the Boonsboro-Harpers Ferry road to the north, and nothing about Franklin's breakthrough into Pleasant Valley just six miles to the north. He also knew nothing about McLaws's withdrawal of his troops from Maryland Heights that night. The only news that Miles received that night was bad.

By 8 p.m., the cavalry was lined up and prepared to leave. Rather than an epic attempt to fight their way out, it was more akin to rats deserting a sinking ship, and it had a demoralizing effect on those of the garrison who knew about it. The route Miles selected for the cavalry crossed the bridge, turned left, and proceeded along the face of Elk Ridge, crossed a shoulder of Elk Ridge, and followed the river to Sharpsburg. Today it is known simply as Harpers Ferry Road. At Sharpsburg, it connected with a variety of roads leading in all directions. This was the very road that General Stuart had warned McLaws about, but McLaws, for whatever reason, had failed to block it.

Unknown to either side, the Union cavalry and the Confederates retreating from Turner's and Fox's Gaps were on a collision course. The retreating Confederates, following their wagon train, were approaching Sharpsburg from the north, and the Union cavalry was approaching Sharpsburg from the east.

The cavalry began crossing the bridge at 8:30 p.m. One might be inclined to picture its leaders as grizzled veterans from the Indian Wars, similar to the type John Wayne portrayed. Wrong! Two of the three leaders were lawyers from Chicago who had been on active duty in the military less than nine months. The senior officer was Col. Arno Voss, commanding officer of the Twelfth Illinois, and his deputy in the regiment was Lt. Col. Hasbrouch Davis. Voss was a thirty-nine-year-old German immigrant who was prominent in the German-American community. He had been editor of a German-language American newspaper, had entered the law, and had risen to the position of district attorney of Chicago. His fellow lawyer from Chicago was thirty-five-year-old Hasbrouch Davis. Davis was a member of a prominent political family. His father had been a longtime senator and governor of Massachusetts. Voss and Davis were active in the militia in Chicago before the war and, when the Twelfth Illinois was formed, were appointed its colonel and lieutenant colonel by the governor. The Eighth New York, however, which was also a part of the departing cavalry, was commanded by a professional officer, albeit of limited experience. This was thirty-year-old Col. B. F. Davis, who had graduated from West Point in 1854 and had been a first lieutenant as late as 1860. Colonel Davis was second in command to Voss. The two Davises and their guide, civilian Thomas Noakes, rode at the head of the column. To describe what followed, we turn to the words of Pvt. Henry Norton of Company H of the Eighth New York:

> On the 14th of September, everything was in readiness for us to get out of the place, if we could. In the evening, about 8 oclock, [we] were drawn up in line . . . We crossed the Potomac

River to the Maryland side on a pontoon bridge. Before we crossed, each captain gave orders to his company that each man must follow his file leader; that no orders would be given. We crossed the river in single file, the 12th Illinois in front, the 8th New York in the rear, while the colonel with his pilot and some 25 soldiers went ahead to clear the road. When the head of the column got across the river they would start off at full speed, so that by the time the last man was across, the head of the line was 10 miles away . . . I was near the end of the line; the way we went was a caution; each horse went as fast as he could go. By that time it was dark—dark was named for it . . . The only way we could tell we were from our file leaders was by the horses' shoes striking fire against the stones in the road . . . We kept it up that way for some five or six miles. The colonel came upon the rebel picket some two miles distant from the river; the picket fired his gun off then retreated. The rebels were surprised to see yankees coming from that direction. They thought we were cooped up in the ferry and did not dare come out.

Some two miles after the pickets were driven in the rebels blockaded the road to stop us. The Colonel knew what the rebels would do, so before he got there he went across lots and gave them the slip. The pilot knew every foot of the ground through Maryland, and the scout knew how Longstreet's corps was situated, having come from there about an hour before we started from the Ferry. The Colonel had his route all mapped out before we started; he was bound to go through or die in the attempt.

He managed to avoid the rebels until he got to Sharpsburg, where the advance guard had a brush with the rebels . . . It did not last long, as the Colonel soon drove them back . . . We learned afterwards by some prisoners taken at Antietam, that the whole of Longstreet's corps stood in line all the rest of the night, expecting to be attacked every minute . . . When the rear of the line got to Sharpsburg, we began to close up; then we had a chance to walk our horses; they were pretty winded, for they had been on a keen scoot ever since we left the river. We had gone through Longstreet's corps. A great many would say it was an impossibility . . . We could not have done it had it not been in the night and the Colonel having managed it just as he did . . .

Just before we got to the pike we halted in a piece of woods; we could hear wagons rumbling on the road ahead of us. The Colonel went ahead to reconnoiter, and when he got to the road he soon found out that it was a rebel wagon train. About a half a mile west from where we were was a fork in the road, the road that branched off running north into Pennsylvania. The Colonel went on ahead and got to the fords before the train. It was yet dark, for it was about 3 oclock in the morning . . . When the head team came along the Colonel told the teamster to turn his team off on the right hand road, so the whole train began to move off in that direction. The rebel teamsters never mistrusted but what everything was all right. It was a big undertaking, for the Colonel might lose this whole command by doing it. As soon as the train began to move off on that road the Colonel sent back for the 8th NY cavalry. We went forward and took possession of the train; the 12th Illinois cavalry was with us. It was done neat and slick . . . We had got the train along a number of miles before daylight. When the rebels found out they were prisoners, were they mad? Mad was no name for it . . . one fellow got off his mule and began to unhitch them from the wagon; another set the straw on fire that the shells were packed in . . . they thought that if they could delay the train it would give the rebels a chance to retake it; we put a stop to that . . . Each man took a team and rode along beside the driver, with a revolver in hand, and each one had orders to shoot the first man who did not obey orders. That quieted them down; so on we went.[1]

The troopers, along with their captured wagons, rode into Greencastle, Pennsylvania, at nine on the morning of the fifteenth—safe, and well beyond the reach of the rebels. Most were to join McClellan at Antietam by the seventeenth.

Private Norton's account was written more than twenty-five years after the event and is highly embellished. It makes the escape sound far more dangerous than it actually was. In fact, there was no force of Confederates on or near their route that was capable of stopping them. They did not ride through Longstreet's corps or encounter any member of it other than the wagon train. That night, half of Longstreet's corps was in Pleasant Valley under McLaws; the other half was retreating to Sharpsburg from Turner's and Fox's Gaps. The fast-moving Union cavalry passed through Sharpsburg well before Longstreet's first men arrived. The only occasional Confederate that the Union column brushed against that night was from Colonel Munford's cavalry brigade. The wagon train that the cavalry captured was not part of the wagon park retreating from Boonsboro to Sharpsburg that night. Rather, it was Longstreet's reserve ammunition train that he had ordered to proceed from Hagerstown to Williamsport when he vacated Hagerstown for South Mountain on the morning of the fourteenth.

The number of wagons actually captured and delivered to Greencastle is in dispute to this day, but it was somewhere between thirty and ninety, which was not an insignificant accomplishment.

In all, 1,594 troopers arrived in Greencastle that morning, having suffered no casualties en route. They had covered more than fifty miles from the time they had left Harpers Ferry at 8:30 p.m. on the fourteenth, until riding into Greencastle at 9 a.m. on the fifteenth. Not bad! Perhaps one of the greatest gains the fleeing cavalry realized was denying General Jackson the capture of 1,594 good cavalry horses. The cavalry's escape route is depicted in map 25.

Upon arriving at Greencastle, Colonel Voss sent the following dispatch to General Wool:

> Greencastle PA
> Sept 15, 1862

Maj General Wool

Harpers Ferry is from all sides invested by a force estimated at 30,000. By order of Colonel Miles I left it last evening at 8 o'clock with the cavalry, about 1,500 strong, to cut my way through the enemy's lines. I succeeded in reaching this place about 9 this morning, having passed the enemy's line about 3 miles northward of Williamsport, and capturing a wagon train of over 60 wagons loaded with ammunition, and 675 prisoners. Colonel Miles intends to hold the Ferry, but is anxiously looking for reinforcements.

Col. Arno A. Voss
Twelfth Illinois Cavalry[2]

Back at Harpers Ferry, cannon fire ceased at dark on the fourteenth, but movement continued throughout the night. General Hill set up artillery on the hill he had captured, opposite

Map 25
Cavalry Escape Route, September 14

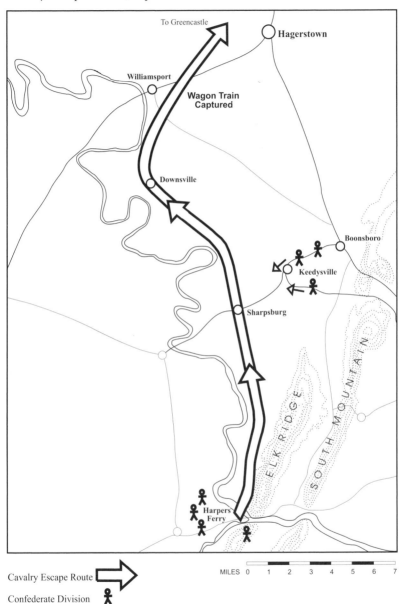

Cavalry Escape Route
Confederate Division

the Union left flank on Bolivar Heights. Two of his brigades continued down to the Shenandoah River and then moved along the river into Harpers Ferry to the flank and rear of the Union line. Hill's other men moved up to within 150 yards of the Union refused line, which extended at an approximate right angle from the Bolivar Heights line. Colonel S. Crutchfield, Jackson's chief of artillery, moved ten cannons across the Shenandoah during the night and set them up on a plateau of Loudoun Heights that took the Union defense line in flank and rear.

If the garrison was loosely surrounded by the end of daylight on the fourteenth, by the end of the night it was tightly boxed in, and the lines were so close that the demoralized defenders could hear the Confederates talking in the dark. To add to the defenders' woes, they were almost out of artillery ammunition other than canister. Lieutenant Binney stated that there were only thirty-six rounds left. The Union defenders clearly under-stood that an infantry assault would come in the morning, and that if they stood up to ward it off they would be swept away by artillery.

By 11 p.m., Lee was becoming more and more worried about McLaws. He was now suggesting various escape routes. At 11:15 p.m., he sent the following dispatch:

> Headquarters Army of Northern VA
> September 14, 1862 11:15 P.M.

Major General McLaws

> General: In addition to what has already been stated in reference to your abandonment of Weverton, and routes you can take, I will mention you might cross the Potomac, below Weverton, into Virginia. I believe there is a ford at Point of Rocks, and at Berlin below, but I do not know whether either is accessible to you. The enemy from Jefferson seems to have forced a passage at Crampton's Gap, which may leave all on the river clear. This por-tion of the army will take position at Centerville, commonly called Keedysville, 2 1/2 miles from Boonsboro, on the Sharpsburg road with a view of preventing the enemy that may enter the gap at Boonsboro turnpike from cutting you off, and enabling you to make a junction with it. If you can pass tonight on the river road, by Harpers Ferry, or cross the mountain below

Sharpsburg, let me know. I will be found at Centreville, or Keedysville, as it is called. By order of General Lee.

R. H. Chilton[3]

Before dawn, Lee became concerned only with McLaws's survival. The capture of Harpers Ferry was no longer an issue. He was now calling for desperate measures by McLaws. He sent the following dispatch:

> Keedysville Md
> Sept 15, 1862
>
> General McLaws
> Commanding Division etc.
>
> General: General Lee desires me to say that he sent several dispatches to you last night; he is in doubt they have been received. We have fallen back to this place to enable you to move readily to join us. You are desired to withdraw immediately from your position on Maryland Heights, and join us here. If you can't get off any other way, you must cross the mountain. The utmost dispatch is required. Should you be able to cross over to Harpers Ferry, do so and report immediately.
>
> I am respectfully your obedient servant.
>
> L. Long
> Colonel and Military Secretary[4]

By the time of these dispatches, Lee had made his decision to make his stand at Sharpsburg. Keedysville, the point of origin of the dispatches, was on the Boonsboro-Sharpsburg road, about midway between the two.

Lee's recommendations to McLaws that night reflected the desperation of the situation. The first dispatch recommended that McLaws attempt to move down the Potomac to Berlin or to Point of Rocks to attempt to make a crossing. This action entailed moving away from, rather than toward, a juncture with Lee. Had McLaws followed this suggestion, he would have required a march of almost sixty miles to join Lee at Sharpsburg and could not have arrived in time to participate in the battle of Antietam.

Map 26
Situation at Daylight, September 15

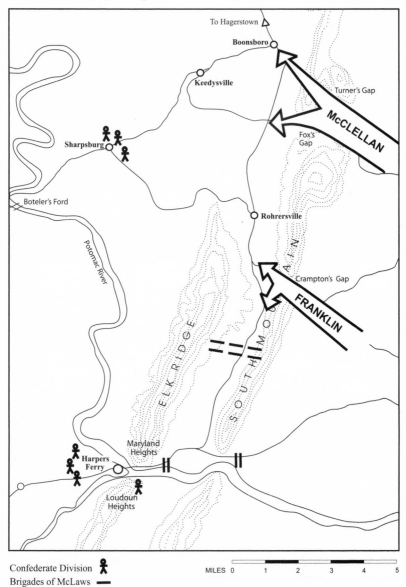

Confederate Division
Brigades of McLaws

MILES 0 1 2 3 4 5

Map 27
Lee's Suggested Escape Routes for McLaws

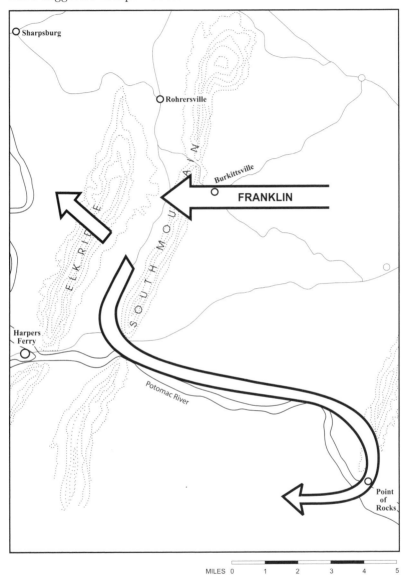

The second dispatch stated that "if you cannot get off any other way, you must cross the mountain." The mountain referred to was Elk Ridge. To cross Elk Ridge, McLaws would have had to abandon his wagons and artillery—and probably his horses as well. In that case, he would have joined Lee as a semi-organized mob, rather than a potent fighting machine.

That night, McLaws sent a courier, accompanied by his aide, Lieutenant Tucker, to Lee, giving his situation. Tucker returned and reported that they had been unable to get through and that the courier had been killed.

By night on September 14, McClellan was already proclaiming victory. At 9:40 p.m., he sent the following dispatch to Halleck:

> Headquarters Army of the Potomac
> Three miles beyond Middletown
> Sept 14, 1862 9:40 P.M.

Major General Halleck
General-in-Chief

> After a very severe engagement, the Corps' of Hooker and Reno have carried the heights commanding the Hagerstown road. The troops behaved magnificently. They never fought better. Franklin has been hotly engaged on the extreme left. I do not yet know the result, except that the firing indicated progress on his part. The action continued after dark, and terminated leaving us in possession of the entire crest. It has been a glorious victory. I cannot yet tell whether the enemy will retreat during the night or appear in increased force in the morning. I am hurrying up everything from the rear, to be prepared for any eventuality. I regret to add that the gallant and able General Reno is killed.

Geo. B. McClellan[5]

As daylight came on September 15, 1862, thirty-six hours of Miles's estimated forty-eight-hour hold-out time had elapsed. The general situation is depicted in map 26. Lee's suggested escape routes for McLaws are depicted in map 27.

Chapter 13

Monday, September 15

Colonel Miles's estimated holdout of forty-eight hours was due to run out at darkness this date. As things turned out, his estimate was overly optimistic. The Confederate artillery barrage on Harpers Ferry opened at daylight. Colonel Trimble was in charge of the Union brigade on the left on Bolivar Heights. The following description of the morning's events is taken from his sworn testimony before the commission investigating the loss of Harpers Ferry:

Question: Was the fire from those batteries that morning a severe one?
Answer: It was perfectly terrific.

Question: Have you been in other engagements besides that one?
Answer: Yes sir; and under artillery fire in three different engagements.

Question: How did that compare with what you had seen in other engagements?
Answer: The others were so perfectly insignificant in comparison with this that there was just no comparison at all.

Question: Did the fires from these different batteries of the enemy command the entire line of ours from every conceivable direction or not?
Answer: It commanded every foot of it around the batteries on the left and along the lines, enfilading that part of the ground, and producing a terrible cross fire. Our position was under their command, every foot of ground; there was not a place where you could lay the palm of your hand and say it was safe. I rode through it all that morning and saw it.

Question: Do you think you would have been destroyed without an assault, simply by long range cannon?

Answer: No, sir; I do not think they could have destroyed us in an hour, or a half a day by their artillery alone, because we could have kept the men under cover, but the very moment they advanced with their infantry in such superior numbers and our men rose to engage them, we would have been swept from the very face of the earth by their artillery . . . The very moment they rose from their position I think there would have been such a destruction of human life without the accomplishment of any good that we would have been held morally responsible by the country for having permitted it.[1]

Between 8 and 9 a.m., the various Union batteries began to report one by one that they were out of long-range ammunition. Colonel Miles stated to General White that they would have to surrender. White recommended calling a council of war among the brigade commanders to get their opinions. A council was quickly convened of White, Miles, D'Utassy, and Trimble. Their opinion was unanimous: surrender was necessary. The time the white flag went up is debatable, but it was before 9 a.m.

White subsequently listed four reasons justifying the surrender:

First. The officer commanding had lost all confidence in his ability to further defend the place, and was the first to advise surrender.

Second. There was no reason to hope that the attenuated line on Bolivar Heights could be maintained, even for half an hour, against the greatly superior forces massed for the assault, supported if necessary by an attack on our rear by Generals Walker and McLaws.

Third. Great as was the disparity in numbers, the disparity in position was greater. Harpers Ferry and Bolivar Heights were dominated by Maryland and Loudoun Heights, and the other positions held by the enemy's artillery. The crest of Maryland Heights is at an elevation of 1060 feet; the southern point, nearest Harpers Ferry, 649 feet; Loudoun Heights 954 feet. The south-west slope of the latter and the grounds nearby, west of the Shenandoah, where batteries of the enemy were placed, were 300 to 600 feet high. The elevation of Bolivar Heights is about 300 feet, while Camp Hill and the town of Harpers Ferry are still lower. Thus all our movements of men or guns during the engagement of the 14th and 15th, as well as the effects of their own plunging fire, were plainly visible from the enemy's signal-station on Loudoun Heights. No effective reply could be made to fire from their elevated positions, no suitable defenses existed from which to resist the assault, and there was no opportunity on the morning of the 15th to change our position, even if there had been a better one to occupy.

Fourth. To await the assault, then impending, with no hope of even a temporary successful resistance, did not seem to justify the sacrifice of life consequent upon such a course—the situation being regarded as one of the unfortunate chances of war, unavoidable under existing circumstances.[2]

General White might have listed reasons five and six: the garrison was out of long-range artillery ammunition, and there were only two days' rations left for the troops.

When the decision to surrender was made, neither Miles nor White nor anyone else in the garrison knew that Franklin's relief force was less than five miles to the north and that Maryland Heights had been all but abandoned. Had they known, they might have decided otherwise.

Despite the talk of terrific bombardments and overwhelming enemy forces, the casualties experienced by the garrison were miniscule. The final figures were 44 killed, 173 wounded, and 12,520 surrendered. Of the 217 killed and wounded, at least 140, or almost 65 percent, were casualties on Maryland Heights during the fighting on the twelfth and thirteenth. Of the 44 killed, at least 28 were killed on Maryland Heights. Of the 173 wounded, at least 109 were wounded on Maryland Heights. To put it another way, no more than 16 were killed and 64 wounded by all of the bombardment and fighting at Harpers Ferry on September 14 and 15. One might suppose that the casualties among the artillery men were disproportionately high. After all, they were up and working while the infantry was seeking shelter, and much of the bombardment was specifically directed at them. The total casualties among the 744 artillery men present were 2 killed and 3 wounded. Ironically, the last man of the garrison to be mortally wounded was none other than the commanding officer, Colonel Miles.

The council of war had just concluded. The white flags had gone up. General White had departed to seek terms, and Colonel Miles and Lieutenant Binney were looking for their horses. Unfortunately, the Confederate bombardment had not entirely ceased. Walker's artillerists on top of Loudoun Heights could not see the white flags through the haze and were still dropping shells into the Union lines. One landed directly behind Miles and exploded, tearing the flesh from his leg to the bone. The wound proved mortal. Miles was carried to his quarters where he lingered until 4:30 p.m. the next day.

What were the Confederate casualties in the battle for Harpers Ferry? Most of the casualties were on Maryland Heights and were as follows: Kershaw's brigade—35 killed, 178 wounded; Barksdale's brigade—2 killed, 15 wounded. The remaining Confederate casualties were as follows: Walker's division—1 killed, 3 wounded; A. P. Hill's division—3 killed, 66 wounded; Lawton's and Jones's division—not reported but insignificant, probably fewer than the fingers on one's hands.

The total Confederate casualties were thus about 300. If we exclude the casualties on Maryland Heights, it was probably safer to have been a Confederate involved in the battle of Harpers Ferry than it would to be a civilian today strolling through Central Park after dark.

The minute Harpers Ferry surrendered, the overall situation between the Union and Confederate forces was completely transformed. McLaws was no longer trapped. He could cross the bridge and join Jackson, or, conversely, Jackson could cross the bridge and reinforce him. McLaws, Jackson, and Walker were also free to rejoin Lee, or vice versa.

If time had been of the essence for the Union to destroy the Confederate components before they reunited, it was now of the quintessence.

Now let us return to Franklin's relief force in Pleasant Valley, five miles to the north. Franklin's two divisions broke through Crampton's Gap before dark on the fourteenth. His third division caught up with him and joined him about 10 p.m. He then had a combined force of more than twenty thousand available for the relief of Harpers Ferry, and the bridge was just six miles down Pleasant Valley. The only obstacles between Franklin and the bridge were one small brigade and darkness. Faced with this situation, Franklin chose to rest his troops.

During the night and early morning, McLaws gathered six of his ten brigades at Brownsville, two miles south of Crampton's Gap on the Boonsboro-Harpers Ferry road and just four miles north of the bridge, to form a defense line against Franklin. These consisted of the three brigades defeated at the gap on the fourteenth (Cobb's, Semmes's, and William Mahone's [led by Parham that day]), the two withdrawn from Maryland Heights

(Kershaw's and Barksdale's), plus Wilcox's. He left only four brigades behind—two to guard the pass between South Mountain and the river to prevent any relief force from reaching Harpers Ferry, and two at Sandy Hook to prevent the garrison from crossing the bridge and approaching his defense line at Brownsville from the rear.

By daylight, he had arranged his forces at Brownsville into two defense lines stretching across Pleasant Valley and facing north. The first line consisted of the fresh brigades of Wilcox, Kershaw, and Barksdale. The backup line consisted of the defeated and decimated brigades of Mahone (Parham), Semmes, and Cobb. This total force consisted of fewer than five thousand men. Pleasant Valley at Brownsville was more than two miles wide. Consequently, the defense lines were extremely thin (see map 28).

Sunrise on September 15 was at 5:40 a.m. Were Franklin's forces ready to attack soon after daylight? Of course they weren't! Let us turn to General Franklin's own words:

> As I was crossing the mountain about 7 A.M., on September 15th, I had a good view of the enemy's force below, which seemed to be well posted on hills stretching across the valley, which is at this place about two miles wide. When I reached General Smith we made an examination of the position, and concluded that it would be suicidal to attack it. The whole breadth of the valley was occupied, and batteries swept the only approaches to the position which, properly defended, would have required a much greater force than ours to have carried . . . The only force available for an attack would have been Smith's division, of about 4500 men, Slocum's division being in no condition to fight that day.[3]

At about 8:30 a.m., Franklin noted that the cannonading from Harpers Ferry had ceased. He concluded that Harpers Ferry must have surrendered and that an attack now by him would be doubly dangerous. McLaws could now be reinforced by Jackson and, if he, Franklin, moved down the valley, he would be moving farther away from McClellan.

In short, the golden opportunities of the Union that morning had been frittered away by excuses and rationalizations. Again, what was possible for the Confederates seemed impossible for the Union. The Confederates could move at night. The Union could not. Confederates defeated on one day could fight the next. Union forces victorious on one day could not fight on the next.

Map 28
Franklin vs. McLaws, Morning of September 15

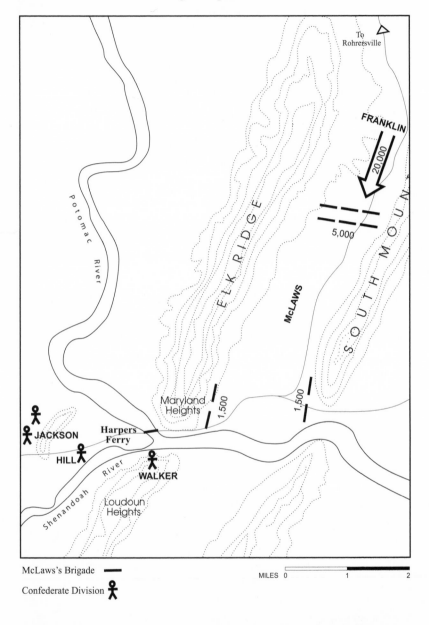

McLaws's Brigade ▬

Confederate Division ☗

Had Franklin attacked early that morning, everything might have been different. It is highly possible that the Harpers Ferry garrison would have heard the sound of the battle and not surrendered. It is also possible that whatever the outcome of the McLaws-Franklin battle, the very fact of the battle might have kept McLaws from rejoining Lee in time for the battle of Antietam—and without McLaws, Lee would have lost.

McClellan retained Franklin's corps at Rohrersville throughout the remainder of the fifteenth. Rohrersville is a small town on the Boonsboro-Harpers Ferry road about three miles north of Crampton's Gap. From there, a road radiates off to the west to Sharpsburg, seven miles distant. At this time, the possibility could not be excluded that Lee, who had retreated to Sharpsburg on the Boonsboro-Sharpsburg road followed by McClellan, would double back on the road to Rohrersville. There, he could meet with Jackson, who was now able to cross the bridge at Harpers Ferry and move up Pleasant Valley to Rohrersville. If this happened, Halleck's worst nightmare would be a reality. The combined Confederate army would be between McClellan and Washington.

Meanwhile, back at Harpers Ferry, General White was seeking General Jackson to surrender Harpers Ferry. Colonel Henry Kyd Douglas of Jackson's staff described what transpired:

> Under instructions from General Jackson, I rode up the pike and into the enemy's line to ascertain the purpose of the white flag. Near the top of the hill I met General White and staff and told him my mission. He replied that Colonel Miles had been mortally wounded, that he was in command and desired to have an interview with General Jackson. Just then General Hill came up from the direction of his line, and at his request I conducted them to General Jackson, whom I found sitting on his horse where I had left him. He was not, as the Comte de Paris says, leaning against a tree asleep, but exceedingly wide awake. The contrast in appearances there presented was striking. General White, riding a handsome black horse, was carefully dressed and had on untarnished gloves, boots and sword. His staff were equally comely in costume. On the other hand, General Jackson was the dingiest, worst dressed, and worst mounted general that a warrior who cared for good looks and style would wish to surrender to. The surrender was unconditional, and then General Jackson turned the matter over to General Hill.[4]

The terms granted by Hill were lenient. They provided that all private property of individuals and the sidearms of officers would be retained by them; all the troops could keep their blankets and overcoats and would be provided two days' rations; all Union troops were to be immediately paroled not to serve again until regularly exchanged; and, refugees were not to be treated as prisoners unless they were deserters from the Confederate army. In addition to these liberal terms, Hill lent White twenty wagons and their teams to haul off officers' private property, with the understanding that the wagons and teams would be returned at the earliest opportunity.

There was only one pontoon bridge across the Potomac, and McLaws needed it to cross his troops into Virginia. White wanted to use it to cross his paroled troops into Maryland on their march to Washington. The Confederates, of course, had priority, and Hill suggested that White's troops ford the Shenandoah and march to Washington via the south bank of the Potomac. After Hill and White together examined possible crossing points and found them unsatisfactory, Hill agreed to allow White to use the bridge during any breaks in the Confederate crossing.

Jackson permitted his three divisions to enter Harpers Ferry. The troops of the Army of Northern Virginia neither plundered nor looted. However, there was one source of goodies that was considered fair game for the winner to take. That was the sutler's supplies. The sutler, although a private merchant, received exclusive permission to accompany a regiment and set up his mobile store at the regiment's camp. He traded in goods that were not part of the standard army ration. These included items such as candies, pastries, canned and fresh fruits, sardines, and oyster crackers, as well as stamps and stationery, reading material, cigars, tobacco, and personal articles such as razors, combs, and various lotions and remedies. Although sutlers were technically forbidden to sell alcoholic beverages, they often sold them under the guise of lotions and remedies. In effect, a sutler's store was a regiment's PX.

When Jackson's men entered town, they loaded their haversacks with sutler's goodies. By the time Walker's and McLaws's troops (and McLaws had done most of the fighting and taken most of the casualties) entered town, the shelves were bare.

As Jackson's men placed a can of peaches or a couple of molasses cookies in their haversacks, none realized that the victorious Confederate troops were now within forty-eight hours of Armageddon, and for many their little delicacies would be the last of their earthly pleasures.

About 10 a.m., General McLaws was advised by courier that Harpers Ferry had surrendered. He ordered the brigades remaining at Sandy Hook to advance their skirmishers to the bridge and directed that all his wagon trains proceed to the bridge. He then sent his aide-de-camp to Harpers Ferry to communicate with General Jackson. The aide returned and reported that Jackson wanted to see McLaws. McLaws, seeing that the Union troops showed no disposition to advance against his defense line at Brownsville, left General Anderson in charge and rode into Harpers Ferry. Jackson ordered McLaws to proceed to Sharpsburg with all possible dispatch. This move would take time, as Jackson's and Walker's troops would occupy the road to Shepherdstown all day and much of the next, and it would take McLaws's troops all that night just to cross the bridge into Harpers Ferry.

McLaws returned and ordered his wagon trains to cross the bridge, with his infantry to follow. He then withdrew his north-ward-facing defense line from Brownsville to the river. Franklin's troops did not molest him and showed no inclination to follow.

To understand the situation in the north following McClellan's breakthrough at Turner's and Fox's Gaps, we must return to the map (see map 29). The National Road crosses South Mountain and continues to Boonsboro. At Boonsboro, there are two roads radiating off to the south. The first is the Harpers Ferry road that goes through Rohrersville. The second goes to Sharpsburg. Near Middletown in the Catoctin Valley, a secondary road angles off the National Road to the southwest. It cuts through South Mountain at Fox's Gap, crosses the Harpers Ferry road, and hits the Boonsboro-Sharpsburg road at a small town called Keedysville. It was at Keedysville that Lee set up his temporary headquarters as his troops retreated to Sharpsburg.

McClellan directed the pursuit of the retreating Confederates as follows. The corps of Sumner, Hooker, and Mansfield were to follow the route to Sharpsburg via Boonsboro. The corps of Burnside (formerly Reno's) and Porter, of which only one division was present, were to follow the lower road to Keedysville. Upon reaching the intersection of the Harpers Ferry road, they were either to turn south to reinforce Franklin or continue to Keedysville as circumstances dictated. McClellan, upon hearing of the Confederate stand at Sharpsburg, ordered Burnside and Porter to continue to Keedysville and thence to Sharpsburg.

One might assume that the retreating Confederates were

Map 29
McClellan's Pursuit of September 15

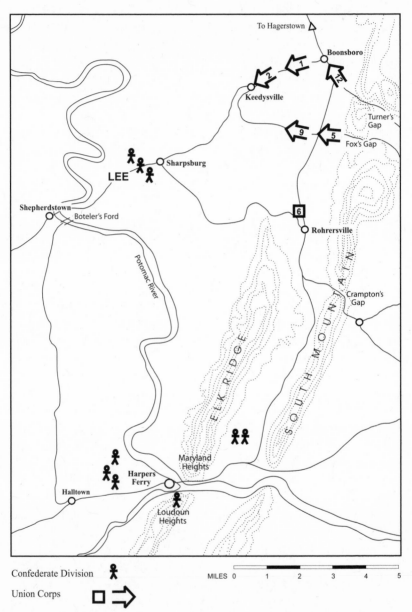

Confederate Division   🧍

Union Corps   □ ⟹

MILES   0   1   2   3   4   5

continually harassed by cavalry and pressed by infantry in the same way Wellington pursued Napoleon on Napoleon's retreat from Waterloo. This was not the case. Except for a sharp clash of cavalry between Fitz Lee and Pleasonton at Boonsboro, the Confederate retreat was unmolested. Excepting the losses at Boonsboro, the retreating Confederates lost not a gun, a wagon, or a man.

The corps of Hooker, which had been in contact with the Confederates on South Mountain, rested while Sumner's corps passed through it, following hours behind the Confederates.

The first division to come up against the Confederates at Sharpsburg was Richardson's division of Sumner's corps. When Richardson found the Confederates deployed to make a stand, he stopped at a respectable distance and waited for reinforcements. When Hooker caught up, he reconnoitered the Confederate position and estimated their number as thirty thousand, which was approximately twice the actual figure.

When McClellan learned of the Confederate stand, he ordered that each corps was to be placed in position for the attack as it arrived—but that no attack was to be made until he arrived on the scene. What followed was described by Maj. Gen. Jacob Cox, commanding the Kanawa division in Burnside's Ninth Corps:

When we approached the line of hills bordering the Antietam, we received orders to turn off the road to the left, and halted our battalions closed in mass. It was now about 3 o-clock in the afternoon. McClellan, as it seemed, had just reached the field, and was surrounded by a group of his principal officers, most of whom I had never seen before. I rode up with General Burnside, dismounted, and was very cordially greeted by General McClellan. He and Burnside were evidently on terms of most intimate friendship and familiarity. He introduced me to the officers I had not known before, referring pleasantly to my service with him in Ohio and West Virginia, putting me upon an easy footing with them in a very agreeable and genial way.

We walked up the slope of the ridge before us, and looking westward from its crest the whole field of the coming battle was before us. Immediately in front the Antietam wound through the hollow, the hills rising gently on both sides. In the background

on our left was the village of Sharpsburg, with fields inclosed
[*sic*] by stone fences in front of it. At its right was a bit of wood
(since known as the West Wood), with the little Dunker Church
standing out white and sharp against it. Farther to the right and
left the scene was closed in by wooded ridges with open farm
lands between, the whole making as pleasing and prosperous a
landscape as can easily be imagined. We made a large group as we
stood upon the hill, and it was not long before we attracted the
enemy's attention. A puff of white smoke from a knoll on the
right of the Sharpsburg road was followed by the screaming of a
shell over our heads. McClellan directed that all but one or two
should retire behind the ridge, while he continued the reconnaissance, walking slowly to the right. I noted with satisfaction the
cool and business-like air with which he made his examination
under fire. The confederate artillery was answered by a battery,
and a lively cannonade ensued on both sides, though without any
noticeable effect. The enemy's position was revealed, and he was
evidently in force on both sides of the turnpike in front of
Sharpsburg, covered by the undulations of the rolling ground
which hid his infantry from our sight.

The examination of the enemy's position and the discussion of
it continued till near the close of the day.[5]

McClellan was looking at three Confederate infantry divisions: that of D. H. Hill, the two of Longstreet, and the cavalry
brigade of Fitz Lee. This was the force he had defeated at South
Mountain the day before and that had fled during the night.
These were the same troops that McClellan, in his victory dispatches for the battle of South Mountain, had declared were
"panicked," "fleeing," "routed," "in disorder," and "whipped."
Two of the three Confederate divisions had marched from
Hagerstown to South Mountain on the previous day, participated in the battle, and then, during the night, had retreated to
Sharpsburg. They must have been totally exhausted. The total
Confederate force before McClellan was probably not more
than fifteen thousand. He already had at least four times that
number on the scene.

McClellan had read Special Order 191. He knew that six
Confederate divisions were at Harpers Ferry. He knew that
Harpers Ferry had fallen that morning. He knew that the six
Confederate divisions at Harpers Ferry would be pounding the

roads to join the three at Sharpsburg. He knew, or should have known, that the Confederate force before him was going to grow rapidly, that time was against him, that the best odds he was going to get were now. Time was golden and fleeting. And yet he frittered away much of the day. It is not known how many hours were wasted before he arrived on the scene. What happened after he arrived on the scene, as described by General Cox, speaks for itself.

Both Jackson and McClellan issued victory messages on the fifteenth—Jackson for his victory at Harpers Ferry, and McClellan for his presumed victories at the South Mountain passes. In fact, McClellan issued several victory proclamations and must have devoted a significant part of the day to writing. Jackson attributed his victory to the Almighty. The Almighty appeared to have played no role in McClellan's victories. Jackson's victory message was addressed to Lee and released at 8 a.m., just about the time the white flag went up. It read as follows:

> General: Through God's blessing, Harpers Ferry and its garrison are to be surrendered. As Hill's troops have borne the heaviest part in the engagement, he will be left in command until the prisoners and public property shall be disposed of, unless you direct otherwise. The other forces can move off this evening so soon as they get their rations. To what point shall they move? I write at this time in order that you may be apprised of the condition of things. You may expect to hear from me again to-day after I get more information respecting the number of prisoners etc.[6]

About twenty-four hours later, Jackson issued the following message:

> Yesterday God crowned our army with another brilliant success in the surrender at Harpers Ferry of Brigadier-General White and 11,000 troops, an equal number of small arms, 73 pieces of artillery, and about 200 wagons. In addition to other stores, there is a large amount of camp and garrison equipage. Our loss was very small. The meritorious conduct of officers and men will be mentioned in a more extended report.[7]

McClellan's first victory message of the day was sent at 8 a.m. and was as follows:

Bolivar Md, Sept 15, 1862 8 A.M.

Maj Gen Halleck
General-in-Chief

I have just learned from General Hooker, in the advance, who states that the information is perfectly reliable that the enemy is making for Shepherdstown in a perfect panic; and General Lee last night stated publicly that he must admit that they had been shockingly whipped. I am hurrying everything foreward [*sic*] to endeavor to press their retreat to the utmost.[8]

He immediately followed up the above with the following:

Bolivar Md, Sept 15, 1862 8 A.M.

Maj Gen Halleck
General-in-Chief

I am happy to inform you that Franklin's success on the left was as complete as that on the center and on the right, and his getting possession of the Burkittsville Gap, after a severe engagement. On all parts of the line the troops, old and new, behaved with the utmost steadiness and gallantry, carrying with but little assistance from our own artillery, very strong positions, defended by artillery and infantry. I do not think our losses very severe. The corps of D. H. Hill and Longstreet were engaged with our right. We have taken a considerable number of prisoners. The enemy disappeared during the night. Our troops are now advancing in pursuit of them. I do not know where he will be found. The morale of our men is now restored.[9]

McClellan then sent the following message to Governor Curtin of Pennsylvania:

Boonsboro, September 15, 1862—8 A.M.

Gov Andrew G. Curtin
Harrisburg:

I have the pleasure of announcing to you that we gained a

complete victory over the enemy yesterday afternoon, and have now entire possession of the South Mountain range. I congratulate you on the gallant behavior of the Pennsylvania Reserves, who as well as all the troops, both old and new, acted with the greatest steadiness and gallantry. The army is moving in pursuit of the enemy.

P.S. I just learned that the enemy are making for Shepherdstown in a perfect panic. Please have any damage done to the Hagerstown road repaired at once, as I shall want to use it for my supplies.[10]

As McClellan warmed to the subject, the battle grew in his mind from a simple victory to a panic to a rout. He took the unusual step of sending a message to old, retired Gen. Winfield Scott after sending his messages to Halleck:

> Camp Near Boonsboro Md
> Sept 15, 1862

Lt. General Winfield Scott
West Point:

We attacked a large force of the enemy yesterday occupying a strong mountain pass, 4 miles west of Middletown. Our troops, old and new regiments, behaved most valiantly and gained a signal victory. R. E. Lee in command. The rebels routed and retreating in disorder this morning. We are pursuing closely and taking many prisoners.[11]

By this time, even Lincoln was caught up in the victory euphoria and sent the following message to the governor of Illinois:

> Wash D. C.
> Sept 15, 1862 3 P.M.

Hon. J. K. Dubois,
Springfield Ill

I now consider it safe to say that General McClellan has gained a great victory over the great rebel army in Maryland, between

Frederick and Hagerstown. He is now pursuing a flying foe.

A. Lincoln[12]

Who won what on September 14-15, 1862? There were three distinct but clearly related battles. These were the battle at Harpers Ferry, the one at Crampton's Gap, and the one at Turner's and Fox's Gaps. The casualties (killed, wounded, captured, and missing) of the three were as follows:

	Harpers Ferry	Crampton's Gap	Turner's/Fox's Gaps
Union	12,737	533	1,183
Confederate	300	840	2,685

The Union casualties are actual. The Confederate casualties are estimates that some consider high. In addition to personnel casualties, material losses must be considered. The Confederates captured seventy-three cannons, more than two hundred wagons, and more than twelve thousand stands of small arms. The Union captured two cannons, the thirty to ninety wagons captured by the Harpers Ferry cavalry, and at most a few hundred stands of small arms.

The battle of Harpers Ferry was unquestionably a resounding Confederate victory. The two battles at the gaps were Union victories only in the sense that the Union captured positions defended by the Confederates and inflicted more casualties than they took. However, the objective of the Union was never to simply occupy the gaps; and the objective of the Confederates was never to defend them indefinitely. The objective of the Union was to destroy the Confederate army in detail before it could reunite. The objective of the Confederates was to defend the gaps until Harpers Ferry fell so that the Confederate army could reunite. In this sense, the battles of the gaps were a resounding success for the Confederates.

In any event, the victory proclamations by the Union were full of exaggerations and half-truths. The Confederates were not panicked, routed (except at Crampton's Gap), or flying; they were not closely pursued; the Union was not capturing large numbers of prisoners; and R. E. Lee was not in personal charge at the scene of any of the three battles.

As day came to a close on Monday, September 15, 1862, the

Map 30
Situation at the End of September 15

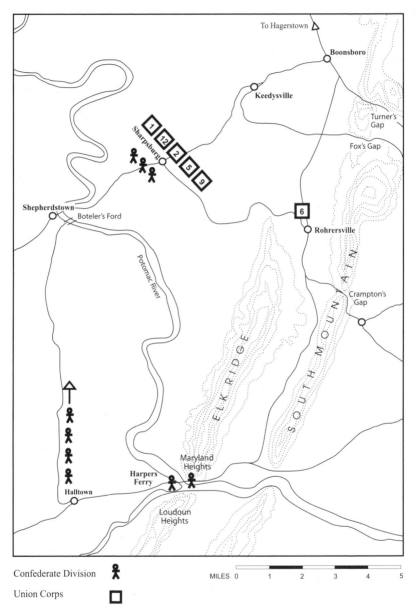

Confederate Division 👤

Union Corps ☐

MILES 0   1   2   3   4   5

corps of Hooker, Sumner, Mansfield, Cox (formerly Reno), and
Porter were taking up positions on Antietam Creek, facing the
division of D. H. Hill and the two divisions of Longstreet.
Franklin's corps was left at Rohrersville in Pleasant Valley.
Jackson, followed by Walker, was preparing for a night march
from Harpers Ferry to Sharpsburg. McLaws's infantry was crossing the bridge at Harpers Ferry, following his wagons to a
bivouac at Halltown. Hill was administering the surrender of
Harpers Ferry.

Fate was inexorably drawing both armies to the little town of
Sharpsburg, where the greatest bloodletting of the war was to
take place. The situation at the end of the fifteenth is as depicted in map 30.

Chapter 14

Tuesday, September 16

The euphoria in Washington created by McClellan's victory proclamations of the fifteenth carried over to the sixteenth. Some now believed it was all over but the mopping up. However, by the afternoon of the fifteenth, McClellan came to the realization that it was not quite over when he found that the Confederates retreating from South Mountain had not continued and fled across the Potomac, as he had supposed they would, but had stopped at Sharpsburg and were facing him, apparently still full of fight.

By dark on the fifteenth, McClellan had drawn up almost his full army before the Confederates, except for Franklin's corps, which he had purposely left at Rohrersville. Even this corps, however, was within supporting distance, as Rohrersville was only eight miles from Sharpsburg. The Confederate force at Sharpsburg was the same as the one that had been defeated at Turner's and Fox's Gaps. It had not yet increased by a man. By the end of the fifteenth then, almost all of McClellan's army of six corps and ninety thousand men was facing or within supporting distance of the fifteen thousand Confederates facing him at Sharpsburg.

The early morning hours of the sixteenth were possibly the most valuable and perishable of the war. Two of Jackson's divisions, followed by Walker's division, were making a forced night march from Harpers Ferry to join Lee. At dawn on the sixteenth, the head of the column was just splashing across the Potomac at Boteler's Ford, four miles south of Sharpsburg. Jackson's troops would be arriving at Sharpsburg all morning, followed by Walker's in the afternoon.

This morning was McClellan's golden opportunity. It was his best and almost his last chance to smash Lee's army in detail before it could reunite.

McClellan had reconnoitered the Confederate position all afternoon on the fifteenth. Was he ready to attack at daylight on the sixteenth before Jackson came up? Of course he wasn't! And why not? Because of the fog, that's why. At 7 a.m., McClellan sent the following message to Halleck:

> Headquarters Army of the Potomac
> Bivouac near Sharpsburg, Md.
> September 16, 1862—7 A.M.

Maj Gen. H. W. Halleck,
General-in-Chief

The enemy yesterday held a position just in front of Sharpsburg. When our troops arrived in sufficient force it was too late in the day to attack. This morning a heavy fog has thus far prevented us doing more than to ascertain that some of the enemy are still there. Do not know in what force. Will attack as soon as situation of enemy is developed. I learn Miles surrendered 8 A.M. yesterday unconditionally. I fear his resistance was not as stubborn as it might have been. Had he held the Maryland Heights he would have inevitably been saved. The time lost on account of the fog is being occupied in getting up supplies, for the want of which many of our men are suffering.

Geo. B. McClellan[1]

After major actions, units of both armies were required to submit written reports covering their units' activities and losses. Numerous reports covering the activity of September 16 at Antietam were written and have survived. The reports of Longstreet, Jackson, Stuart, and Jones make no mention of fog. The reports describing the crossing of the river bottom at dawn make no mention of fog. Hooker's report makes no mention of fog. The reports of artillery units that were active that morning, and whose business it was to observe and fire at enemy positions, make no mention of fog; and the reports of signal units, whose duty it was to occupy high places and observe and report battlefield conditions, made no mention of fog. Most amazing of all, McClellan's report of the activity on September 16 made no mention of fog. McClellan's only comments concerning the morning of the sixteenth in his report are as follows:

The morning of the sixteenth (during which there was considerable artillery firing) was spent in obtaining information as to the ground, rectifying the position of the troops, and perfecting the arrangements for the attack.[2]

If McClellan's dispatch said there was fog, there must have been fog. However, it appears that it was not sufficiently unusual to be worthy of note or remark by anyone, nor sufficiently intense to significantly interfere with anyone's activities.

One might assume that Lee was nervously pacing back and forth and biting his fingernails during the morning, wondering whether McClellan would attack before Jackson arrived. The head of Walker's column overtook the rear of Jackson's column, and Walker and Jackson together reported their arrival to Lee about noon at Lee's headquarters on the south edge of Sharpsburg. Walker described the meeting:

> A little past the hour of noon on the 16th of September, 1862, General "Stonewall" Jackson and myself reached General Lee's headquarters at Sharpsburg and reported the arrival of our commands. I am thus particular in noting the hour of the arrival of my division for the reason that some writers have fallen into the error of mentioning my arrival as coincident with that of McLaws' division, which was some twenty two hours later.
>
> The thought of General Lee's perilous situation, with the Potomac River in his rear, confronting with his small force, McClellan's vast army, had haunted me through the long hours of the night's march, and I expected to find General Lee anxious and careworn. Anxious enough, no doubt, he was, but there was nothing in his look or manner to indicate it. On the contrary, he was calm, dignified, and even cheerful. If he had had a well equipped army of a hundred thousand veterans at his back, he could not have appeared more composed and confident. On shaking hands with us, he simply expressed satisfaction with the result of our operations at Harpers Ferry, and with our timely arrival at Sharpsburg; adding that with our reinforcement he felt confident of being able to hold his ground until the arrival of the divisions of R. H. Anderson, McLaws and A. P. Hill, which were still behind, and which did not arrive until the next day.[3]

Why was Lee so confident when the odds were so heavily

stacked against him? Probably for at least two reasons. First, he probably knew, in his heart of hearts, although his charitable nature would prevent him from saying so, that his opponent was an incompetent. Second, he occupied a strong defensive position.

Lee's position, in the most simplistic form, is depicted in map 31. His front line was an arc to the east of Sharpsburg with Sharpsburg as the focal point. The two extremities of the arc, about four miles apart, were firmly anchored on topographical features to prevent him from being flanked. The left of the arc was anchored on a hill near the Potomac, and the right of the arc ran along Antietam Creek, which ran into the Potomac. Inasmuch as Lee was inside the arc and McClellan outside, Lee could move his forces from point to point along the front by moving them along chords of the arc. McClellan, on the other hand, had to move his along the perimeter. In addition, the roads inside the arc facilitated Lee's capability to concentrate troops at any point, but the diverging roads outside the arc were useless to McClellan for the same purpose. In short, Lee could concentrate his forces at any point on the perimeter much faster than McClellan could.

In addition, the arc incorporated topographic features that were favorable to the defense. To the west of the Hagerstown road, there were stone outcroppings that could serve as breastworks. To the north of the Boonsboro road, there was a sunken farm road that ran along the perimeter for about a half a mile that could serve as a shallow trench. From just north of the Rohrersville road, the perimeter ran along the Antietam Creek, and the only bridge over the creek in this area was the one on the Rohrersville road. On the Union side of the bridge, the ground was flat, and troops approaching the bridge were exposed. On the Confederate side of the bridge, there was a steep hill that provided an unobstructed view right down the length of the bridge. Standing on the hill and looking down the length of the bridge it is not surprising that it took Union troops so long to get across the bridge but rather that they were able to get across at all.

Four miles behind the center of the arc lay Boteler's Ford, which provided Lee a sheltered line for the receipt of reinforcements, as well as a potential line of retreat. All in all, Lee's position was formidable. But yet, on the morning of the sixteenth, he was outnumbered almost six to one.

Map 31
Lee's Position at Sharpsburg

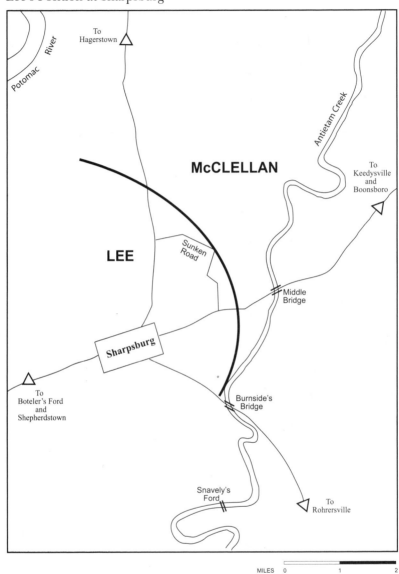

With the arrival of Jackson and Walker, Lee had his army reunited, except for McLaws's divisions (his own and that of Anderson) and that of A. P. Hill. When we last left McLaws at midnight on the fifteenth, his wagons were still crossing the bridge into Harpers Ferry, and his infantry was waiting to follow. We now turn to McLaws's words:

> On the morning of September 16, my command, consisting of my own division and that of General Anderson, marched through Harpers Ferry from Pleasant Valley, and halted near Halltown [see map 30] and a short distance from the road which turned to the right toward Shepherdstown, which was on the way to Sharpsburg, to which place I had been directed to march by orders direct from General Lee and afterward from General Jackson. The entire command was very much fatigued. The brigades of General Kershaw and Barksdale had been engaged on Maryland Heights on the 12th, 13th and 14th, and on the 15th had been marched from the heights to the line of battle up the valley, formed to oppose that of the enemy below Crampton's Gap. Those of Generals Cobb, Semmes and Mahone [Colonel Parham] had been engaged and badly crippled at Crampton's Gap, and all the others had been guarding important points under very trying circumstances. A large number had no provisions, and a great portion had not had time or opportunity to cook what they had. All the troops had been without sleep during the night previous, except while waiting in line for the wagon trains to pass over the pontoon bridge at Harpers Ferry. I had ridden on to Charlestown to look after the sick and wounded from Pleasant Valley, when notice was sent me to hasten the troops to Sharpsburg. I returned to camp and started the command at 3 P.M. Halted after dark (and the night was very dark) within 2 miles of Shepherdstown, when, receiving orders to hasten forward, again commenced the march at 12 o'clock that night, many of the regiments still without provisions. I may here state that the crossing at Harpers Ferry was very much impeded by the paroled prisoners passing over the bridge whenever there was an opportunity offered by any accident to the bridge causing temporary halt in the trains or batteries, which was of frequent occurrence, and the streets of Harpers Ferry town were crowded with prisoners and wagons, all of which prevented me from halting, even for a moment, in the town to obtain provisions there.[4]

Thus, as the night of the sixteenth was approaching the seventeenth, the head of McLaws's tired column was nearing Boteler's Ford, four miles from Lee's headquarters at Sharpsburg.

The only remaining troops of Lee's army were in A. P. Hill's division at Harpers Ferry. Hill had been entrusted not only with arranging the surrender of the troops at Harpers Ferry, but also with taking charge of the captured materiel. This involved much more than arms and wagons. It also included equipage, medical, veterinary, quartermaster, ordnance, and commissary supplies. To give an idea of the magnitude of the task, following is an inventory of captured commissary stores:

Salt-pork	1,315 pounds
Salt-beef	1,545 pounds
Bacon	19,267 pounds
Hard bread	155,954 pounds
Rice	628 pounds
Coffee	4,930 pounds
Sugar	209 pounds
Candles	67 pounds
Soap	280 pounds
Beans	9 bushels
Salt	154 bushels
Vinegar	180 gallons
Molasses	80 gallons[5]

Hill had not started for Sharpsburg as of the close of September 16.

On the fifteenth, a change in the Union command structure was required because of the nature of the deployment of the Union forces against Lee. When McClellan started moving out from Washington to encounter Lee, he had his corps arranged into three wings under three "wing commanders." The right wing consisted of the First Corps (Hooker's) and Ninth Corps (Reno's) under Wing Commander Burnside. In the case of the other two wings, the senior corps commander simply assumed the dual functions of corps and wing commander. However, Burnside, who was normally the Ninth Corps commander, preferred to turn over the Ninth Corps to its senior division commander and assume the position of wing commander as a separate function. When the various corps arrived at Sharpsburg, they were assigned their positions in accordance with their order of arrival. Thus, Burnside's First Corps ended up on McClellan's far right and his Ninth Corps on McClellan's far left, with the other corps

in between. In consequence, it was no longer practicable for
Burnside to serve as commander of both, and Hooker was
ordered to report directly to McClellan. Burnside thus again
became de facto commander of the Ninth Corps, rather than
wing commander.

By late on the sixteenth, problems began to arise between
George McClellan and his good friend, Ambrose Burnside.
McClellan sent the following dispatch to Burnside. To lessen the
pain, McClellan sent it in the third person and had it signed by
his aide-de-camp and acting assistant adjutant general.

Headquarters Army of the Potomac
September 16, 1862

Major General Burnside
Commanding Ninth Corps etc.

General: The general commanding has learned that, although
your corps was ordered to be in a designated position at 12 m. today, at or near sunset only one division and four batteries had
reached the ground intended for your troops.

The general has also been advised that there was a delay of
some four hours in the movement of your command yesterday. I
am instructed to call upon you for explanations of these failures
on your part to comply with the orders given you, and to add, in
view of the important military operations now at hand, the commanding general cannot lightly regard such marked departure
from the tenor of his instructions.

I am, general, very respectfully, your obedient servant.

Lieutenant-Colonel, Aide-de-Camp and
Acting Asst. Adjt. Gen.[6]

On the next day, the crucial day of the seventeenth, the
Burnside-McClellan problems were to grow far worse.

McClellan finally decided on his plan sometime after noon on
the sixteenth. In McClellan's words, the plan was as follows:

The design was to make the main attack upon the enemy's
left—at least to create a diversion in favor of the main attack,
with the hope of something more by assailing the enemy's

right—and, as soon as one or both of the flank movements were fully successful, to attack their center with any reserve I might then have on hand.[7]

Whatever McClellan's plan was, he took his first step toward implementation sometime between 1 and 2 p.m. on the sixteenth, when he issued instructions to Hooker, commander of the First Corps. This was more than twenty-four hours after McClellan first appeared on the scene.

We will now turn to Hooker's own words to describe what followed:

Between one and two o'clock [p.m.] the day following [the sixteenth], I received instructions from the major-general commanding the Army of the Potomac to cross the river [Antietam Creek] with the First Corps and attack the enemy on his left flank, Meade's and Rickett's divisions crossing the bridge near Keedysville, and Doubleday's at the ford just below it.

As soon as I saw my command underway, I rode to the head-quarters of the commanding general for any further orders he might have to give me, when I was informed that I was at liberty to call for reinforcements if I should need them, and that on their arrival they would be placed under my command, and I returned and joined my troops on their march. Our direction was nearly perpendicular to the river we had crossed, my object being to gain the high ground or divide between the Potomac and Antietam Rivers, and then incline to the left, following the elevation toward the left of the rebel army. Two regiments of Meade's division were thrown forward as skirmishers, followed by a squadron of Owen's Cavalry, and all supported by Meade's division. We had not proceeded over a half a mile before the commanding general with his staff joined me, apparently to see how we were progressing. Among other subjects of conversation, I said to the general that he had ordered my small corps, now numbering between 12,000 and 13,000 (as I had just lost nearly 1,000 men in the battle of South Mountain), across the river to attack the whole rebel army, and that if reinforcements were not forewarded [*sic*] promptly, or if another attack was not made on the enemy's right, the rebels would eat me up. Pretty soon after this interview, my skirmishers became engaged with the enemy's advanced post, and the firing was continued incessantly until dark, we advanced slowly, the enemy retiring before us. During the last part of the time the resistance became formidable, and we all slept on our arms that night.[8]

Hooker's attack on the Confederate left constituted the start of the battle of Antietam. The exact time at which the shooting started is not known, but Longstreet reported it as "late Tuesday evening." Thus, McClellan wasted the entire day of the sixteenth as two of Jackson's divisions and Walker's divisions arrived and Lee consolidated his position.

Meanwhile, back at Harpers Ferry, Tuesday, September 16, was to be Colonel Miles's last day on earth. When he was hit by artillery shrapnel on the morning of the fifteenth, he knew his wounds were fatal. He was carried in a blanket by six volunteers to his quarters where his wounds were dressed. He was in and out of lucidity for his remaining hours, and in great pain. He was perplexed at McClellan's failure to relieve the garrison and knew nothing of Franklin's presence in Pleasant Valley. He was never to see a single Union soldier from the outside reach the beleaguered garrison.

Lieutenant Binney, Miles's devoted aide, remained beside Miles almost continuously from the time he was wounded until the time he died. Other staff officers came to pay their respects. Miles was effusive in his praise for General White and hoped he would receive due recognition. Miles said he could not understand why the government was so slow in sending him assistance. He thought that the army must have known of his situation, and that the tremendous cannonading must have been heard by McClellan. Miles said that he only regretted that he could not live to do justice to the gentlemen so closely connected with him (his staff) for their bravery in carrying his orders over the field, and to his artillery officers.

Lieutenant Binney and Maj. Henry B. McIllvaine, his chief of artillery, reported Miles's last words, or near last words, somewhat differently. Binney said that Miles remarked that "he had done his duty; he was an old soldier and willing to die."[9] McIllvaine reported his last words as, "I have done my best, and what I thought to be my duty. This is a fitting end for a soldier."[10] Miles expired at 4:30 p.m., September 16, 1862.

Now that Miles was dead and could no longer defend himself, his name was to be dragged through the mud. The charges against him went beyond incompetence. By some, he was actually accused of being a traitor, a Benedict Arnold, who was in collusion with the Confederates and who willingly turned over Harpers Ferry to them after a token resistance. But, more about that subject later.

Miles came within an inch of immortality. Had he held out just one more day and then died in the defense of Harpers Ferry rather than during its surrender, he would have become one of the greatest heroes of the war. The Confederate army under Lee would not have had time to reunite before its destruction. In that case, we might well visualize statues of Miles today, the inscription of which might read, "Colonel Dixon Miles, whose death during the gallant defense of Harpers Ferry facilitated the destruction of the Confederate Army."

General Hill indicated that he would take care of the transportation of Miles's body, but he failed to follow through. Lieutenant Binney and Major McIllvaine managed to secure a team and wagon and transported Miles's body to his home in Baltimore.

Before Miles's body was even in the ground, the war was moving beyond Harpers Ferry. All Confederate troops, except those of A. P. Hill, had departed for Sharpsburg by daylight on the seventeenth. The Union Sixth Corps, under Franklin, was still at Rohrersville at the head of Pleasant Valley. McClellan had kept it there on the remote possibility that Lee might join Jackson at Harpers Ferry rather than Jackson joining Lee at Sharpsburg. However, as the sixteenth progressed, it became more and more evident that the Confederates were headed for Sharpsburg. Consequently, that night McClellan ordered that Franklin, with the divisions of Smith and Slocum, proceed to join him on Antietam Creek and that Franklin's third division, under Couch, proceed down Pleasant Valley and occupy Maryland Heights. However, before Couch reached Maryland Heights, he too was called to join McClellan. Ironically, it seems that less than two days after the surrender of Harpers Ferry, no one was interested in it.

Back in the White House, Lincoln was uneasy. After seeing McClellan's messages of the fifteenth reporting that he was pursuing a fleeing enemy that had been "shockingly whipped" and was fleeing in a "perfect panic," Lincoln was anxiously awaiting a message from McClellan reporting the coup de grace. For some reason, as of noon, Lincoln still had not seen McClellan's 7 a.m. "fog" message and could contain himself no longer. He sent the following message to his friend, Governor Curtin of Pennsylvania, who always seemed to have the latest information via his intrepid telegrapher at Hagerstown:

Washington D. C.
September 16, 1862—Noon

Governor Curtin
Harrisburg

What do you hear from General McClellan's Army? We have nothing from him today.

A. Lincoln[11]

Governor Curtin answered promptly as follows:

Harrisburg, Pa
September 16, 1862
[Received 1:30 P.M.]

His Excellency the President

We have no definite news. Our telegrapher operator at Hagerstown reports that a battle is progressing near the Potomac, between Sharpsburg and Williamsport. What success did McClellan meet with yesterday? We have not heard, and should know, in order to use our forces that are now being pushed into Maryland.

A. G. Curtin[12]

Lincoln, in the meantime, had read McClellan's fog message and responded as follows:

Washington D. C.
September 16, 1862—2:35 P.M.

Governor Curtin:

Since telegraphing you, dispatch came from General McClellan, dated 7 o'clock this morning. Nothing of importance

Map 32
Situation at the End of September 16

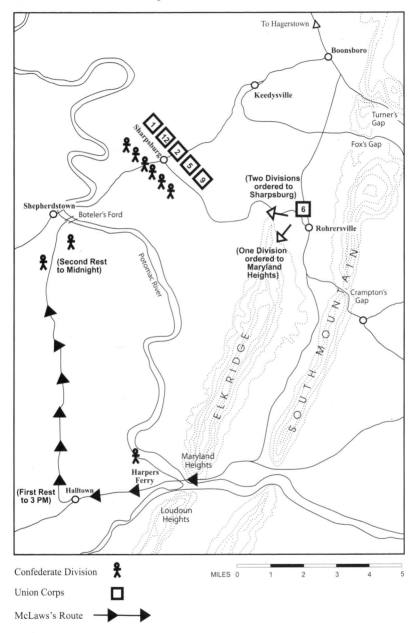

Confederate Division

Union Corps

McLaws's Route

MILES 0   1   2   3   4   5

happened with him yesterday. This morning he was up with the
enemy at Sharpsburg, and was waiting for heavy fog to rise!

A. Lincoln[13]

Three hours later, Governor Curtin followed up with the
message Lincoln wanted to hear:

> Harrisburg, Pa
> September 16, 1862—5:30 P.M.

President Lincoln:

The following just received from Hagerstown: "Jackson has
recrossed the Potomac, and General McClellan has engaged him
with a large force a few miles this side of Sharpsburg, 10 miles
from here. The whole rebel army in Maryland will probably be
annihilated or captured tonight. McClellan is on the battle-field."

A. G. Curtin[14]

McClellan's reputation was growing by leaps and bounds
again, entirely on the basis of his own messages proclaiming his
"victories." Lincoln probably slept soundly that night, believing
that the "Young Napoleon" had taken care of everything and
that it was now all over in the East but the mopping up. In fact,
as of the close of the sixteenth, McClellan was frittering away his
second day, as Lee's army reunited in front of him. The morrow
was to bring McClellan's supreme test—and the bloodiest day of
the war.

About noon on the sixteenth, the second of Porter's divisions,
that of George Morell, caught up with McClellan and joined
him. Porter's third division, that of Andrew A. Humphreys, was
still en route and would not arrive until the eighteenth.

After dark, McClellan ordered Franklin and two of his divisions at nearby Rohrersville to proceed at dawn to join him. He
ordered Franklin's third division, that of Couch, to proceed
down Pleasant Valley toward Harpers Ferry and occupy
Maryland Heights.

The situation at the end of the sixteenth is depicted in map 32.

Chapter 15

Wednesday, September 17—Antietam

The events of Wednesday, September 17, 1862, in the vicinity of the small town of Sharpsburg, Maryland, and nearby Antietam Creek were forever after known in the South as the battle of Sharpsburg and in the North as the battle of Antietam. This date was to have the dubious distinction of being the bloodiest day on the North American continent—and this includes the events on September 11, 2001. Neither battle name is exactly correct as the battle actually took place in the farmland area to the northeast of the town and between the town and Antietam Creek.

The area of the battle today looks much as it did in September 1862. There has been no commercialization. The area appears totally at odds with its bloody reputation. It is an area that exudes beauty, peace, and tranquility. Mountains can be seen in the distance, and the area itself is one of quaint farms with cornfields, wheat fields, pastures, orchards, and patches of woods. Antietam Creek meanders through the area to its junction with the nearby Potomac. As if to accentuate the beauty of the area, the centerpiece is a picturesque, white clapboard country church, which was known locally as the Dunker Church. (The name "Dunker" was applied by the locals because the church belonged to a German Baptist sect that used total immersion for baptism; that is, they "dunked" the supplicant.) All in all, the area could well have served as the locale for Beethoven's *Pastoral Symphony.*

The name "creek" for the stream that meandered through the area is somewhat misleading. One usually visualizes a creek as something one could step over, jump over, or at least wade across. This was not the case with Antietam Creek. In most areas of the county, it would have fully justified the name "river." The Antietam was sixty to one hundred feet wide and could normally only be crossed on a bridge or at a ford; and as of September 17, 1862, the ford at issue was waist deep.

The town of Sharpsburg itself was insignificant but yet was an important road junction. Boonsboro was six miles to the northeast, at the junction with the National Road, and Shepherdstown was four miles to the southwest, across the Potomac via Boteler's Ford, at the junction of the Harpers Ferry-Martinsburg road. Then (as now), both Shepherdstown and Boonsboro were significant-sized towns, and Shepherdstown, then (as now), was a college town. At Sharpsburg, a road radiated off to the north to Hagerstown, one to the southeast to Rohrersville, and one to the south to Harpers Ferry. The question remains, why did the battle take place at Sharpsburg? The answer is that, once the Confederates had been driven from South Mountain and Lee decided to make his stand in Maryland, it could have been at no other place.

The Confederate defense line did not run in its entirety along Antietam Creek (see map 33). Rather, it extended along an arc from north of Sharpsburg to the east and southeast where it hit the Antietam between the middle bridge on the Boonsboro Pike and the lower bridge (later called Burnside's Bridge). The line then continued along the Antietam until it entered the Potomac. Thus, only the southernmost sector of the Confederate line and the Union line were separated by the Antietam. Under this somewhat unusual arrangement, both sides of the middle bridge were under Union control, and here a Union soldier could cross the Antietam without molestation. A little farther down, however, any crossing would be contested to the death.

At daylight on the seventeenth, McClellan's chances to destroy the Confederate army before it reunited still existed but were rapidly running out. Six of the nine Confederate divisions were already present, but McLaws's two divisions were still approaching Boteler's Ford and could not be in action before about 9 a.m.; A. P. Hill's division was still seventeen miles away at Harpers Ferry. As of 6:30 a.m., Hill was just reading his orders to proceed to Sharpsburg with all haste. McClellan had his entire vast Army of the Potomac in hand, except for two of Franklin's divisions, which were expected to arrive that morning, and Humphreys's and Couch's divisions, which would not arrive until the eighteenth.

A couple of things should have been obvious to McClellan at daylight on the seventeenth. First, the best chance he was going to get to attack and defeat Lee was before 9 a.m. And second, it was not a good idea to attack piecemeal or in phases, as Lee had interior lines and could easily move men from one sector to

Map 33
McClellan's Deployment, September 17

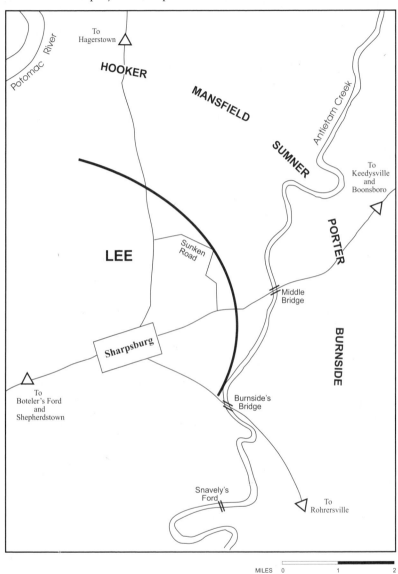

another. Thus, even if Lee had fewer men (which McClellan did not believe), the attacker could always expect to meet his match at the point of conflict in a phased attack.

However, McClellan was not a simple man who was governed

by the obvious or logical, as were men such as Lincoln and Grant. The obvious could be seen by the simple, and, in McClellan's eyes, war was a complex chess match that could only be understood by the few and the trained, such as himself. So McClellan set in motion that morning a series of piecemeal and phased attacks that did not reach their maximum intensity until after McLaws's divisions had reached the battlefield.

When the sun came up on the seventeenth, it was hard to believe that only twelve days had elapsed since Miles's men had reported the Confederates splashing across the Potomac at White's Ford in their invasion of the North. So much had happened in those twelve days. Miles had been killed, and Harpers Ferry had been lost, but McClellan had brought order out of chaos. He had rebuilt, revitalized, and strengthened the Army of the Potomac. He had won the battle of South Mountain, and now it was Lee's army, and not Washington, that was endangered. McClellan had literally risen phoenix-like out of the ashes of the Peninsula campaign and was again the indispensable man. The "Young Napoleon" was back. But today was to be his supreme test. It all came down to Antietam.

Until McLaws would arrive later in the morning, the odds were about three to one in McClellan's favor—seventy-five thousand for McClellan, twenty-five thousand for Lee. After McLaws's two divisions arrived for Lee at about 9 a.m., and Franklin's two divisions arrived for McClellan between 10 and 11 a.m., the odds in McClellan's favor would be slightly lessened—eighty-nine thousand for McClellan, and thirty-three thousand for Lee. And eventually, after A. P. Hill's division finally arrived for Lee, the odds in favor of McClellan would be lessened again.

At daylight, McClellan's troops were deployed as indicated in map 33. Hooker's First Corps was astride the Hagerstown Pike on McClellan's far right, next came Mansfield's Twelfth Corps, then Sumner's Second Corps, then Porter's Fifth Corps astride the Boonsboro road, and finally, Burnside's Ninth Corps along Antietam Creek, centered on what later became known as "Burnside's Bridge." Only Burnside fronted on the creek, with it between him and the enemy. When Franklin's two Sixth Corps divisions arrived, McClellan placed them behind Sumner.

McClellan opened the battle at daylight with Hooker's First Corps advancing down the Hagerstown Pike. About 7:30 a.m., when Hooker's corps was spent and pushed back, and Hooker was wounded and carried from the field, McClellan threw in Mansfield's Twelfth Corps. Mansfield had no sooner entered combat than he was shot dead from the saddle. This event punctuated another maxim that was already becoming commonly accepted, namely, don't go into combat riding on a horse. Longstreet, among others, had already learned that lesson by firsthand experience. During the battle, Longstreet and Lee were inspecting their position on foot when Gen. D. H. Hill rode up. We will now turn to Longstreet's words as he addressed Hill:

> "If you insist on riding up there and drawing the fire, give us a little interval so that we may not be in the line of fire when they open up on you." General Lee and I stood on the crest with our glasses, looking at the movement of the Federals on the rear left. After a moment I turned my glass to the right. As I did so, I noticed a puff of white smoke from the mouth of a cannon. "There is a shot for you," I said to General Hill. The gunner was a mile away, and the cannon shot came whisking through the air for three or four seconds, and took the front legs off the horse that Hill sat on.[1]

Depending on one's views, fortunately or unfortunately, Hill was not hurt.

Mansfield's attack fared little better than Hooker's and, between 8 and 9 a.m., after Mansfield's had faltered, McClellan ordered Sumner and his three divisions to enter the fray. Up to this time, the attack had been piecemeal by corps. Now it became piecemeal by divisions. Sumner's divisions attacked in phase, with the last not arriving before the first was destroyed. As might be expected, Lee, with his interior lines, moved his troops about to meet the point of each attack. First, he moved Walker's division, which had been on his far right facing Burnside, to his left. Then, he threw in McLaws's troops, who had just arrived in time to hit Sumner's lead division (under Sedgewick) in the flank and disperse it within minutes. Before 11 a.m., the conflict, which had all been on the Union right and right center up to this point, subsided and was not to be renewed. The fighting thus far had been largely of the now obsolete type with rows of standing, unprotected men blazing away at each other at point-blank range. McClellan could see his own losses but, unknown to him, Lee's were almost as bad. Furthermore, Lee, unlike

Map 34
McClellan's Attack, September 17

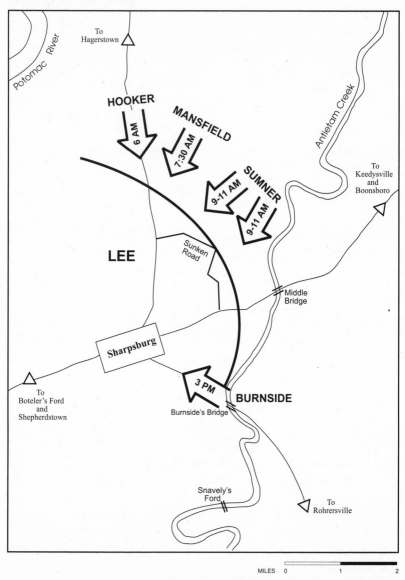

McClellan, had no reserves to throw in, and one more push would probably have been fatal. See map 34 for the positions of the morning's attacks.

McClellan's attention now shifted to Burnside, whose men

had been sitting idly by observing the events as best they could to their far right. At approximately 10 a.m., McClellan, by courier, ordered Burnside to cross the Antietam and make a diversionary attack.

There was one bridge in Burnside's sector. This was the so-called lower bridge, later to be infamously known as "Burnside's Bridge." It was a three-span stone structure, just wide enough for eight men to advance abreast. A hill rose abruptly up on the Confederate side of the bridge, into which the Confederates had dug rifle pits that sheltered approximately four hundred Confederate riflemen in near invulnerability. The Confederates looked directly down the length of the bridge, on which no more than eight of the enemy could face them at one time. To add to Burnside's problem, the approach to the bridge on his side of the creek was completely open, and it was murderous even to approach the bridge. Confederate cannon fire was zeroed in on the bridge approaches, and the lay of the land was such that there was no good place to locate Union artillery to respond.

To put yet another layer on Burnside's leaden mantle, the four hundred Confederate troops entrenched in the hill were commanded by Brig. Gen. Augustus Toombs, a diehard rebel who had no intention of letting the Yankees get across the bridge. Toombs had been a prewar representative and then senator from Georgia and, at the formation of the Confederacy, had been a leading contender for its chief executive. Toombs, however, ended up in the third position, as secretary of state. However, even though he had no military training or experience, he gave up his high position to accept a brigadier generalship in the Confederate army so as to have an opportunity to kill Yankees. Toombs had the reputation of being a brilliant intellectual, a spellbinding orator, and a big boozer. This was to be his big day.

As Burnside surveyed his options, he was bombarded with ever more strident demands from McClellan to cross the Antietam. There are those today who view Burnside as a hapless idiot who was obsessed with forcing the bridge when his men could have splashed across the Antietam knee deep almost anywhere. This was not really the case.

Engineers had examined the creek for crossings and local residents had been interrogated. The consensus was that a crossing that day would not have been easy. It was determined that there was a ford almost one air mile (but twice that by creek miles) downstream from the bridge called Snavely's Ford. Burnside dispatched one of his divisions, under Brig. Gen. Isaac P. Rodman, to attempt to make a crossing there as he continued attempts to force the bridge. Burnside was fully aware that he probably could not carry the bridge unless he was aided by a crossing elsewhere. Burnside made at least five attempts to rush the bridge as Rodman headed south; all ended in failure.

McClellan was becoming increasingly exasperated with Burnside's failure to get across the Antietam and sent one more demand at about 1 p.m. This one was accompanied by McClellan's inspector general, who was empowered to relieve Burnside from command if necessary. By this time, circumstances began to conspire against Toombs and his defenders. They were running short of ammunition. Rodman's force (although Rodman had been killed) succeeded in getting across at Snavely's Ford and was approaching from the south. Finally, a rush by two volunteer regiments, the Fifty-first New York and the Fifty-first Pennsylvania, carried the bridge. Toombs and his men fled, and Burnside was firmly across the Antietam. It was now 1 p.m., three hours after Burnside had first been ordered to cross. Burnside retained his command.

Was McClellan, in his frustration, trying to cast the blame for his lack of success up to this point on his friend Burnside? Or was he merely acting on what he considered to be the best interests of the country in his apparent readiness to humiliate Burnside? No one will ever know—but it was probably the latter. McClellan was not known as a mean or vindictive man but, to the contrary, was always loyal to and considerate of his subordinates. In any event, it appears that the McClellan-Burnside friendship did not suffer from this incident.

How deep really was the water in Antietam Creek that day? There is no way of knowing now, but Capt. David L. Thompson, of Company G of the Ninth New York Volunteers, crossed the Antietam that day and stated that it was waist deep—at the ford.

With Burnside across the creek, it was now time for McClellan to renew his attack on his other wing. At about 1 p.m., he sent a courier to Sumner, the senior officer on his right, to renew the attack with his and Franklin's newly arrived troops. When Sumner read the order, he said to the courier:

> Go back young man, and tell General McClellan I have no command. Bank's [Mansfield's] command and Hooker's command

Major General Ambrose Burnside USV
Of Burnside's Bridge Fame

are all cut up and demoralized. Tell him General Franklin has the only organized command in this part of the field.[2]

McClellan appeared in person immediately after his courier. After discussing the situation with Sumner, he agreed and called off the attack. Had he carried through with the attack, there is no doubt he would have achieved a smashing victory.

Now that McClellan had decided not to commit Sumner and Franklin, Burnside's corps became the main engine of the attack rather than a diversion. McClellan then ordered Burnside to seize the town of Sharpsburg and continue down the Boonsboro-Shepherdstown road to seize Boteler's Ford in Lee's rear, cutting off his retreat. In fact, there was little in Burnside's path to stop him. There was only one small division of about two thousand men, including those of Toombs, between him and Sharpsburg.

However, Burnside's lead troops were spent and nearly out of ammunition. He decided to replace those who had crossed the creek with his reserve division who had not yet crossed. This replacement of troops took time, crossing and recrossing the bridge. Burnside was not ready to advance on Sharpsburg until 3 p.m. There was little in Burnside's path, and, once he seized the town and the ford, Lee would have been cut off from all means of retreat.

As Burnside's men moved off at 3 p.m., Lee's army was not yet fully reunited. Hill had received his orders at 6:30 that morning at Harpers Ferry to proceed posthaste to Sharpsburg. He left Colonel Thomas with one brigade to complete the removal of captured property, and, with the remainder of his division, was on the road by 7:30 a.m. He had seventeen long miles to go on a hot day but kept up a killing pace, despite the fact that men were falling out by the wayside, unable to continue. By 2:30 p.m., the lead of his column was already in sight of the battlefield, and he rode ahead to report to Lee.

When Burnside's men first sighted Hill's men, there was some doubt as to whether they were friend or foe. Hill's men had shed their rags for new blue uniforms that they had acquired at Harpers Ferry. Burnside quickly realized that they were foe as they hit his advancing troops in the flank and drove them back to the river. The arrival of Hill's men had constituted the final reuniting of Lee's army. And their timely arrival saved the day—but not quite yet.

McClellan had not yet committed Porter's corps, which was

standing by in his center, straddling the Boonsboro road. McClellan's initial plan had been to stretch the two Confederate flanks and then commit his reserves down the middle. Here we come to an account by Capt. Thomas M. Anderson of Porter's corps, who was on the Confederate side of the middle bridge as Burnside was being driven back by Hill:

> At the battle of Antietam I commanded one of the batallions [*sic*] of Sykes's division [Porter's corps] of regulars, held in reserve on the north of Antietam Creek near the stone bridge. Three of our batallions were on the south side of the creek, deployed as skirmishers in front of Sharpsburg. At the time that A. P. Hill began to force Burnside back upon the left, I was talking with Colonel Buchanan, our brigade commander, when an orderly brought him a note from Captain Blunt, who was the senior officer with the batallions of our brigade beyond the creek. The note, as I remember, stated in effect that Captain Dryer, commanding the 4th Infantry, had ridden into the enemy's lines, and upon returning had reported that there were but one confederate battery and two regiments in front of Sharpsburg, connecting the wings of Lee's army. Dryer was one of the coolest and bravest officers in our service, and on his report Blunt asked instructions. We learned afterward that Dryer proposed that he, Blunt and Brown, commanding the 4th, 12th and 14th Infantries, should charge the enemy in Sharpsburg instanter [*sic*]. But Blunt preferred asking for orders. Colonel Buchanan sent the note to Sykes [Porter's corps], who was at the time talking with General McClellan and Fitz John Porter, about a hundred and fifty yards from us. They were sitting on their horses between Taft's and Weed's batteries a little to our left. I saw the note passed from one to the other in the group, but could not, of course, hear what was said. We received no orders to advance, however, although the advance of a single brigade at the time [sunset] would have cut Lee's army in two.
>
> After the war, I asked General Sykes why our reserves did not advance upon receiving Dryer's report. He answered that he remembered the circumstances very well and that he thought that McClellan was inclined to order in the Fifth Corps, but when he spoke of doing so Fitz John Porter said: "Remember, General: I command the last reserve of the last army of the Republic."[3]

If Captain Anderson's recollection is accurate, McClellan followed bad advice, contrary to his inclinations, twice during the day—first from Sumner, then from Porter. These decisions were to prove costly to him and probably cost him the command of the Army of the Potomac and, possibly, the presidency of the United States. Had McClellan followed his own inclinations in either instance, he would have won a decisive victory over Lee.

As of the end of September 17, Lee's and McClellan's armies stood approximately where they stood at dawn that day. Lee's army was now fully reunited. McClellan had failed to destroy it piecemeal and, from this point on, would proceed without any inside knowledge of Confederate intentions that the copy of Special Order 191 had provided him up to this point.

Why did not McClellan, with his vast superiority, succeed in crushing Lee's army? For the simple reason that McClellan and Sumner and Porter and others believed that they were facing 120,000 and not 35,000 men. Even when on the verge of winning, they were afraid to commit their reserves, in the fallacious belief that Lee still possessed sufficient reserves for a massive counterattack.

The losses of this date were appalling. Every building, barn, and shed for ten miles around was crammed with wounded; the medical force available to care for them was completely overwhelmed.

The Union casualties for the day were 12,469. The Confederate casualties are only estimates, but were around 11,000. In the whole Revolutionary War, the American casualties were 10,623 killed and wounded. In the War of 1812, the American casualties were 6,765 killed and wounded. On the single day of September 17, 1862, the American casualties consisted of an estimated 23,469, of which 19,402 were killed or wounded. The remaining 4,069 missing undoubtedly included mostly prisoners, but also included many killed but not identified.

Although the total Union casualties were greater than those of the Confederates, the percentage of those present who became casualties from the Union was far less. For the Confederates, the percentage of those present who became casualties was 31 percent. For the Union, it was only about 14 percent.

The Union casualties varied widely between corps and were as follows:

	Total	Killed	Wounded	Missing
First Corps (Hooker's)	2,619	348	669	95
Second Corps (Sumner's)	5,209	860	3,801	548

Fifth Corps (Porter's)	130	21	102	2
Sixth Corps (Franklin's)	447	70	344	33
Ninth Corps (Burnside's)	2,293	432	1,741	120
Twelfth Corps (Mansfield's)	1,743	247	1,38	485
Cavalry	28	5	23	0

(Note: Any discrepancies in total figures is likely due to the total for prisoners, which is not included in the official records.)

It can be seen from the above figures that the Fifth and Sixth Corps, which never participated in the attack, were hardly bloodied. The big loser was Sumner's Second Corps, whose three divisions conducted a poorly coordinated attack during the morning, without a proper preliminary examination of the field.

Among the Union dead of September 17 was Maj. Gen. Israel Richardson. It was Richardson who had brought Col. Dixon Miles's budding career to a sudden halt in July 1861 when he, then a colonel, accused Miles of being drunk during the battle of First Bull Run. Thus, Richardson was to meet his Maker within twenty-four hours of Miles.

Before leaving the matter of casualties, let us return and examine a bit more closely what actually happened at Burnside's Bridge. Both sides agree that Burnside began his attempt to force the bridge with successive rushes at about 10 a.m. and succeeded at about 1 p.m. Beyond that, there is considerable divergence in the accounts by the two sides. From the Union perspective, it overcame almost insurmountable obstacles through the bravery and gallantry of its troops. From the Confederate perspective, a tiny force of its troops conducted a heroic defense against an overwhelming force of the enemy.

The actual Confederate defense force, in a position to shoot at the oncoming Union attackers, consisted of only two regiments of Toombs's brigade. These were the Second Georgia, which had only 97 men, and the Twentieth Georgia, which had a maximum of 347 men. The two regiments at the bridge were deployed approximately three-fourths of a mile in front of the main Confederate line and so could not be easily reinforced or resupplied with ammunition. In the eyes of the Confederates, the Antietam was fordable both above and below the bridge, and if so forded, their two regiments would be flanked and could be cut off from the main body. The on-scene commander for the

Confederates, a Toombs subordinate, was Col. Henry L. Benning.

By 1 p.m., most of Colonel Benning's men were out of ammunition, and he observed two Union regiments with fixed bayonets rushing the bridge, as well as Union columns fording the creek both above and below the bridge. In addition, a Union battery located upstream was now enfilading his men. Consequently, Benning decided to give up his position and ordered his men to retreat to the main Confederate line. His casualties consisted of 42 killed and wounded in the Second Georgia and 68 killed and wounded in the Twentieth Georgia, for a total of 110. This number constituted about one-third of his force.

What were the Union casualties on the bridge and its approach? A Confederate sergeant reported to Benning that he saw piles of bodies on the bridge and its approach, and estimated the dead to be from five hundred to a thousand. This estimate was high. All of the casualties incurred in seizing the bridge were from the Ninth Corps; the total casualties for the Ninth Corps for the entire day of the battle were 432 dead, 1,741 wounded, and 120 missing. Some of these casualties were suffered at Snavely's Ford, and others after the corps had crossed the Antietam. A reasonable estimate for the casualties at the bridge might be around 250 dead, and, inasmuch as the ratio for wounded to killed was about four to one that day, 1,000 wounded. Thus, in the contest for the bridge, approximately 1,250 Union troops were shot trying to force the bridge, while 110 Confederates were shot defending it.

McClellan was to make up his losses of September 17 much more quickly than Lee. Within hours of the end of the battle, on September 18, General Humphreys's division of Porter's corps was to join McClellan; General Couch of Franklin's corps, whom McClellan had recalled from Maryland Heights, was to rejoin. The addition of Humphreys and Couch would fully make up for McClellan's losses. Lee was not so fortunate. No organized units were to join in the days following the battle. However, stragglers were rejoining in large numbers, and it is estimated that at least three thousand rejoined within twenty-four hours of the battle.

McClellan was unusually subdued at the close of the seventeenth. In his report to Halleck, he did not claim victory. His report is as follows:

The battle of yesterday continued for fourteen hours, and until after dark. We held all we gained, except a portion of the extreme left; that was obliged to abandon a part of what it had gained. Our losses very heavy, especially in general officers. The battle will probably be renewed today. Send all the troops you can by the most expeditious route.[4]

It took time after the sobering events of September 17 for McClellan to regain his chutzpah and verbally transform the drawn battle into another great McClellan victory.

Chapter 16

The Aftermath

At the close of the fighting on the seventeenth, Lee listened to the reports of his generals in his usual imperturbable manner and then, to the surprise of many, sent them back to their troops with the announcement that they would stay and contest McClellan on the morrow.

By darkness on Wednesday the seventeenth, when the shooting had stopped, the idyllic, bucolic scene of the morning had turned into a fit competitor for Dante's *Inferno*. The dead and dying lay in rows where they had stood in line of battle, and in piles where they had defended points such as the sunken road. Let us now turn to the words of Col. Henry Kyd Douglas of Jackson's staff, who rode out onto the battlefield that night:

> The dead and dying lay as thick over it as harvest sheaves . . . The pitiable cries for water and appeals for help were much more horrible to listen to than the deadliest sounds of battle. Silent were the dead, and motionless. But here and there were raised stiffened arms; heads made a last effort to lift themselves from the ground; prayers were mingled with oaths, the oaths of delirium; men were wriggling over the earth; and midnight hid all distinction between blue and grey.
>
> My horse trembled under me in terror, looking down at the ground, sniffing the scent of blood, stepping falteringly as a horse will over or by the side of human flesh; afraid to stand still, hesitating to go on, his animal instinct shuddering at this cruel human mystery. Once his foot slid into a little shallow filled with blood and spurted a little stream on his legs and on my boots. I had a surfeit of blood that day and I couldn't stand this. I dismounted and giving the reins to my courier I started in to the wood of Dunker Church.[1]

Soon after the heat of the day arrived on Thursday, September 18, the corpses began to blacken and bloat in the hot

September sun. A Federal officer declared that "many were as black as negroes . . . heads and faces hideously swelled, covered with dust until they looked like clods. Their attitudes were wild and frightful."[2] These dust-covered clods were the friends, comrades, brothers, sons, fathers, and husbands of yesterday.

The field was also sprinkled with dead, dying, and maimed horses. These dumb animals that had no part in the decision process that caused it all, shared in full the terror, pain, and death of those who brought them there. The horses, unlike their masters, could neither crouch nor bend nor hide from the hail of lead that engulfed them. When once they fell, they could not be moved easily and putrefied where they had fallen, thus adding to the odor of death that permeated the field.

As the day of the seventeenth came to a close, the nation, from the president on down, became aware that a great battle was in progress and assumed that it would continue on Thursday, the eighteenth. Details outside the battle were sparse, but McClellan's reputation, as a result of his victories at South Mountain, was sky high, and he was undoubtedly visualized as performing devilishly clever maneuvers as he completed the destruction of Lee's army. Anything that McClellan said he needed was equivalent to a decree from the Almighty and had to be provided regardless of cost or inconvenience. After dark, when things quieted down on the night of the seventeenth, McClellan sent the following modest request for ammunition to the chief of ordnance in Washington:

> Headquarters Army of the Potomac
> Via Hagerstown Md
> September 17, 1862

Brigadier General Ripley
Chief of Ordnance

    If you can possibly do it, force some 20 pounder Parrott ammunition through tonight, via Hagerstown and Chambersburg, to us near Sharpsburg, Md.

Geo. B. McClellan
Major General
Commanding[3]

A Parrott gun was merely a particular type of cannon invented by a French officer named Parrott. The firing chamber was protected by an extra band of metal so that it could withstand a larger powder charge and, hence, deliver a projectile to a greater distance. The delivery of McClellan's Parrott ammunition became the supreme task of the nation. To deliver the ammunition, a train would have to proceed along a circuitous route from Washington to Baltimore to Harrisburg, Pennsylvania, to Hagerstown, a distance of almost two hundred miles, and would have to pass over the tracks of three separate railroad companies.

Despite the fact that it was in the middle of the night when McClellan's message arrived, it received the personal attention of the president of the United States, the secretary of war, an assistant secretary of war, three railway presidents, the governor of Pennsylvania, and numerous lesser officials. By 1:30 a.m. on the eighteenth, the train was already loaded and ready to leave Washington, and all the tracks of all three railroads were being cleared all the way to Hagerstown. The train then proceeded at the then breathtaking speed of forty miles per hour and delivered its cargo to Hagerstown ahead of schedule. Whether anyone actually picked up the cargo at Hagerstown and transported it the final ten miles to Sharpsburg is unknown. In any event, the ammunition was not used on the eighteenth.

As day broke on the eighteenth, nothing happened. And as the day continued to progress, nothing continued to happen. Lee finally decided that, if McClellan was going to do nothing, maybe he would do something. He called in his most experienced artillerist, Col. Stephen Dill Lee (no relation), and told him to report to Jackson. He tasked Jackson with determining whether, with total artillery support from Lee, he could turn McClellan's right flank (Hooker's sector) and roll up McClellan's army. After a careful examination of the position by Jackson and S. D. Lee, Jackson decided that it was not feasible, and so advised Lee. This was the only known instance in which Jackson and Lee failed to see eye to eye on a bold scheme. Lee, who would not go against the opinion of Jackson, then gave up the scheme.

As the day wore on, McClellan received reinforcements. First, Couch's division of Franklin's corps joined him from Maryland Heights. Then, Humphreys's division of Porter's corps joined him from Frederick. Lee's army continued to be rejoined by large numbers of stragglers during the day, but not in sufficient numbers to match McClellan's reinforcements. By late in the day, Lee decided to retire across the Potomac at Boteler's Ford after dark. At this point, it could not be considered an actual retreat but, rather, a tactical move.

Lee's intentions at the moment were that, once he was across the Potomac, he would take the road westward to Martinsburg and then north to Williamsport. At Williamsport, he would cross back into Maryland. To this end, he ordered his cavalry to seize Williamsport. At Williamsport, he would not only be back in Maryland, but he would be on the main north-south valley road (US 11) that extended to his supply base in the South and to his objectives in Hagerstown and Harrisburg in the North. This, after all, had been his original intention when he entered Maryland at White's Ford, fifty miles to the east, in the first place. (See map 35.)

Lee's precarious retirement across the Potomac at the narrow ford that night was completely successful and unmolested. He lost neither gun nor wagon nor man to enemy action. However, he did have to leave behind his dead and those wounded too seriously to move.

As he took the road to Martinsburg, Lee left a rear guard at Shepherdstown. This detail consisted of two small infantry brigades comprising six hundred men and forty-four cannon under his chief of artillery and friend, Gen. Nat Pendleton, part-time general and full-time clergyman.

At dawn on the nineteenth, when McClellan realized that Lee had gone, leaving his dead and desperately wounded behind, the idea grew in his mind by leaps and bounds that he had won, and that he had won big. He had driven Lee from Maryland. He had crushed the Confederate invasion.

McClellan's first claim to a complete victory was sent at 8:30 a.m. on the nineteenth and read as follows:

Headquarters Army of the Potomac
September 19, 1862—8:30 A.M.
(Received 11 A.M.)

Major General H. W. Halleck
General-in-Chief

But little occurred yesterday except skirmishing, being fully occupied in replenishing ammunition, taking care of wounded etc. Last night the enemy abandoned his position, leaving his

Map 35
Lee's Withdrawal, September 18-19

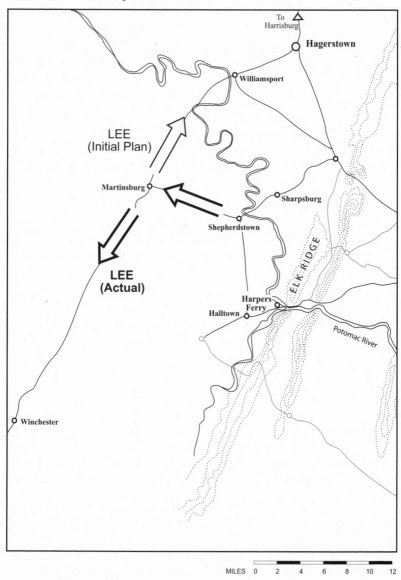

dead and wounded on the field. We are again in pursuit. I do not
yet know whether he is falling back to an interior position or
crossing the river. We may safely claim a complete victory.

Geo. B. McClellan
Major General[4]

McClellan quickly followed up the above message with the following:

> Headquarters Army of the Potomac
> September 18, 1862—10:30 A.M.
> (Received 11 A.M.)

Major General Halleck
General-in-Chief

Pleasonton is driving the enemy across the river. The enemy is driven back into Virginia. Maryland and Pennsylvania are now safe.

Geo. B. McClellan
Major General[5]

Halleck's response to McClellan's victory proclamations contained one more feeble reiteration of Halleck's favorite theme—that Lee was purposely luring McClellan away to the west with the intention of slipping back south of the Potomac and seizing Washington from the south. Halleck's response was as follows:

> Washington D. C.
> September 19, 1862 12:30 P.M.

Major General McClellan

Yours of 8:30 A.M. and 10:30 A.M. just received. All available troops from railroad guards sent to you yesterday. Stoneman's provision division, unless ordered otherwise by you, is still guarding fords below Point of Rocks. So long as the river remains low there is much danger of a movement below your left. Letters received here give it as part of Lee's original plan to draw you as far as possible up the Potomac, and then move between you and Washington. Perhaps his defeat may be such as to prevent the attempt.

H. W. Halleck
General-in-Chief[6]

By the time Lee reached Martinsburg, he had concluded that his army was really in no condition to resume the invasion of

Maryland, and, instead of turning north to Williamsport, he turned south to his supply base at Winchester to rest, reinforce, and refit his army.

McClellan slowly advanced to the river on the nineteenth where he confronted Pendleton on the opposite shore. During the night, five hundred Union volunteers crossed over the river, seized four cannons from the surprised Pendleton, and brought them safely back to the Union side. Thus emboldened, McClellan, on the following day, ordered a much larger reconnaissance force of three brigades of Porter's corps to cross the river.

At this point, General Jackson decided that enough was enough and ordered Gen. A. P. Hill back to the river to drive them off. Hill, by this time, had become Lee and Jackson's fireman. If some crisis arose, and the solution was battle, their immediate response was to send Hill. A. P. Hill was a sickly young man of thirty-seven who only rose to his full potential at times of stress and violence. As battle approached, Hill would don a bright red shirt so that his men could find him. It is said that in both Lee's and Jackson's deathbed ramblings, when they were mentally transported back to the battlefield, both sent for Hill. This was the case even though Hill had long since preceded Lee to the grave.

The Union brigades withdrew before Hill, but not fast enough. The last Union regiment, the 750-man 118th Pennsylvania, was pinned against the river with an eighty-foot high cliff at their backs. Hill literally drove them into the river, exacting 269 casualties while suffering few of his own. This so-called battle of Shepherdstown cooled the Union ardor for the time being, and there was no further molestation of the Confederates on their retreat to Winchester.

On September 29, McClellan submitted a report covering his losses and the estimated Confederate losses for the battle of the South Mountain passes and the battle of Antietam. Throughout the campaign, at every point he had overestimated the number of Confederates facing him by at least a factor of two. Now, he overestimated their losses by a factor of two. Furthermore, when he enumerated the Federal losses, he made no mention of the major losses at Harpers Ferry, which he, incidentally, was responsible for relieving before it surrendered.

Halleck responded to McClellan's report with the following congratulatory message:

Washington D. C. Sept 30, 1862

Major General McClellan; Commanding etc.

General: Your report of yesterday, giving the results of the battles of South Mountain and Antietam, has been received and submitted to the President. These were hard-fought battles, but well-earned and decided victories. The valor and endurance of your army in the several conflicts which terminated in the expulsion of the enemy from the loyal state of Maryland are creditable alike to the troops and to the officers who commanded them. A grateful country, while mourning the lamented dead, will not be unmindful of the honors due to the living.

H. W. Halleck
General-in-Chief[7]

A close reading of Halleck's message reveals that, while it gave credit to the troops and the officers who commanded them, it gave no personal credit to McClellan at all. This was very much in conflict with McClellan's personal views, wherein the real credit for the victories belonged not to the troops, but to George B. McClellan. McClellan's true views are probably best expressed in his private correspondence with his wife:

> I feel some little pride in having, with a beaten and demoralized army, defeated Lee so utterly and saved the north so completely . . . Those in whose judgment I rely tell me that I fought the battle splendidly and that it was a masterpiece of art.[8]

One of the main objectives of the Confederate invasion of Maryland in September 1862 was to gain foreign recognition and support for the South. The Lincoln administration, of course, correspondingly wanted to forestall this possibility. Lincoln had prepared a draft of the Proclamation of Emancipation. This was in fact not a humanitarian or principled gesture but, rather, a political gesture to facilitate the prosecution of the war. It was intended to gain foreign and domestic sympathy for the Union cause by seemingly seizing the high moral ground. In fact, the proclamation, as then worded, did not free all the slaves, but only those under Confederate control.

It exempted the slaves in the border states, such as Maryland, which both sides were continuing to woo.

As of mid-September 1862, Lincoln had not published the draft because the circumstances were not propitious. If he published it with the Confederates invading the North and seemingly winning, it would look like nothing more than a cynical, desperate measure of a loser. Lincoln had to await a more favorable military situation—and McClellan was to give it to him. By September 19, 1862, McClellan had created the perception that he had driven the Southern army from all Northern territory and was pursuing the loser to destruction. The perception, created by McClellan's "smoke and mirrors" victories was as good as the fact, and, on September 22, Lincoln published the document. The publication undoubtedly contributed to the ultimate Northern victory—and none other than George B. McClellan made the publication possible.

But McClellan's glory days were to be short-lived. There were now rumors in Washington that he did not actually want to destroy the Confederate army, but that he was a pacifist who preferred a negotiated peace to the war. As McClellan did little after the battle of Antietam, the rumors intensified. When Washington appeared to be in danger, McClellan was constantly cautioned that he was moving too far too fast. Now that Washington appeared safe, the criticism shifted 180 degrees, and he was berated for not going far enough fast enough. On September 22, McClellan began to move his corps from Antietam to Harpers Ferry.

On October 1, Lincoln paid McClellan a surprise three-day visit. The visit had many aspects of the ceremonial. Lincoln visited the wounded, reviewed the troops, and toured the battlefield. However, he also had discussions with McClellan, both private and in the company of others.

Lincoln's visit is reminiscent of President Harry Truman's visit with Gen. Douglas MacArthur in Honolulu during the Korean War. This visit was a political move that preceded Truman's sacking of MacArthur. Like the Truman-MacArthur visit, there are conflicting versions of what was said. To McClellan, it appeared to consist of a mere exchange of pleasantries and platitudes. To others, it appeared that Lincoln read McClellan the riot act for not pursuing Lee more vigorously. In any event, McClellan's days as commanding general of the Army of the Potomac were now running out.

When we last left Harpers Ferry on the morning of Wednesday, September 17, Gen. A. P. Hill, as he hit the road for Sharpsburg with the remainder of his division, had left behind a brigade under Colonel Thomas. Thomas's function was to take away what he could of the useable government property and to destroy what he could not.

The first information that the Union received on the state of affairs at Harpers Ferry was on Thursday, the eighteenth, when a survey party under William C. Hall, which was inspecting the railroad and telegraph wires, arrived at Sandy Hook. Hall reported that the railway and telegraph wires as far as the bridge were intact, and that there were fewer than two hundred rebel troops remaining. He further reported that the Union dead on Maryland Heights remained unburied, that the railway bridge had been burned but that the piers remained good, and that, as he was leaving late that afternoon, the rebels were busy destroying the pontoon bridge.

The next information acquired was from another party that visited the site the following day, September 19. It reported that the pontoon bridge was destroyed, that all useable property had been carted off, and that there was no longer a Confederate garrison, but small parties of Confederates were still intermittently visiting the site.

On the twentieth, there was a report from a Union cavalry patrol that actually entered the city. They found no Confederates but discovered three hundred Union sick and wounded who had been left behind when the parolees departed on the fifteenth and sixteenth. Harpers Ferry was now available for reoccupation by the Union without a fight.

Rufus Ingalles, McClellan's chief quartermaster, decided that the Army of the Potomac could not be sustained where it was and that the most suitable base for future offensive operations against Lee was Harpers Ferry. However, this decision necessitated the laying of a new pontoon bridge, rebuilding the railway bridge, putting the canal back in operation, rebuilding the vehicular bridge across the Shenandoah, and putting the Harpers Ferry-Winchester railroad spur back into operation. Beginning on the twenty-second, McClellan began moving his troops into Harpers Ferry from the Antietam, corps by corps.

And so, for the poor citizens of Harpers Ferry, yet a new cycle of rebuilding to be followed by destruction was put in motion.

Chapter 17

The Commission

The surrender of Harpers Ferry was almost immediately looked upon as a disgrace because of the small number of casualties suffered in its defense. Within days of the surrender, once the garrison parolees were back in Union hands, Secretary of War Edwin Stanton ordered four of the senior members of the garrison placed under arrest. These included Colonel Ford, who had lost Maryland Heights, and the three officers who had attended the council of war with Colonel Miles and agreed to the surrender. These were General White and Colonels D'Utassy and Trimble. Another, although less obvious, officer who was vulnerable was old General Wool, head of the Middle Department. It was in the Middle Department that Harpers Ferry was located, and Wool bore overall responsibility for what transpired there.

Having placed the four officers under arrest, Stanton convened a military commission to investigate the loss and fix responsibility. Stanton appointed three generals to the commission. These were Maj. Gen. David Hunter, U.S. Volunteers president; Maj. Gen. G. Cadwalader, U.S. Volunteers; and Brig. Gen. C. C. Augur, U.S. Volunteers.

Major General Hunter, the president, was sixty years old and had graduated from West Point in 1822, two years before Colonel Miles and seven years before Robert E. Lee. Hunter was one of the "old army" colonels. He had been a colonel in the prewar army when the other colonels included Dixon Miles, Voss Sumner, and Robert E. Lee.

Hunter had been enmeshed in controversy much of his life—and it was his latest controversy that made him available for appointment to the commission. In March 1862, he had been appointed commander of the Department of the South. In this capacity, he commanded Federally occupied areas of South Carolina, Georgia, and Florida. On May 7, 1862, Hunter issued his own proclamation of emancipation, well before that of

Lincoln, to free all of the slaves in his area. For this action, and other actions that exceeded his authority, he was relieved of command and ordered to Washington to await orders. Hunter had become a pariah in the South, only to be trumped later by Generals Benjamin Butler and William Tecumseh Sherman. Had Hunter fallen into Southern hands, he probably would have been executed.

Major General George Cadwalader, the next senior man on the commission, was a fifty-five-year-old lawyer-general who had been in and out of the military since 1826. His duties since the beginning of the war had consisted primarily of serving on various boards and committees and as advisor to the president and the secretary of war.

The third general on the commission, and junior member, was Brig. Gen. Christopher Columbus Augur. Augur was a forty-year-old graduate of West Point, class of 1842. Augur had considerable combat experience, having participated in the Mexican War, the Indian Wars, and the early battles of the Civil War. It was, in fact, his convalescence from a war wound that caused him to be available in Washington for appointment to the commission. Augur, the combat commander, nicely balanced Cadwalader, the lawyer, on the commission.

The commission convened in Washington, D.C., on September 23, 1862, just eight days after the surrender of Harpers Ferry. The judge-advocate stated that the matters that the secretary of war desired to be submitted for the investigation of the commission were the circumstances attending the late evacuation of Maryland Heights under the command of Colonel Ford and the subsequent surrender of Harpers Ferry by Colonel Miles, then in command. The secretary desired the commission to diligently inquire and faithfully report all the facts bearing, in their judgment, upon the conduct of the commanding officers or their subordinates in making the evacuation and surrender.

The commission took sworn testimony from forty-four witnesses. Colonel Miles, who died one day after the surrender, of course could not testify. However, Miles was well represented by his young aide, Lt. Henry M. Binney. Binney had been with Miles almost constantly throughout the period of the inquiry and was able to, apparently accurately, testify as to what Miles had said and done.

Among the witnesses called were General Wool, General White, Colonel Ford, brigade commanders Colonels D'Utassy, Trimble,

and Ward; independent commanders Colonels Downey and
Maulsby; Lt. Col. Hasbrouck Davis of the escaping cavalry, and
Thomas Noakes, their guide; and Captain Russell, who had successfully penetrated the Confederate lines on the night of the thir-
teenth and delivered Miles's message, first to General McClellan
and then to General Franklin. Last, and possibly least, General
Halleck was called and testified. Neither General McClellan nor
General Franklin was called, and not one single individual from
the Army of the Potomac was called. Also, unfortunately, Major
Cole, the second courier to elude the Confederate lines on the
night of the thirteenth and successfully carry Miles's message to
General McClellan, was not called; Col. Arno Voss, who commanded the escaping cavalry, was not called either.

By the time the commission met, allegations and rumors and
hearsay were swirling about the reputation of Colonel Miles. It was
said that he was stupid, a swaggering moron, that he drank, and
that he was actually disloyal, a traitor like Benedict Arnold.
Witnesses were questioned on all these aspects. Let us address
them individually. First, we will look at the allegation that he was
little more than a bumbling fool. The following are excerpts from
the sworn testimony of Lt. John L. Willmon, one of his aides:

> Question: What were the characteristics of Colonel Miles in
> regard to doing business; did he seem to understand his business;
> was he systematic?
>
> Willmon: I always admired his way of doing business; he was
> very exact.
>
> Question: Did he seem to have control of all of his faculties?
>
> Willmon: Yes, sir; that was one thing I admired in him; no mat-
> ter how much he was pressed, he did everything as I thought, in
> admirable style.
>
> Question: Did you ever see Colonel Miles, during this time,
> when you thought he had not the control of his faculties, all his
> senses?
>
> Willmon: No, sir.[1]

The commission was unable to elicit one word of criticism as to Miles's leadership capabilities from any member of his staff. All appeared to admire him. Furthermore, General White never criticized Miles's competence as a leader and, in fact, even long after the war, defended his decision to defer to Miles, alleging that under the circumstances that then prevailed, Miles was the correct choice for the top job.

Next, we come to the question of Miles's drinking. For the commission to delve into Miles's drinking habits was completely logical and appropriate. Miles was known to have had a drinking problem in the past and, in fact, was found drunk on duty during the battle of First Bull Run. Did Miles remain on the wagon since that time, or did he have a relapse? If so, did drinking affect his decisions? The following is from the testimony of Lieutenant Binney, his aide:

Question: State whether you ever noticed Colonel Miles in a state of intoxication at any time during the siege of Harpers Ferry; and, if so, at what time.

Answer: No, sir. Since I have been with him, in February last, I have never known him to use any intoxicating drink in any shape, kind or form. I have visited with him the different camps of the different regiments, and we have always been invited to dismount and go in. When we have done so, Colonel Miles has always refused to drink. Even at a private party on the 4th of July he refused to drink champagne with the ladies there.

Question: You never suspected that he drank privately?

Answer: No, sir; I never saw him under the influence of liquor, and never saw any liquors about his quarters, and I knew all his rooms. I know that General Rosecrans came there at one time and asked for something to drink, and Colonel Miles said he had kept none about him.

Question: Did you ever see his nerves affected by want of liquor?

Answer: No, sir; I never saw him except when he was calm and cool, under all circumstances, and seemed to be equal to all emergencies that might arise, except on Monday morning, the morning of the surrender. I think that then, surrounded as he was, and attacked on all sides, he seemed to be a little flustered, and hardly to know how to act. At all other times he seemed to be perfectly cool and calm. That is the only time that I ever saw him when he seemed to be excited. As far as liquor is concerned, I am willing to make oath that he never used it while he was at Harpers Ferry. I have often heard him make the remark to some of the colonels when asked to take something to drink, that he begged to be excused; that he had had enough said about his drinking at Bull Run, and since that time he had never allowed liquor to pass his lips. I know he has had presents of liquors, wines etc., but they were put in his closets and cupboards, and were there after his death. I never saw empty bottles, even, about his quarters, unless it was in the rooms of some of his staff.[2]

Now we come to the question of Miles's loyalty. To start with, Miles was a native Marylander, and most Marylanders probably favored the Confederacy. However, the real suspicion probably started with the Lieutenant Rouse affair. In August, shortly before the Confederate siege of Harpers Ferry, a cavalry patrol from the garrison captured a Confederate officer named Rouse. Lieutenant Rouse was brought to Miles for interrogation, and to some it appeared that Miles knew Rouse. In any event, Miles closeted himself privately for half an hour and then ordered Rouse released under parole. This action surprised many, as Rouse had seen too much of the defenses. In any event, Rouse was released and a few days later, on September 15, when the garrison surrendered, Rouse reappeared in full uniform with General Hill. To some, this incident raised the suspicion that Miles had come to some arrangement with Rouse wherein the garrison would be surrendered after a token defense.

Much later, another element was added to the suspicion. Major Cole had left besieged Harpers Ferry during the night of the thirteenth, attempting to get through to McClellan to seek help. Without question, he got through to McClellan. McClellan asked Cole to try to get back to Harpers Ferry with a message to Miles stating that help was on the way; he should not surrender but should reoccupy Maryland Heights if he could. From this point the story becomes contested. There were those who later claimed that Cole got back and delivered the message to Miles but that Miles told no one. This version was not yet circulating at the time of the commission, and Cole, unfortunately, was never called as a witness. Others, however, who should have known, like Colonel Miles's aide and shadow, Lieutenant Binney, testified categorically, under oath, that Cole never returned. In any event, the commission did pursue a line of questioning that related to Miles's loyalty. The consensus of those closest to Miles was that he was not only not disloyal but, to the contrary, was unusually patriotic.

Lieutenant Binney was with Miles when he died. Following are excerpts of his testimony:

> Question: You say that you were with Colonel Miles from the time he was wounded until he died?

> Answer: Yes, sir.

> Question: Did his mind wander any during that time?

> Answer: It did at times; at other times it was very clear.

> Question: You heard everything he said?

> Answer: Yes, sir.

> Question: He uttered no disloyal expressions at all?

> Answer: No, sir; and directly the reverse.[3]

Next to Miles, the commission spent the most time in examining the conduct of Colonel Ford. It was Colonel Ford who had lost Maryland Heights. Much of the testimony concerning Ford was actually favorable. However, there was one fatal omission in his performance that he could not overcome. He was not present and in charge at the site of the battle on the morning and early afternoon of the thirteenth as he should have been. It is interesting to note that Ford never introduced his malady into his defense as a matter of mitigation.

The commission then turned its attention to the conduct of the 126th New York at the battle of Maryland Heights. The loss of the battle was largely attributable to the fact that the raw regiment broke and ran. The regiment's commander, Colonel Sherrill, was seriously wounded while gallantly exposing himself to danger just before the fiasco. Thus, he became immune to criticism. Major Baird, the next senior officer, was left standing there and in command when the rout occurred. This fact placed Baird in a vulnerable position before the commission and made him a logical choice as scapegoat.

Next to Ford and Miles, the three primary targets of the commission were Brigadier General White, Colonel D'Utassy, and Colonel Trimble. It was these three who, with Miles, had attended the council of war immediately before the surrender and who had all agreed to the surrender. All three had been placed under arrest as soon as they returned to Union control.

General White, unlike the others, was politically connected. He was a friend of Lincoln's. D'Utassy was one of the real characters of the war. He was a Hungarian émigré who achieved his colonelcy in large part because of his experiences in the Hungarian wars of liberation. Among other things, D'Utassy had been a trick circus rider, a phony self-proclaimed nobleman, and a crook. Within a year of the commission, D'Utassy became a resident of Sing Sing prison for other matters. Be that as it may, the commission could find no fault with the conduct of any of the three during the siege. All had, at every point, appeared to be brave, conscientious, and competent officers. D'Utassy had actually appeared to go the extra mile. After Maryland Heights had been evacuated, he had volunteered to go back and recover the cannons left behind, which he did. Furthermore, he had twice volunteered to attempt to recapture Maryland Heights but was overruled by Miles.

The commission next turned its attention to old General Wool, in whose department Harpers Ferry was located. Actually, even this inquiry was questionable in that on September 12, three days before the surrender, Halleck had sent a message to McClellan for delivery to Miles that transferred Miles's command from Wool to McClellan. The message was never delivered. Be that as it may, Wool had been responsible for maintaining Miles in command and for everything that Miles and his command did.

The commission called Henry Halleck as a witness. In deference to Halleck's position, the questions were put to him in writing in advance. They were as follows:

Will you state to the commission at what time General McClellan was ordered to advance and repel the enemy invading the State of Maryland; at what time he did actually advance; the average number of miles marched by him per day in pursuit of the invading enemy, and if, in your opinion, General McClellan should not have relieved and protected Harpers Ferry?

Halleck provided dates, times, and places for the answer to the first part of the question. For the second part regarding his opinion about the possible relief of Harpers Ferry, he answered as follows:

It is not easy to answer the latter part of the question of the Commission without a full knowledge of the position and forces of the enemy. General McClellan has not made any report of his operations in Maryland, nor have I seen any report of his subordinate officers. But judging from all the information I could obtain from scouts, spies, deserters, and prisoners of war on these matters, I am of opinion that it was possible for General McClellan to have relieved and protected Harpers Ferry, and that he should have done so.

The commission next asked Halleck if his message to Colonel Miles of September 7 indicated that it was the intention of the government that Miles remain as permanent commander there. The message read as follows:

Washington D. C. September 7, 1862

Colonel Miles, Harpers Ferry:

Our army is in motion. It is important that Harpers Ferry be held to the latest moment. The government has the utmost confidence in you, and is ready to give you full credit for the defense it expects you to make.

H. W. Halleck
General-in-Chief

It is this message that Colonel Miles showed to General White upon White's arrival at Harpers Ferry on September 12 as evidence that Washington desired Miles to remain in command; it is this message that was the clincher in convincing White to cede command to Miles. Halleck answered the commission as follows:

So far as the telegram is concerned, there was no intention
about it. It was a communication to the commanding officer of
the post, and applied equally to his successor, should he have
one.[4]

So in Halleck's brief testimony to the commission, he managed to nimbly sidestep his responsibility for retaining Miles in
command; failed to mention that it was he who twice refused to
evacuate the garrison (as McClellan had requested); and last,
based on unnamed spies, scouts, and deserters, cast the blame
for the loss on McClellan, who, as he said, could have and should
have relieved the garrison. Neither McClellan nor any member
of his staff or army was called as a witness, so McClellan had no
opportunity to respond to the accusation.

The commission issued its final report on November 3, 1862.

Final Report of the Commission

The Commission, consisting of Maj. Gen. D. Hunter, U. S.
Volunteers, president; Maj. Gen. G. Cadwalader, U. S.
Volunteers; Brig. Gen. C. C. Augur, U. S. Volunteers; Capt. Donn
Piatt, assistant adjutant-general of Volunteers; Capt. F. Ball, jr.,
aide-de-camp, U. S. Army; Col. J. Holt, Judge-Advocate-General,
called by the Government to investigate the conduct of certain
officers connected with, and the circumstances attending, the
abandonment of Maryland Heights and the surrender of
Harpers Ferry, have the honor to report as follows:

On the 3d day of September, General White entered Harpers
Ferry, with his command, from Winchester. The next day he was
ordered to Martinsburg, to take command of the forces at that
place. On the 12th of September he again returned to Harpers
Ferry, where he remained until its surrender, without assuming
command.

On the 7th of September, General McClellan (the larger portion of his command having preceded him) left Washington,
under orders, issued some days previously, to drive the enemy
from Maryland. He established that night his headquarters at
Rockville, and from which place, on the 11th of September, he
telegraphed to General Halleck to have Colonel Miles ordered
to join him at once.

On the 5th of September, Col. Thomas H. Ford, of the

Thirty-second Ohio, took command of the forces on Maryland Heights.

Forces were placed at Solomon's Gap and Sandy Hook. Those at Sandy Hook, being under Colonel Maulsby, retired, by order of Colonel Miles, to the eastern slope of Maryland Heights two or three days previous to their evacuation by Colonel Ford.

On the 11th of September the force at Solomon's Gap was driven in by the enemy. Colonel Ford called upon Colonel Miles for reinforcements, and on Friday, the 12th of September, the Thirty-ninth and One hundred and twenty-sixth New York Regiments were sent him, and on the morning of the 13th he was further reinforced by the One hundred and fifteenth New York and a portion of a Maryland regiment under Lieutenant-Colonel Downey.

Colonel Ford made requisition for axes and spades to enable him to construct defenses on the heights, but obtained none, and on the 12th, with twelve axes belonging to some Maryland regiment, being all he could obtain, a slight breastwork of trees was constructed near the crest of the heights, and in front of which for a short distance a slashing of timber was made.

The forces under Colonel Ford were stationed at various points on Maryland Heights, the principal force being on the crest of the hill near the breastwork and lookout. Skirmishing commenced on Friday, the 12th, on the crest of the hill.

Early in the morning of the 13th the enemy made an attack on the crest of the hill, and after a short engagement, the troops retired in some confusion to the breastwork, where they were rallied. About 9 o'clock a second attack was made, which the troops behind the breastwork resisted for a short time, and until Colonel Sherrill, of the One hundred and twenty-sixth New York, was wounded and carried off the field, when the entire One hundred and twenty-sixth Regiment, as some witnesses testify, with the exception of two companies, as Major Hewitt states, broke and fled in utter confusion. Both men and most of the officers fled together, no effort being made to rally the regiment except by Colonel Ford and Lieutenant Barras, acting adjutant, and some officers of other regiments, directed by Colonel Miles, who was then on the heights.

Soon after, the remaining forces at the breastwork fell back under a supposed order from Major Hewitt, who himself says that he gave no such order, but merely sent instructions to the captains of his own regiment that, if they were compelled to retire, to do so in good order. Orders were given by Colonel Ford for the troops to return to their position, and they advanced some distance up the heights, but did not regain the breastwork.

That morning Colonel Miles was on Maryland Heights for some hours, consulting with Colonel Ford. He left between 11 and 12 o'clock without directly ordering Colonel Ford to evacuate the heights, but instructing him, in case he was compelled to do so, to spike his guns and throw the heavy siege guns down the mountain. About 2 o'clock, perhaps a little later, by order of Colonel Ford, the heights were abandoned, the guns being spiked according to instructions.

On Sunday, Colonel D'Utassy sent over to the Maryland Heights four companies, under Major Wood, who brought off without opposition four brass 12-pounders, two of which were imperfectly spiked, and also a wagon-load of ammunition.

General White, on his return to Harpers Ferry on the 12th of September, suggested to Colonel Miles the propriety of contracting his line on Bolivar Heights so as to make a better defense; but Colonel Miles adhered to his original line of defense, stating that he was determined to make his stand on Bolivar Heights. General White also urged the importance of holding Maryland Heights, even should it require the taking [of] the entire force over there from Harpers Ferry. Colonel Miles, under his order to hold Harpers Ferry to the last extremity, while admitting the importance of Maryland Heights, seemed to regard them as applying to the town of Harpers Ferry, and that to leave Harpers Ferry even to go on Maryland Heights would be disobeying his instructions.

General McClellan established his headquarters at Frederick City on the morning of the 13th of September.

On the night of the 13th, after the evacuation of Maryland Heights, Colonel Miles directed Captain (now Major) Charles H. Russell, of the Maryland cavalry, to take with him a few men and endeavor to get through the enemy's line and reach some of our forces, General McClellan if possible, and to report the condition of Harpers Ferry; that it could not hold out more than forty-eight hours unless reinforced, and to urge the sending of reinforcements. Captain Russell reached General McClellan's headquarters at Frederick at 9 am on Sunday, the 14th of

September, and reported as directed by Colonel Miles. Immediately upon his arrival, General McClellan sent off a messenger, as Captain Russell understood, to General Franklin. At 10 am Captain Russell left for General Franklin's command, with a communication to General Franklin from General McClellan. He reached General Franklin about 3 o'clock that afternoon, and found him engaged with the enemy at Crampton's Gap. The enemy was driven from the gap, and the next morning, the 15th, General Franklin passed through the gap, advancing about a mile, and, finding the enemy drawn up in line of battle in his front, drew his own forces up in line of battle. While there stationed, the cannonading in the direction of Harpers Ferry, which had been heard very distinctly all the morning, Harpers Ferry being about 7 miles distant, suddenly ceased; whereupon General Franklin sent word to General McClellan of the probable surrender of Harpers Ferry by Colonel Miles, and did not deem it necessary to proceed farther in that direction.

The battle of South Mountain was fought on Sunday, the 14th, and on the same day, during the afternoon, the enemy at Harpers Ferry attacked the extreme left of the line on Bolivar Heights, but, after some time, were repulsed by the troops under the command of General White. On Sunday night the cavalry at Harpers Ferry made their escape, under Colonel Davis, of the Twelfth Illinois Cavalry, by permission of Colonel Miles, and reached Greencastle, Pa., the next morning, capturing on their way an ammunition train belonging to General Longstreet, consisting of some 50 or 60 wagons.

The Commission regard this escape of cavalry as being worthy of great commendation to the officers conducting the same.

Several of the infantry officers desired permission to cut their way out at the same time the cavalry made their escape, but Colonel Miles refused, upon the ground that he had been ordered to hold Harpers Ferry to the last extremity.

On the morning of the 15th the enemy opened their batteries from several points, seven to nine, as estimated by different witnesses, directing their attack principally upon our batteries on the left of Bolivar Heights.

The attack commenced at daybreak; about 7 o'clock Colonel Miles represented to General White that it would be necessary to surrender. General White suggested that the brigade commanders be called together, which was done. Colonel Miles stated that the ammunition for the batteries was exhausted, and he had about made up his mind to surrender. That was finally agreed to by all present, and General White was sent to arrange articles of capitulation. The white flag was raised by order of Colonel Miles, but the enemy did not cease firing for some half or three-quarters of an hour after. Colonel Miles was mortally wounded after the white flag was raised. The surrender was agreed upon about 8 am on Monday, the 15th of September.

The following was the testimony of officers commanding batteries:

At the time of the surrender, Captain Von Sehlen had some ammunition; could not tell what amount, but mostly shrapnel; had lost about 100 rounds on Saturday, the 13th, by the explosion of a limber, caused by one of the enemy's shells.

Captain Rigby had expended, during the siege of Harpers Ferry, about 600 rounds, being all that he had with the exception of canister.

Captain Potts had expended about 1,000 rounds, being all that he had with the exception of canister.

Captain Graham had but two guns of his battery under his immediate command on the morning of the surrender; had probably 100 rounds of all kinds, but no long-time fuses.

Captain Phillips had expended all his ammunition except some 40 rounds of canister and some long-range shells, too large for his guns.

Captain McGrath's battery had been spiked and left on Maryland Heights on Saturday.

It appears that during the siege, and shortly previous, Colonel Miles paroled several Confederate prisoners and permitted them to pass through our lines. During the week previous to the evacuation of Maryland Heights, a Lieutenant Rouse, of the Twelfth Virginia Cavalry, who had been engaged in a raid upon a train from Harpers Ferry to Winchester a short time before, was captured and brought into Harpers Ferry. He escaped while on the way to the hospital, he pretending to be sick, but was retaken. He was paroled, but returned in command of some rebel cavalry on the morning of the surrender. The attention of General A. P. Hill was called to the fact that Lieutenant Rouse was a paroled prisoner, but no attention was paid to it. Lieutenant Rouse himself, on being spoken to about it, laughed at the idea of observing his parole.

On Saturday, the day of the attack upon and evacuation of Maryland Heights, Colonel Miles directed the 16 confederate prisoners be permitted to pass through our lines to rejoin the rebel army at Winchester. Other cases are testified to, but the above-named are of most importance.

Brigadier-General White and Colonels D'Utassy and Trimble

Of the subordinate officers referred to in this case, with the exception of Col. Thomas H. Ford, the Commission finds nothing in their conduct that calls for censure. On the contrary, General Julius White merits its approbation. He appears from the evidence to have acted with decided capability and courage.

In this connection the Commission calls attention to the disgraceful behavior of the One hundred and twenty-sixth New York Infantry, and recommend that Major Baird, for his bad conduct, as shown by the evidence, should be dismissed [from] the service. Some of the officers of this regiment, Lieutenant Barras, acting adjutant, and others, not known by name to the Commission, behaved gallantly, and should be commended.

Col. Thomas H. Ford

In the case of Colonel Ford, charged with improper conduct in abandoning Maryland Heights, the Commission, after a careful hearing of the evidence produced by the Government, and that relied on by the defense, and a due consideration of the arguments offered by counsel, finds:

That on the 5th of September Colonel Ford was placed in command of Maryland Heights by Colonel Miles; that Colonel Ford, finding the position unprepared by fortifications, earnestly urged Colonel Miles to furnish him means by which the heights could be made tenable for the small force under his command should a heavy one be brought against him. These reasonable demands were, from some cause unknown to the Commission, not responded to by the officer in command of Harpers Ferry; that subsequently, when the enemy appeared in heavy force, Colonel Ford frequently and earnestly called upon Colonel Miles for more troops, representing that he could not hold the heights unless reinforced; that these demands were feebly, or not at all, complied with; that, as late as the morning of the 13th of September, Colonel Ford sent two written demands to Colonel Miles for reinforcements, and saying that, with the troops then under his command he could not hold the heights, and, unless relieved or otherwise ordered, he would have to abandon them; that, as late as 11 o'clock a. m. of the 13th, a few hours previous to the abandonment of this position, Colonel Miles said to Colonel Ford that he (Colonel Ford) could not have another man, and must do the best he could; and, if unable to defend the place, he must spike the guns, throw them down the hill, and withdraw to Harpers Ferry in good order.

The Commission is, then, satisfied that Colonel Ford was given a discretionary power to abandon the heights or not, as his better judgment might dictate, with the men and means then under his command; and it is believed from the evidence, circumstantial and direct, that the result did not, to any great extent, surprise, nor in any way displease, the officer in command at Harpers Ferry.

But this conclusion, so much relied upon by the defense, forces the Commission to consider the fact: Did Colonel Ford, under the discretionary power thus vested in him, make a proper defense of the heights, and hold them, as he should have done, until driven off by the enemy?

The evidence shows conclusively that the force upon the heights was not well managed; that the point most pressed was weakly defended as to numbers, and, after the wounding of the gallant colonel of the One hundred and twenty-sixth New York Infantry, it was left without a competent officer in command, Colonel Ford, himself, not appearing nor designating any one who might have restored order and encouraged the men. That the abandonment of the heights was premature is clearly proven. Our forces were not driven from the field, as full time was given to spike the guns and throw the heavier ones down the precipice, and retreat in good order to Harpers Ferry. The loss in killed and wounded does not indicate a desperate conflict, and the opinion of officers sustaining the abandonment is weakened by the fact that the next day a force returning to the heights found them unoccupied, and brought away, unmolested, four abandoned guns and a quantity of ammunition.

In so grave a case as this, with such disgraceful consequences, the Commission cannot permit an officer to shield himself behind the fact that he did as well as he could, if in so doing he exhibits a lack of military capacity. It is clear to the Commission that Colonel Ford should not have been placed in command on Maryland Heights; that he conducted the defense without ability, and abandoned his position with out sufficient cause, and has shown throughout such a lack of military capacity as to disqualify him, in the estimation of the Commission, for a command in the service.

Col. D. S. Miles.

The Commission has approached a consideration of this officer's conduct, in connection with the surrender of Harpers Ferry, with extreme reluctance. An officer who cannot appear before any earthly tribunal to answer or explain charges gravely affecting his character, who has met his death at the hands of the enemy, even upon the spot he disgracefully surrendered, is entitled to the tenderest care and most careful investigation. These this Commission has accorded Colonel Miles, and, in giving an opinion, only repeats what runs through our nine hundred pages of evidence, strangely unanimous upon the fact that Colonel Miles' incapacity, amounting to almost imbecility, led to the shameful surrender of this important post.

Early as the 15th of August he disobeys orders of Major-General Wool to fortify Maryland Heights. When it is attacked by the enemy, its naturally strong positions are unimproved, and, from his criminal neglect, to use the mildest term, the large force of the enemy is almost upon an equality with the few men he throws out for their protection.

He seemed to have understood and admitted to his officers that Maryland Heights was the key to the position, and yet he placed Colonel Ford in command with a feeble force; made no effort to strengthen him by fortifications, although, between the 5th and 13th of September, there was ample time to do so; and to Colonel Ford's repeated demands for means to intrench and reinforcements to strengthen the position, he made either inadequate return or no response at all. He gave Colonel Ford discretionary power as to when he should abandon the heights, the fact of the abandonment having, it seems, been determined only in his own mind, for, when the unhappy event really occurred, his only exclamations were to the effect that he feared Colonel Ford had given them up too soon. This, too, when he must have known that the abandonment of Maryland Heights was the

surrender of Harpers Ferry. This leaving the key of the position
to the keeping of Colonel Ford, with discretionary power, after
the arrival of the capable and courageous officer who had
waived his rank to serve wherever ordered, is one of the more
striking facts illustrating the utter incapacity of Colonel Miles.

Immediately previous to and pending the siege of Harpers
Ferry he paroled rebel prisoners, and permits, indeed, sends
them to the enemy's headquarters. This, too, when he should
have known that the lack of ammunition, the bad conduct of
some of our troops, the entire absence of fortifications, and the
abandonment of Maryland Heights were important facts they
could, and undoubtedly did, communicate to the enemy.
Sixteen of these prisoners were paroled on the 12th, and a pass
given them in the handwriting of Colonel Miles, and some of
them left as late as the 14th; while a rebel officer, by the name of
Rouse, after an escape, is retaken, and subsequently has a private
interview with Colonel Miles is paroled, and after the surrender
appears at the head of his men, among the first to enter Harpers
Ferry.

It is not necessary to accumulate instances from the mass of
evidence that throughout scarcely affords one fact in contradic-
tion to what each one establishes, that Colonel Miles was unfit to
conduct so important a defense as that of Harpers Ferry.

This Commission would not have dwelt upon this painful subject were it not for the fact that the officer who placed this inca-
pable in command should share in the responsibility, and in the
opinion of the Commission Major-General Wool is guilty to this
extent of a grave disaster, and should be censured for his conduct.

The Commission has remarked freely on the conduct of
Colonel Miles, an old officer, killed in one of the battles of our
country, and it cannot, from any motives of delicacy, refrain
from censuring those in high command when it thinks such censure deserved. The General-in-Chief has testified that General
McClellan, after having received orders to repel the enemy
invading the State of Maryland, marched only 6 miles per day on
an average when pursuing the invading enemy. The General-in-
Chief also testifies that, in his opinion, General McClellan could,
and should, have relieved and protected Harpers Ferry, and in
this opinion the Commission fully concur.

The evidence thus introduced confirms the Commission in

the opinion that Harpers Ferry, as well as Maryland Heights, was prematurely surrendered. The garrison should have been satisfied that relief, however long delayed, would come at last, and that 1,000 men killed in Harpers Ferry would have made a small loss had the post been secured, and probably save 2,000 at Antietam. How important was this defense we can now appreciate. Of the 97,000 composing at that time the whole of Lee's Army, more than one-third were attacking Harpers Ferry, and of this the main body was in Virginia. By reference to the evidence, it will be seen that at the moment Colonel Ford abandoned Maryland Heights his little army was in reality relieved by Generals Franklin's and Sumner's corps at Crampton's Gap, within 7 miles of his position, and that after the surrender of Harpers Ferry no time was given to parole prisoners even, before 20,000 troops were hurried from Virginia and the entire force went off on the double-quick to relieve Lee, who was being attacked at Antietam. Had the garrison been slower to surrender or the Army of the Potomac swifter to march, the enemy would have been forced to raise the siege or have been taken in detail, with the Potomac dividing his forces.

D. Hunter,
Major-General, President

J. Holt
Judge-Advocate-General[5]

In addition to its judgments of Miles, Ford, White, D'Utassy, and Trimble, the commission recommended that Major Baird be dismissed from the service and that old General Wool be censured.

Did Harpers Ferry hold out as long as it could have? There were those with better military credentials than Generals Hunter, Cadwalader, and Augur who thought so. These included Robert E. Lee and Stonewall Jackson.

Chapter 18

Whose Fault Was It?

As of the end of September 17, 1862, Lee's army was fully reunited, and the golden opportunity provided to the Union by the finding of Special Order 191 was gone with the wind. The Union had been provided four precious days to act, with an unsurpassed knowledge of the Confederates' intentions and vulnerabilities. In those four days, if it had destroyed any one of the detached pieces of the Confederate army, it undoubtedly would have prevailed over the remainder. Those four days provided a real prospect, not only for the destruction of the Army of Northern Virginia, but for the capture or deaths of Lee, Longstreet, and Jackson. Had this happened, there would have been no Fredericksburg, Chancellorsville, or Gettysburg.

Who was responsible for this failure? Let us start at the top with President Lincoln. When McClellan first moved out from Washington to Rockville on September 7 to confront the Confederate forces invading Maryland, he did not know whether the Confederate invasion was a feint or the main effort. He did not know how many Confederates there were, how they were deployed, or what their intentions were. Consequently, to hedge his bets, he left three of his corps behind (those of Porter, Sigel, and Heintzelman) to bolster the already formidable garrison troops of Washington.

By September 11, McClellan had come to the realization that he had the main Confederate army in front of him and that, if it was in front of him, it could not be threatening Washington behind him. He explained all this to Halleck in his letter of the eleventh and then requested that the corps of Porter, Sigel, and Heintzelman be sent to him. Lincoln intervened and answered McClellan's request by granting him Porter, with a vague promise of more to follow. In the event, Sigel and Heintzelman were retained and did not join McClellan. Subsequent events vindicated McClellan's judgment. Washington was not threatened; Sigel and Heintzelman were not required for its defense, and they contributed little, if anything, to the events of September 1862. On the other hand, had they been sent to McClellan, they could have tipped the balance in a number of instances.

One obvious instance where Sigel's and Heintzelman's corps could have proved decisive for McClellan was in the final phase of the battle of Antietam. McClellan's original plan was to stretch the two flanks of the Confederate position and then to commit his reserves down the middle. When it came time to commit the reserves during the afternoon of the seventeenth, after Burnside had crossed the bridge, McClellan backed out and withheld Porter's and Franklin's corps for fear of a Confederate counterattack. Had he had two additional corps and committed any two of the four available, he would have won decisively. Blame for the fact that he did not have the additional two can be put at the feet of Abraham Lincoln.

We now come to Henry Halleck, General in Chief, U.S. Army. The loss of the garrison at Harpers Ferry can be attributed directly to Halleck. Sometime between September 3 and September 6, McClellan first proposed to Halleck, in Halleck's bedroom in the presence of Secretary of State William Seward, that Harpers Ferry be abandoned. Halleck peremptorily rejected the proposal without explanation—probably for the simple reason that McClellan recommended it. At the time, the garrison could unquestionably have been withdrawn to the north via Hagerstown.

McClellan next recommended to Halleck on September 11 that the garrison be evacuated and join him. Halleck replied that this was no longer possible and that McClellan would have to forcibly relieve the garrison. Again, examining the situation on the basis of what we now know, McClellan was probably right and Halleck wrong, and the garrison could have been evacuated.

Strictly speaking, Halleck's refusal to evacuate the Harpers Ferry garrison at McClellan's first request could not be related to actions following the finding of Special Order 191, because if the garrison had been evacuated before September 8, there would have been no Special Order 191. However, Halleck's refusal to evacuate the garrison on or after September 11 did influence the events following the discovery of Special Order 191, because Special Order 191 was issued on September 9. How the events would have played out if the garrison had been evacuated on the eleventh is simply unknown. However, McClellan would have been fortified by nine thousand additional troops, and his prospects would have been commensurately enhanced.

Our next candidate for those who contributed most to the failure to capitalize on the finding of Special Order 191 is cavalry commander Brig. Gen. Alfred Pleasonton. Of the things the Union failed to do or did wrong after the finding of Special Order 191, the one that stands near the top of the list is the failure to establish contact with the garrison at Harpers Ferry after telegraphic communications were cut on the eleventh.

As the days went by, the garrison felt increasingly isolated and uninformed. They did not know if they were going to be relieved, and if they were, when, or from which direction. They did not know whether Union forces were approaching or being driven back. By the thirteenth, they knew they were besieged in all directions. They believed they were besieged by vastly superior forces and considered that, ultimately, they would have to surrender. They knew nothing of the finding of Special Order 191, nor did they know that the fate of Harpers Ferry was directly related to a larger scheme, or that their holding out just an extra twenty-four hours would contribute enormously to the destruction of the Confederate army. It was imperative that they be informed of these matters so that they not consider that prolonging their resistance would result in nothing more than a useless effusion of blood.

Colonel Dixon Miles clung tenaciously to the literal reading of the last order he had received—to hold Harpers Ferry to the last extremity—and he considered that Maryland Heights was not Harpers Ferry. Despite the obvious advantages of moving the center of gravity of his defenses to Maryland Heights at the potential cost of losing Harpers Ferry, he refused to do so. Had he been directly ordered to hold Maryland Heights at all costs, even at the expense of losing the city of Harpers Ferry, it would all have worked out differently—and vastly more favorably to the Union.

Contact with Harpers Ferry was lost on the eleventh, and between that time and the surrender on the morning of the fifteenth, no courier from the outside got through to Colonel Miles. Could couriers have gotten through to Miles if a determined effort had been made? Certainly they could have!

The perimeter that Miles was defending was almost ten miles long, and the area was thickly wooded and mountainous. Pleasonton had troopers available who lived in the area and were intimately familiar with the terrain. By the eleventh, Union cavalry patrols were operating within ten miles of the perimeter, and neither Jackson nor McLaws nor Walker had yet arrived. Close encirclement was not accomplished until the afternoon of the thirteenth, and even then it was porous. After the close encirclement, exactly 1,605 members of the garrison (1,594 cavalry, Russell's group of 10, and Cole) attempted to make their way through the Confederate lines—and 1,605 succeeded. Not one was killed, and not one was wounded or captured.

Furthermore, by the thirteenth, the Union had reoccupied the signal station at Point of Rocks (see map 36). This station was within easy visual signaling distance of Maryland Heights. Thus, if Miles had still held Maryland Heights, or if he had been made aware of the reoccupation of Point of Rocks, continuous contact with the outside world could have been reestablished.

What do we know of McClellan's and Pleasonton's efforts to reestablish contact with Miles? Not as much as we would like to—but enough to indict both. The first firm indication we have was on the eleventh, shortly after contact was lost. At 12:30 p.m., McClellan sent the following dispatch to Pleasonton: "Can you without too much risk, send a small party to communicate with Harpers Ferry by the south side of the Potomac."[1] Admittedly, this was an anemic order, more in the form of a suggestion. Yet a good, energetic officer would have picked it up and run with it.

At 10 p.m. on the evening of the eleventh, McClellan ordered Pleasonton to report to him in person at Clarksburg (thirteen miles southeast of Point of Rocks) on the morning of the twelfth. We do not know what words were exchanged at this meeting, but from later events it is clear that they included McClellan's tasking Pleasonton with contacting Harpers Ferry.

At 1:45 p.m. on the twelfth, Halleck telegraphed McClellan: "Is it not possible to open communications with Harpers Ferry so that Miles can cooperate with you?"[2] At the same time, Halleck forwarded a message to McClellan for Miles to be delivered when McClellan reestablished contact. The message was as follows:

1:45 P.M.
Headquarters of the Army
Washington D.C. Sept 12, 1862

Colonel Dixon Miles
Harpers Ferry

Map 36
Reestablishing Communications with Harpers Ferry

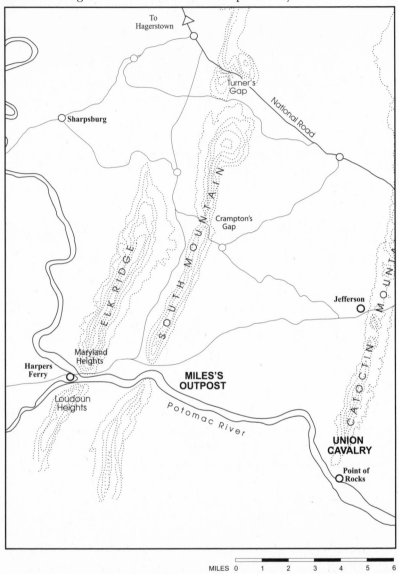

MILES 0   1   2   3   4   5   6

You will obey such orders as General McClellan may give you.
You will endeavor to open communications with him and unite
your forces to his at the earliest possible moment. His army is now
near the line of the Monocacy.

Henry W. Halleck
General-in-Chief[3]

McClellan responded at 6 p.m. as follows:

> Headquarters Army of the Potomac
> Near Urbana Maryland
> September 12, 1862 6 P.M.

Major General Halleck

I learn nothing reliable as to the enemy south of the Potomac. I this morning ordered cavalry to open communications with Harpers Ferry, and in my orders of movement for tomorrow have arranged so that I can go or send to his (Miles) relief, if necessary. I have heard no firing in that direction, and, if he resists at all, I think I can not only relieve him, but place the rebels who attack him in great danger of being cut off. Everything moves at daylight tomorrow. Your message to him this moment received. Will forward by first opportunity.

Geo. B. McClellan
Major General, Commanding[4]

Halleck's message to Miles was never delivered.

Note that McClellan stated in his reply that he "this morning" ordered the cavalry to open communications with Harpers Ferry; it was "this morning" that he had his meeting with Pleasonton. To further validate that McClellan ordered Pleasonton at their morning meeting to open communications with Harpers Ferry, we have McClellan's summary of the situation that he sent to Lincoln at 9 p.m. In it, he stated that "I have taken all possible means to communicate with Harpers Ferry."[5]

The next and last specific reference we have to an attempt to get a courier through to Miles was on the fourteenth. As previously discussed, Maj. Henry Cole, from Harpers Ferry, succeeded in penetrating the Confederate lines and reached McClellan on the afternoon of the fourteenth, with the message that Miles could hold out for only forty-eight hours from the time Cole left (i.e., until dark on the fifteenth). McClellan then asked Cole to try and get back with a message. The message was that help was imminent, that Miles should attempt to recover Maryland Heights, and that Miles should not surrender. McClellan claimed that, in addition to Cole, he gave the same message to three separate couriers. The question is, who were these messengers and what happened to them? This mystery remains. But what is known is that none arrived in Harpers Ferry before the surrender.

If McClellan, via Pleasonton, had established contact with Miles, what would he have told him? At a minimum, he would have given him Halleck's message advising Miles that he was now under McClellan's command and that Miles was to unite his forces with those of McClellan. We also know from McClellan's subsequent words and actions that he would have told Miles that help was en route, that it would arrive via Pleasant Valley, and, consequently, it was imperative that Miles maintain a position north of the river. If he had lost Maryland Heights, he must try to regain it. And last, but not least, Miles would probably have been informed of the larger situation and of his role within it. He would have been informed that McClellan was in hot pursuit of Lee's army and that, for each additional hour that Miles kept Jackson, McLaws, or Walker from rejoining Lee, McClellan's prospects for destroying Lee would be commensurately enhanced.

Had this information been available to Miles, it is all but certain everything would have worked out differently. A likely scenario would have been as follows: Miles would have abandoned Harpers Ferry and moved his troops north of the river and destroyed the bridge behind him. Lee would have recalled Jackson or Walker and left McLaws to his own devices to escape as he could. McLaws's eight thousand would have been sandwiched between Franklin's twenty thousand and Miles's fourteen thousand. If McLaws had escaped at all, it would have had to be in a direction away from Lee, and consequently he could not have joined Lee in time for the battle of Antietam. Had McLaws not rejoined Lee, Lee would have been decisively defeated.

Before leaving the subject of establishing communications with Harpers Ferry, let us look at several other scenarios that "might have taken place" had Miles been kept advised of the larger situation surrounding him. On the night of the fourteenth, Miles's potent cavalry force left at dark with the sole objective of avoiding capture on the following day when the garrison surrendered. The route the cavalry selected proceeded westward along the north bank of the Potomac to Sharpsburg and points beyond. The cavalry, by chance, bumped into and captured Longstreet's ammunition train near Williamsport, which earlier in the day had left Hagerstown for the ford at Williamsport. Although this capture was a significant accomplishment for the Union, it pales into insignificance when compared to what the cavalry might have accomplished that night had it been aware of the larger situation.

During the day of the fourteenth, McClellan attacked the forces of D. H. Hill and Longstreet, which were defending Turner's and Fox's Gaps in South Mountain. This attack put the entire Confederate army wagon park and artillery reserve, located at Boonsboro just on the other side of the mountain from McClellan, in jeopardy. Consequently, Lee ordered the wagons and artillery reserve to proceed south from Boonsboro to Sharpsburg. Then, after dark, he withdrew his exhausted troops from the mountain passes to follow the wagons and artillery to Sharpsburg. The objective was to take a defensive position behind Antietam Creek, just north and west of Sharpsburg. Thus, during the night of the fourteenth, by pure chance, the escaping Union cavalry passed through Sharpsburg heading west, just as Lee's wagons, followed by his tired troops, approached Sharpsburg from the north.

Now, it is every cavalryman's dream to be rampaging through a retreating enemy's wagon train. This possibility was presented to the Union cavalry on a platter the night of the fourteenth, under the most favorable circumstances. The Union cavalry was in front of the wagon train, and its protection behind it. But the Union cavalry knew nothing of the approaching Confederates and continued on its flight to the west as the wagon train crossed Antietam Creek unmolested.

To speculate about other scenarios that "might have taken place" a bit further: Could Miles's infantry have left the night of the fourteenth as his cavalry did? This question was brought up by the military commission that investigated the loss of Harpers Ferry. Let us turn to the testimony of Capt. Samuel C. Means, commanding officer of the Loudoun Rangers, which left Harpers Ferry that night:

Question: Will you give the Commission your judgment as to whether the infantry could have effected their escape the night the cavalry cut their way through?

Means: I do not think there would have been any difficulty in the world.

Question: You think they could have passed over the road you passed over?

Means: Yes sir; the infantry could have done it well and easy. It was through the mountain; a rough road. It would have been bad for the artillery to have gotten over, it is very true, but infantry could have done it.[6]

When it was pointed out to Means that there was only a sin- gle bridge over the Potomac, and that the cavalry required more than two hours to cross it, Means replied that the water was so low that night that the cavalry could have forded the river, leaving the bridge for the exclusive use of the infantry. Means also testified that, under forced march, the infantry could have covered the first twelve miles in three hours, thus putting the head of the column through Sharpsburg before midnight.

Let us suppose that McClellan had directed Miles to withdraw his infantry that night to Sharpsburg and that when the exhaust- ed Confederate column reached Antietam Creek, instead of find- ing the succor they expected, they found fourteen thousand Union troops across their path, and McClellan's vast army coming up behind. What would have happened then? All this is, of course, speculation, and no one knows if it would have been possible to withdraw the Union infantry from Harpers Ferry in the dark without Jackson or Hill becoming aware of it. Yet, these are additional possibilities, highly favorable to the Union, that might have occurred had there been communications for concerted action between McClellan and the garrison.

There is still another instance where contact with the outside might have been of inestimable value to the Union. During the night of the fourteenth, McLaws, becoming fully aware that the pri- mary threat to him was Franklin's force in his rear, withdrew all of his troops from Maryland Heights, except for a single small regi- ment of two hundred. Thus, Maryland Heights was practically free for the retaking by Miles—but he knew nothing of this situation and so did nothing about it.

From all of this, we can see that if McClellan had established communications with Miles, a variety of scenarios were possible, all highly favorable to the Union. At an absolute minimum, it is possible that the garrison would have held out longer than it did; in which case, not all of the besieging Confederates would have gotten back in time for the battle of Antietam, and Lee would have been decisively defeated.

Thus, we can conclude that one of the greatest mistakes of the Union commanders was their failure to open communications with the garrison. This mistake can be laid at the feet of General Pleasonton for failing to do so, and at the feet of General McClellan for failing to see that Pleasonton did so.

Our next candidate for the incompetent who contributed most to the Union's failure to capitalize on the finding of Special Order 191 is Gen. William Buel Franklin, commander of the Sixth Corps. General Franklin was a strong contender, but then the competition was fierce.

It was Franklin who was specifically tasked with relieving the garrison at Harpers Ferry. Franklin received his orders at about 7 p.m. on September 13 while he and two of his divisions were camped just east of Jefferson. Jefferson was about ten road miles from Burkittsville, which was at the foot of Crampton's Gap (see map 36). Crampton's Gap led to Pleasant Valley, and it was just six miles down Pleasant Valley to the bridge at Harpers Ferry. There were no Confederates between Franklin and Crampton's Gap, and the only Confederates on the other side of the gap were McLaws's two divisions, which were mostly tied down facing Harpers Ferry. McLaws's total force was about 8,000, while Franklin's two divisions at Jefferson constituted 12,300. In addition, Franklin had a third division of more than 7,000 closing up from the east, about a half-day's march behind.

McClellan's orders to Franklin outlined the contents of Special Order 191 in its entirety and then directed Franklin to seize Crampton's Gap and relieve Harpers Ferry.

The following chronology of events speaks for itself:

Saturday, September 13, 7 p.m.
  • Franklin reads McClellan's orders at Jefferson.
Sunday, September 14, 12 Noon
  • Franklin's two divisions reach the base of Crampton's Gap (ten miles from Jefferson).
  • A messenger from McClellan arrives telling Franklin to hurry, as Harpers Ferry is in mortal danger.
  • Crampton's Gap is defended by about 500 Confederate cavalry under Col. Thomas Munford.

• Franklin reconnoiters the Confederate position.

Sunday, September 14, 3 p.m.

• Another messenger from McClellan arrives (Captain Russell) who repeats the message that Franklin should hurry, as Harpers Ferry is in mortal danger.

• Colonel Munford is reinforced by Colonel Parham with about 300 infantry. The total Confederate defense force is now about 850.

• Franklin initiates attack.

Sunday, September 14, 5 p.m.

• Confederates are hard pressed. Colonel Munford calls to General Cobb, whose brigade is at Brownsville two miles to the south, for help. Cobb puts his brigade of about 1,200 on the road for Crampton's Gap.

Sunday, September 14, 6 p.m.

• Cobb's troops begin arriving, but Confederate defenders are flanked at both ends. Confederates are routed and flee down Pleasant Valley toward Harpers Ferry.

• Franklin now holds Crampton's Gap and has free access to Pleasant Valley and is within six miles of bridge at Harpers Ferry. However, he does not pursue fleeing Confederates because of approaching darkness. He rests his troops.

Sunday, September 14, 9 p.m.

• Franklin is joined by his third division and now has about 20,000 men.

Monday, September 15, 5:50 a.m.

• Confederates have formed a new defense line across Pleasant Valley at Brownsville, two miles south of Crampton's Gap. The line consists of Confederates defeated at the Gap on the fourteenth, Kershaw's and Barksdale's brigades that were bloodied in the fight for Maryland Heights on the thirteenth, and Wilcox's brigade withdrawn from Sandy Hook. The total Confederate defense line contains about 5,000 troops.

Monday, September 15, 6-8:30 a.m.

• Franklin reconnoiters Confederate line and decides that it is too strong to attack.

• Harpers Ferry surrenders.

General Franklin's own words condemn him. In describing

the events of the morning of the fifteenth, Franklin states, "As I was crossing the mountain [Crampton's Gap] about 7 A.M., September 15, I had a good view of the enemy below [etc., etc., etc.]"[7] Crossing the mountain at 7 a.m. indeed! Franklin had possession of the gap by 7 p.m. on the fourteenth and should have been in position in the valley to attack McLaws at daylight—and sunup that day was before 6 a.m. Franklin's real mission was to rescue a drowning man, which he perfectly well knew because of the repeated urgings of McClellan. But at no point did his words or deeds show an appreciation of urgency.

Franklin later attempted to justify his decision not to attack on the early morning of the fifteenth by stating that General Slocum's division, which bore the brunt of the fighting at the gap on the fourteenth, was in no condition to fight on the morning of the fifteenth. It would seem that the battle of Crampton's Gap was a strange victory for Franklin when his victorious troops were not able to fight on the morrow, but the vanquished were.

The moral of these events of September 13 to 15 is that if a person's house is on fire, and General Franklin is the chief of the firehouse on the next block, the owner had better put it out himself.

Now we come to Maj. Gen. George B. McClellan. When the Confederates began to give way at Turner's and Fox's Gaps on the night of September 14, McClellan had essentially his whole army in hand except for Franklin's corps, which was six miles to the south near Rohrersville, and two divisions of Porter's corps that had not yet caught up.

When the Confederates' withdrawal began, it was, or should have been, no secret to him where they were going. The nearest place where they could unite with the troops at Harpers Ferry was Boteler's Ford, near Sharpsburg. There were three routes to Sharpsburg: the one through Fox's Gap to Keedysville, where it hit the Sharpsburg road; the National Road to Boonsboro, where it intersected with the Sharpsburg road; and the road from Rohrersville to Sharpsburg (see map 37). The Confederates had access to two of the roads. McClellan had access to all three.

Most of the retreating Confederate infantry were exhausted. Longstreet's two divisions had made a forced march of fifteen miles from Hagerstown that day and entered directly into action. Now, without respite, in the middle of the night, they were going to have to make a forced march to Sharpsburg.

Map 37
McClellan's Routes to Sharpsburg

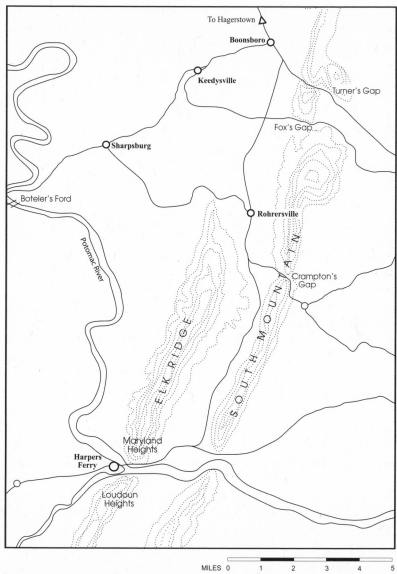

McClellan had troops on the scene that had not even marched that day. Be that as it may, McClellan's pursuit did not begin until after daylight on the fifteenth. He gave the tired Confederates a free start of at least eight hours.

By the time the Union troops began bumping up against the

Confederate troops at Sharpsburg at noon on the fifteenth, the Confederates had already assumed a defense posture with Boteler's Ford in their rear, awaiting reinforcements from Harpers Ferry. The Confederates knew, and McClellan should have known, that the Confederates' first reinforcements could not arrive before the sixteenth.

Although the Confederates had little time to dig in, were greatly outnumbered, and McClellan's objective was obvious (the ford in the Confederates' rear), he persisted in the cosmetic folderol of making a personal battlefield reconnaissance. He ordered that no attack be made until he arrived on the scene, made a personal reconnoitering of the Confederate position, and then directed the attack. No attack of any kind was made on the fifteenth.

On the sixteenth, McClellan continued to procrastinate, first blaming his delay on the fog. Jackson's two divisions arrived during the morning to reinforce Lee, and Walker's arrived in the afternoon. After wasting the whole day, McClellan began an anemic attack against the Confederates' left flank with only Hooker's corps, just before dark, when it was too late in the day to achieve any significant results.

If McClellan's wasting of the fifteenth was bad, his wasting of the sixteenth was criminal. By the end of the sixteenth, Lee was only lacking McLaws's two divisions and A. P. Hill's division, and McLaws's divisions were already en route.

On the big day, the seventeenth, instead of committing all of his troops early in the day, McClellan attacked in phases, one corps at a time. This gave Lee ample time to introduce the arriving troops of first McLaws and then Hill, to frustrate each phase. Achieving a smashing victory, which would have been easily possible for McClellan on the fifteenth or sixteenth, proved beyond his reach on the seventeenth.

McClellan never learned what Lee, Longstreet, and Jackson had learned early: there are three armies marching, and the third is time—and time is often the decisive one.

Finally, we come to the real and main culprit. It was General McClellan's intelligence organization. General Nathaniel Banks made a study of Lee's army in 1862 using all sources of available information, including deserters and the interrogation of prisoners. Banks concluded that there were approximately 96,000 men subordinate to Lee. The Union commanders knew from their own experiences that no more than about half this number could be present in an active, mobile army at any one time. Hence, the data indicated that Lee's invasion force could consist of no more than about 50,000 men. This figure was actually somewhat high, but within reasonable range of the precise number.

McClellan, based on his own sources, believed that he was facing a minimum of 120,000 Confederates. McClellan's beliefs permeated all echelons of the command of the Army of the Potomac. At every point in every battle of the Army of the Potomac in September 1862, the on-scene Union commander considered that he was dealing with at least twice the number of Confederates actually facing him—and acted accordingly.

At the battles of Turner's and Fox's Gaps, as General Hill looked down on the approaching Union army, he stated, "I knew my little force could be brushed away as well as a strong man can brush to one side the wasp or the hornet."[8] But Hill's force was not brushed aside because the Union commanders considered that there were vast numbers of Confederates (nonexistent) lurking in the woods, waiting to ambush them. Had the Union army "brushed" Hill aside, their cavalry could have pounced on the Confederate wagon train that was just on the other side of the pass and destroyed it. In addition, the Union army could have placed itself squarely between Lee and Jackson.

The same sad tale was repeated at the battle of Antietam. By early afternoon, McClellan had all but won the battle, and he had two corps in reserve and the Confederates had none. Longstreet later stated,

> It was easy to see that if the Federals broke our line there, the Confederate army would be cut in two and probably destroyed, for we were already badly whipped and were only holding our ground by sheer force of desperation.[9]

If McClellan had put in either or both of his corps at this point, he would have won decisively. However, he committed neither on the false belief that the Confederates had huge reserves for a counterattack.

General Franklin's actions matched those of his master. When he encountered Colonel Munford's tiny force at Crampton's Gap on the afternoon of the fourteenth, he frittered away much of the afternoon in a reconnaissance on the false belief that he was facing a major force. On the following morning, he repeated his performance. When he encountered McLaws's scratch force across Pleasant Valley with his own, vastly superior force, he procrastinated until it was too late, in the false belief that he was outnumbered.

Why did General Grant later succeed where General McClellan failed? Grant was probably not as smart as McClellan, probably not as good an organizer, and probably not as charismatic a leader. Grant succeeded because he always had a realistic assessment of the forces facing him and acted accordingly. McClellan failed because he always had a grossly inflated assessment of the forces facing him and acted accordingly.

Chapter 19

Did It Make a Difference?

Even with Special Order 191, McClellan failed to destroy the Confederate army before it reunited. Had he destroyed any one of the four components, he could have easily prevailed against the remainder. Had he destroyed the Army of Northern Virginia in September 1862, the worst of the war might have been over. Without the Army of Northern Virginia, Richmond would have been available for the taking. But it was not to be. Ninety percent of the war's casualties were still ahead. To take Richmond, the Union ultimately had to fight the Army of Northern Virginia for two and a half more years. The battles of Fredericksburg, Chancellorsville, Gettysburg, the Wilderness, Spotsylvania, Cold Harbor, and the siege of Petersburg were all still ahead. All this might have been avoided.

Did the losing of Special Order 191 by the Confederates and its finding by the Union, then, make a difference? And if so, in whose favor? Indeed, it did make a difference—a profound difference, and in favor of the Union. Had McClellan not read Special Order 191, he would not have attacked the Confederates at South Mountain on September 14. Had he not attacked the Confederates at South Mountain on the fourteenth, there would have been no battle of Antietam on the seventeenth.

Had McClellan not read Special Order 191, what would he have done? We cannot answer this with certainty, but we can establish a good probability by looking into the future. In June-July 1863, there occurred what was largely a repeat of the situation of September 1862. The Army of Northern Virginia again invaded the North. Again, it used the Shenandoah-Cumberland Valleys as its supply line. Again, the army moved up the valleys toward Harrisburg. Again, its objectives were to cut the B & O and Pennsylvania rail lines, to secure foreign recognition for the Confederacy by achieving a victory on Northern territory, and to convince the Northern electorate that it was in their best interest to recognize the secession of the Confederate states. In this

278

invasion, McClellan was no longer in command of the Army of the Potomac. Its new commander was George Gordon Meade, whom Lincoln and Stanton considered to be more aggressive than McClellan. But Meade was subjected to the same political pressures as McClellan had been, and he acted in much the same way. He considered that his primary objective was to protect Washington, Baltimore, and Philadelphia. To achieve this objective, he visualized taking a defensive position along Pipe Creek in Maryland. He had no intention of attacking the Confederate army. It was only as a result of an unintended, chance encounter with the Confederates at Gettysburg that Meade was shifted to the offensive and Lee to the defensive. In short, like Meade, it is probable that McClellan would have remained on the defensive to protect Washington, Baltimore, and Philadelphia. In fact, we know from McClellan's own words that he attacked the Confederates at South Mountain only as a result of his reading Special Order 191.

What scenario would have unfolded had McClellan not attacked on the fourteenth? Probably as follows: Harpers Ferry would have fallen. The Confederates would have reunited at Hagerstown. There, they would have awaited the rejoining of their stragglers and the arrival of reinforcements from Richmond. Then they would have proceeded up the Cumberland Valley toward Harrisburg in accordance with their plan. They might have succeeded in reaching the Susquehanna and cutting the Pennsylvania railroad. They might have captured Harrisburg. They might have secured foreign recognition. If so, the European powers would have been able to ship armaments intended for the Confederacy in their own ships to their Caribbean dependencies. In this case, the Confederate blockade runners would have had only an overnight trip, and the trickle of armaments to the Confederacy might have grown into a flow. Last, but not least, the Confederates might have convinced the Northern electorate that peace with secession was in their best interest.

But none of these dire things were to happen to the Union. They were not to happen because, as a result of reading Special Order 191, McClellan attacked the Confederates at South Mountain. As a result of his seizing the South Mountain passes, the Confederates reunited at Sharpsburg. As a result of their reuniting at Sharpsburg, the battle of Antietam took place. And as a result of the battle of Antietam, the Confederate invasion was ended.

McClellan's dubious "victories" at South Mountain and Antietam created the appearance of a great Union success—and the appearance or perception of a success was as good as the fact. As a result, Lincoln issued the Proclamation of Emancipation and thus seized the moral high ground for the war. There was to be no foreign recognition of the Confederacy and thus no flood of armaments. There was to be no increase in the clamor for peace among the Northern electorate, and even Maryland declined to join the Confederacy. All of these benefits accrued to the Union because, after reading Special Order 191, McClellan decided to switch to the offensive and attacked at South Mountain.

In short, the loss of Special Order 191 by the Confederates and its finding by the Union proved to be disastrous for the Confederacy and of enormous benefit to the Union. Those of the Union to be commended, and to whom the nation owes a debt of gratitude, include Cpl. B. W. Mitchell, who found it; Sgt. John M. Bloss, who recognized its significance; Capt. S. E. Pittman, who was able to vouch for its authenticity; and last, but not least, the young Napoleon, Maj. Gen. George B. McClellan, who acted upon it.

And yet, the execution of the Confederate plan contained in Special Order 191 was a smashing Confederate success. As visualized by the plan, the Union garrison at Martinsburg was swept into the bag at Harpers Ferry. As visualized by the plan, the entire bag at Harpers Ferry was captured and, as visualized by the plan, the entire Confederate army was reunited in time to confront McClellan.

In a sense, the execution of the plan even exceeded expectations. At Harpers Ferry, the Confederates inflicted almost thirteen thousand Union casualties (including prisoners) for a loss of three hundred casualties of their own. The victory at Harpers Ferry constituted the most lopsided Confederate victory of the war and entailed the biggest bag of Union prisoners for any single engagement of the war. In addition to the personnel casualties inflicted, the Confederates also made their biggest bag of Union artillery for any engagement of the war.

Despite the above, as a final irony, the losing of Special Order 191 inflected the totality of events so as to accrue to the disadvantage of the Confederates, and possibly even fatally so. Whoever lost the order probably did more damage to the Confederate cause than any other individual.

Chapter 20

Who Lost Special Order 191?

Before leaving the subject, let us more carefully examine the question: who lost Special Order 191? To answer that question, let us start with the facts of the situation and then proceed to logic.

Fact 1. General Jackson did not know that Colonel Chilton of Lee's staff was going to send a copy of Special Order 191 directly to General Hill. Consequently, Jackson copied the order and sent a copy to Hill over his own signature. Thus, two separate copies of the same order were destined for Hill by two different routes and two separate couriers. Hill, of course, could not have known this fact until he received both copies.

Fact 2. The copy of the order that was lost and recovered by the Union was the copy addressed to General Hill and signed by Colonel Chilton.

Fact 3. General Hill, who was known as an especially religious man and a man of integrity, denied until his dying day that he ever saw or received Chilton's copy. Major J. W. Ratchford, Hill's chief of staff, also denied that he ever saw or received Chilton's copy.

Fact 4. When found, the single-page document was in an envelope and wrapped around three cigars. There were no other papers in the envelope and no marks on the envelope.

Fact 5. The only signature on the document was that of Colonel Chilton, and there were no notes of a personal nature on the document.

Fact 6. The usual method of receipting for a secret document in the Army of Northern Virginia was for the recipient to sign the envelope and for the courier to return the envelope to the originator.

Fact 7. The Confederate command did not know that the document was lost until months later. In the spring of 1863, General McClellan testified before a joint committee of Congress and mentioned the finding of the document. This fact appeared in the Northern press, which was avidly read by General Lee and other Confederate generals. Thus, newspaper

accounts constituted the Confederates' first certain knowledge
of the loss.

Fact 8. Inasmuch as the Confederates did not know the document was lost, they conducted no investigation at the time.

Fact 9 (near certain). Colonel Chilton did not put any cigars
for Hill in the envelope.

Fact 10. At the time of the delivery of the document, Lee's
headquarters and the headquarters of all the involved Confederate
generals (except Walker) were in and around Frederick,
Maryland, and were within a few miles of each other and within
easy conferencing distance.

The first conclusion we may draw from these facts is based on
simple logic. If the document was lost before delivery, it was lost
by the courier. If it was lost after delivery, it was lost by someone
on Hill's staff, if not by Hill himself.

Some allege that the fact that the document was found in
an envelope constitutes *prima facie* evidence that it was never
delivered; had the document been delivered, the courier would
have returned the signed envelope. This theory can be countered with the argument that had the courier not returned with
the signed envelope, headquarters would have known that the
document had not been delivered, and this fact they did not
know. We cannot exclude the possibilities that the envelope in
which the document was found was not the same one that the
courier had been provided for delivery, or that, in this instance,
a receipt other than the signed envelope was employed. In any
event, it appears that the courier must have brought back
something that caused headquarters to accept that the document
had been delivered and that there was no cause to raise an alarm.

But, some counter, the courier could have lost the document,
panicked, and returned a receipt with a forged signature. There
are a number of objections to this hypothesis. First, as any professional officer knows (and Colonel Chilton was the epitome of a
professional officer), military officers do not hand a super-sensitive
document to just anyone to serve as a courier for delivery. Couriers
are selected for their trustworthiness, reliability, and integrity. For
example, in the U.S. Navy, only commissioned officers with
appropriate security clearances can act as couriers, and even then,
all material presented to them is doubly wrapped and sealed.
Second, the courier must have realized that to forge a signature
and conceal the loss would constitute a much greater crime than

the carelessness of losing the document, and would subject him to much greater punishment; that not reporting the loss would preclude his superiors from taking steps to repair the damage, and thus could result in irreparable loss to his country. Last and not least, the courier must have realized that any concealment on his part would quickly become evident since all the senior officers were within conferencing distance, and Hill's lack of knowledge of the contents of the envelope would likely be quickly revealed.

For those who believe the courier lost the document, there is another factor of relevance. The distance from Lee's headquarters to Hill's was short—no more than a couple of miles. The time required for delivery should have been a half hour or less. Thus the opportunity for loss through tedium, inattention, boredom, or stopovers was limited.

Only one who has served as a courier for a vital secret document, the loss of which could be disastrous, can fully understand the burden the custody of the document imposes. It is like having sole custody of someone else's baby. The person responsible can relax only when custody is duly turned over to someone else in rightful authority.

There was yet another factor that must have added to the mental burden of the courier. The Confederate army was not in friendly territory. If the document was lost, there was a high likelihood that it would end up in Union hands. Although much of Maryland was pro-Confederate, this was not the case for the part of Maryland in which Lee's army was located. This situation must have been evident even to the rank and file by September 9. Longstreet even used this fact in his argument against the plan contained in the special order. He contended that because they were in unfriendly territory, any movements of the army would quickly be made known to Union headquarters.

What is the likelihood that Colonel Chilton waived the security requirements and either gave the document to an untested courier, or waived the requirement for a receipt? Not very likely. This was probably the most sensitive document that Chilton ever handled, and we know from the comments of the recipients that each immediately recognized its extreme sensitivity. Colonel Chilton would hardly have achieved his top position on Lee's staff had he been a careless man. That very month, he was promoted to inspector general of the army, where it was his job to see that others obeyed the regulations. Colonel Chilton was a seasoned professional officer who had graduated from West Point in 1837 and had spent all of the intervening twenty-five years on active duty in the army. Furthermore, for many of those twenty-five years, he had served as paymaster. If there was one job that demanded habits of accuracy, adherence to regulations, detailed precision, and strict accountability—that was it.

In 1874, twelve years after the event, Chilton was questioned about his role in the lost order. His answers were extremely vague, and he claimed that he did not remember at this late date to whom he gave the message for delivery. It must be remembered that at the time of the dispatching of the order, neither Chilton nor any other Confederate, other than the unknown culprit, knew anything was amiss. Chilton's recollection, or lack thereof, suggests that everything that day progressed in a routine manner and that there were no memorable exceptions. To expect Chilton to remember the details would be equivalent to asking a witness to describe the suspect he passed on the street before he knew the murder had been committed.

If we accept the hypothesis that the courier lost the document, we must accept as fact that the very man who was selected as inspector general of the army entrusted what was probably the most sensitive document of his career to an individual who, knowing that he was in unfriendly territory, (1) managed to lose the document within one half hour; (2) failed to find it by retrieving his steps; (3) decided to conceal the loss, even though such concealment could be catastrophic to his comrades and country, and knowing that the concealment would inevitably be exposed; and, (4) managed to convince headquarters and Colonel Chilton that the document had been delivered even though he lacked a valid receipt. We would also have to believe that Colonel Chilton, having experienced these major alterations in routine and procedure, would fail to remember any of it.

Before we leave the question of the courier, let us address the question of what constructive steps the Confederates could have taken had the courier manfully reported the loss, as he should have done immediately upon its discovery, if he were indeed aware that it had been lost.

First, the Confederates controlled all the area the courier had to traverse on the ninth, but conceded the area to the slowly oncoming Union army after the tenth. They thus had ample time to search for the lost order. Since the loss had to have occurred along the route the courier traversed, the chances of recovery were excellent. Second, the Confederates could have cancelled or altered the plan, which was what Longstreet wanted to do anyway. Third, they could have translated the loss into a "trick of war" wherein they planned their operations in anticipation of the Union's finding and reading the order. As a matter of fact, this is precisely what the Union high command suspected upon finding and reading the order.

Now we come to the matter of the three cigars. Were they wrapped in the document before or after it was delivered? It would seem only logical that Colonel Chilton did not put them in the envelope. The courier would hardly be likely to open a sealed envelope to use the contents to wrap his cigars. If the envelope were not sealed, it would represent extreme careless-ness and a security violation of almost laughable proportions. Any number of persons could then read the document between the time Chilton surrendered it and Hill received it, and there would be no way of knowing who or how many. However, even if the envelope were unsealed, the courier would hardly be likely to use the contents as a cigar wrapper.

If the cigars were placed in the envelope before its delivery, it most likely occurred between the time Chilton signed the document and the time it was handed to the courier. Let us assume it was done so by some highly placed individual at Lee's headquarters who was a friend of Hill or wanted to send Hill a token gift as a mark of his esteem. Had the cigars been placed in the envelope by the friend, presumably the friend would want Hill to know the source of the gift, otherwise the gesture would be meaningless. However, there were no notes of a personal nature in the envelope, and the only signature on the only paper in the envelope was Chilton's. Had Hill received the cigars, he could only have concluded they were from Chilton, which they were not.

There is no reason to believe that Chilton and Hill were par-ticular friends. Chilton had graduated from West Point well before Hill arrived, and they had no known prewar association. Hill left the army to follow the profession of educator, while Chilton remained as a career officer.

Long after the war, the circumstances of the lost order were widely discussed in periodicals of interest to veterans, but no one ever came forward as the source of the cigars. In conclusion, we can make a fairly convincing case that the cigars were not placed in the envelope before its delivery.

Now let us visualize another scenario. Let us say that Jackson's courier arrived at Hill's headquarters well before Chilton's courier, delivered his document, obtained his receipt, and left. Hill read the document, discussed it with his staff, and gave proper protection to the document. After the group dispersed, Chilton's courier arrived and got some member of Hill's staff to sign for it and left with his receipt. The staffer read the document, determined that, except for the signature, it was a duplicate of what they had already discussed and saw no need to immediately get it to Hill. Hill could have been in a conference, asleep, away, or whatever at the time. It is logical to conclude at this point that a belatedly arriving duplicate is far more likely to get careless treatment than a startling original. Let us say that the staffer wanted to put the document in his pocket for later delivery to Hill. But, he had cigars in his pocket, so he wrapped the document around the cigars, stuck the package in an envelope, and put the envelope in his pocket. He subsequently lost it, we know not how, and it ended up in the meadow where Corporate Mitchell picked it up. A likely time for the loss of the document was when the army packed up to move out, in accordance with the plan, on September 10, 1862.

For completeness, let us mention two accounts of the loss of the order that have little credibility. The first was a report that General Hill was seen to drop a paper, presumably the lost order, in the street. The second was an account that the Comte de Paris, who was an observer with Lee's army, said that the order was found in a house in Frederick that had been occupied by Hill. Both of these accounts are easily refuted. First, the document was not found on or near a street, and second, Hill never occupied a house in Frederick. His headquarters were always in a tent.

In 1897, thirty-five years after the event, Confederate major general Thomas L. Rosser alleged that he knew who the guilty party was—that it was the courier, and that the courier was a member of General Jackson's staff. However, Rosser did not reveal the name of the individual. Rosser was not a principal in the fateful events of September 9, 1862, and it is not known if he knew, or merely thought he knew; and if he knew, how he knew.

There are three problems with the Rosser story. First, why would Colonel Chilton select a member of Jackson's staff as a courier rather than a member of Lee's staff. Second, how would Rosser know anything about the situation? At the time, he was colonel in command of the Fifth Virginia Cavalry of Hampton's brigade of Stuart's cavalry command. He was not only not personally involved, but was not even a member of any of the commands involved. Third, if there were such a courier who had lost the plan and then failed to report the loss while there was still time for constructive action, he would thereby have shown a willingness to subject his comrades, and even the entire army, to disaster, destruction, and death rather than face the reprimand or punishment he so richly deserved. Such an individual would be looked upon by his comrades-in-arms as a total scoundrel, beneath contempt. It is hard to see why Rosser or any Confederate would want to protect the reputation of such a man by withholding his name.

We will never know for sure who lost Special Order 191, how it was lost, or when it was lost. We cannot even absolutely eliminate the possibility that the Confederates were so careless with this most sensitive of sensitive documents that they did not require receipt of it. We cannot even absolutely eliminate the possibility that the document was lost during the pack-up on September 10, and that the individual responsible for its loss did not even realize its loss. There is simply not enough evidence to indict anybody.

We will end by turning to the fourteenth-century logician, William of Occam, and his famous Occam's Razor, which contends that when multiple explanations for an event are possible, the correct one is the simplest one. The simplest explanation in this instance is that the document was delivered to Hill's headquarters where it was lost by someone on Hill's staff, if not by Hill himself.

Chapter 21

What Happened to Them?

Last, we address the question, what happened to each of the principal players in this drama? We will start with the lost order itself. Its drafter was Col. Robert Hall Chilton, chief of staff to and personal friend of Robert E. Lee. Colonel Chilton is the logical starting point in determining who lost Special Order 191. He drafted it and handed it to someone. That someone either handed it to someone else or lost it. Chilton, to his dying day, feigned poor memory and claimed that he could not remember the circumstances of that fateful day.

In October 1862, shortly after the event, Chilton was appointed brigadier general and assumed new duties as the inspector general of the Army of Northern Virginia. Chilton remained in this post until the end of the war. Following the war, he became president of a manufacturing company in Columbus, Georgia, and died there in 1879 at the age of sixty-three.

The Union man who first touched the lost order was Cpl. B. W. Mitchell. Mitchell's picking up the order proved to be the most costly act in his life, for he was seriously wounded in the battle of Antietam. Had he not picked it up, there would have been no battle of Antietam. Mitchell spent eight months in the hospital, was discharged, returned home, and died three years later.

In 1879, Mitchell's son sent a letter to George McClellan, long since out of the army, advising McClellan that it was Mitchell who had found the lost order, informing him that Mitchell's family was destitute, and requesting McClellan's help in securing a pension. McClellan responded as follows:

Trenton, New Jersey
November 18, 1879

W. A. Mitchell, Esq.
La Cynge, Kansas

Dear Sir:

Your letter of the 9th inst. has reached me. I cannot, at this interval of time, recall the name of the finder of the papers to which you refer—and it is doubtful whether I ever knew the name. All that I can say is that on or about 13th of September, 1862—just before the battles of South Mountain and Antietam, —there was handed to me by a member of my staff a copy [original] of one of General Lee's orders of march, directed to General D. H. Hill, which order developed General Lee's intended operations for the next few days, and was of very great service to me in enabling me to direct the movements of my own troops accordingly. This order was stated to have been found on one of the abandoned campgrounds of the Confederate troops by a private soldier, and as I think, of an Indiana regiment. Whoever found the order in question and transmitted it to the headquarters showed intelligence and deserved marked reward, for he rendered an infinite service. The widow of that soldier should have her pension without a day's delay. Regretting that it is not in my power to give the name of the finder of the order, I am very truly yours.

George B. McClellan[1]

After Mitchell, the next Union man to handle Special Order 191 was 1st Sgt. John M. Bloss. After the event, Bloss rose in rank to captain, participated in the battles of Antietam, Chancellorsville, and Resaca, and was wounded. Bloss was mustered out in October 1864 and began a highly successful career as an educator. He served as a teacher, school principal, district superintendent of schools, and Indiana state superintendent of schools.

The next Union man to handle the lost dispatch was Col. Silas Colgrove, commanding officer of Mitchell's and Bloss's regiment, the Twenty-seventh Indiana. Colgrove participated in the battle of Antietam, where his horse was shot out from under him, but he was unhurt. He was then transferred to the Western theater where he participated in the battles around Atlanta and was severely wounded. Colgrove recovered and was brevetted brigadier general in August 1864. Following the war, he served as a judge for many years, and also as a railway president. His final job was with the Federal Pension Bureau in Washington,

D.C., where he retired in 1893. Colgrove died in Lake Kerr, Florida, in 1907 at the age of ninety-one.

Colgrove gave the lost order to the acting assistant adjutant general of the Twelfth Corps, Capt. S. E. Pittman. It was Pittman, the bank teller become officer, who recognized Colonel Chilton's signature. After the event, Pittman was transferred to the Western theater where he rose in rank to lieutenant colonel. After the war, he was active in veterans' fraternal organizations in Michigan and as late as 1903 was still enthralling crowds at veterans' reunions with a recitation of his role in the recovery of the lost order.

Now let us look at what happened to the man to whom the lost Special Order 191 was addressed, Maj. Gen. D. H. Hill. Then and now, it was widely assumed that Hill was somehow responsible. To the end of his life, Hill vehemently denied that he had ever received the order. He considered it grossly unfair to be considered the culprit merely because he was the addressee. In fact, no one ever presented any evidence to indicate that he did receive it.

General Hill played a prominent role in both the battle of South Mountain and the battle of Antietam and added to his reputation as a fine combat commander. In February 1863, Hill was given command of troops in North Carolina and was then promoted to lieutenant general and given command of a corps in Gen. Braxton Bragg's Army of Tennessee. Hill, at best a difficult man, had a falling out with his new commander and as a result failed to gain confirmation of his promotion in the Senate and reverted to the rank of major general. In the final phases of the war, Hill served under Gen. P. G. T. Beauregard at Petersburg and later under Gen. Joseph Johnston in his final operations against Gen. William T. Sherman.

After the war, Hill returned to his profession as an educator, first as president of Arkansas Industrial University, and then Middle Georgia Military and Agricultural College. He died of cancer in September 1889 at the age of sixty-eight.

Now let us turn to the siege of Harpers Ferry—first to the vanquished, then to the victors. What was left of Col. Dixon Miles's reputation was firmly destroyed by the military commission, and, of course, Miles was no longer alive to defend himself. However, it is just possible that those who served under him who were able to walk safely back into their homes at the end of the war were thankful it was Miles they served under—a man who refused to waste lives when he considered that there was nothing more to gain—rather than some glory-seeking diehard.

The commission had also destroyed the reputation of Col. Thomas H. Ford, loser of Maryland Heights, who was dismissed from the service. However, upon presidential review, Ford was exonerated and his rank restored. Once Ford had achieved this restoration of his honor, he resigned and returned to the practice of law in Ohio, where he died in 1868.

Brigadier General Julius White, who was not only exonerated by the commission but found to merit its approbation, was released from arrest and restored to duty. White's service throughout the remainder of the war was largely under Gen. Ambrose Burnside. He served in Burnside's Knoxville campaign and with him at Petersburg. White was brevetted major general on March 13, 1865. After the war, he served briefly as U.S. minister to Argentina. White died in 1890 at the age of seventy-four.

Col. William H. Trimble was also exonerated and restored to duty by the commission. Trimble, however, was colonel of the Sixtieth Ohio, and both he and the Sixtieth had only a one-year commitment that was soon to expire. Trimble was released from further active duty on November 13, 1862.

Col. Frederick D'Utassy, the flamboyant Hungarian adventurer, was also exonerated by the commission and restored to duty. However, his good fortune was to be short-lived. In less than a year, D'Utassy was charged with fraudulent activities, court-martialed, convicted, and sentenced to one year in the federal penitentiary at Sing Sing. He entered Sing Sing as a convict in May 1863, less than a year after his glory days when his troops retrieved the cannons left behind on Maryland Heights. D'Utassy completed his one-year sentence, rose from the ashes, and became a success in the insurance business. In 1895, at the age of sixty-eight, he was found dead in a gas-filled hotel room in Wilmington, Delaware. It is unknown whether his death was a suicide or an accident.

The commission also added to the disgrace of the 126th New York, whose cowardly conduct led to the loss of Maryland Heights. However, its colonel, Eliakim Sherrill, escaped criticism inasmuch as he was carried from the field, seriously wounded in the face, before the break came. Sherrill returned to duty before his wound had fully healed and was mortally wounded at the head of his regiment at Gettysburg, July 2, 1863.

Maj. William H. Baird had been made the scapegoat for the 126th, and the commission had recommended his dismissal from the service. However, upon presidential review, the commission's verdict was overturned, and Baird was restored to his rank. Baird's subsequent conduct more than justified the review's decision. Baird rose in rank to lieutenant colonel and contributed greatly to the full restoration of the regiment's reputation. Baird was mortally wounded at Petersburg in 1864 and died at the age of thirty-three.

The two senior officers in the escape of the cavalry from Harpers Ferry the night of September 14 were Col. Arno Voss of the Twelfth Illinois and Col. B. F. "Grimes" Davis of the Eighth New York. The glory the two acquired for this feat was to be short-lived. On August 8, 1863, Brig. Gen. John Buford dismissed Colonel Voss in the field as not competent to command a regiment. The dismissal was endorsed by both chief of cavalry, Maj. Gen. Alfred Pleasonton, and commanding general of the Army of the Potomac, Maj. Gen. George G. Meade. To save face, Voss was later allowed to resign. Voss died in 1886 at the age of sixty-three. Colonel Benjamin Franklin "Grimes" Davis, commanding officer of the Eighth New York, was promoted to brigade command but was killed at the battle of Brandy Station on June 9, 1863, at the age of thirty-one.

Lieutenant Colonel Stephen Downey, commanding officer of the Third Regiment of the Maryland Potomac Home Brigade, was all of twenty-two years old in September 1862. Downey had entered the service on September 12, 1861, as a private and amazingly, by May 1, 1862, had reached the rank of lieutenant colonel. It was Downey who nearly captured Stonewall Jackson in his daring raid in Boonsboro, and it was Downey who was responsible for ruining Henry Kyd Douglas's new plumed hat. It was Downey who was also one of the most intrepid defenders of Maryland Heights. With the surrender of Harpers Ferry, Downey was captured, paroled, and testified before the Harpers Ferry military commission in October 1862. Downey then resigned from the army in November 1862, thus completing a most adventuresome, exciting, and successful army career of just fourteen months.

Downey proved to be as adventuresome and successful a civilian as he had been an officer. After practicing law in Washington until 1869, he set out for Laramie, Wyoming, in the heart of what was then the wild, wild West. Downey opened a survey office and worked his way up to deputy U.S. surveyor. He became one of the leading citizens of the territory and was ultimately elected delegate to Congress. Downey was among the first to recognize the oil potential of Jackass Springs and was the first to put in a land claim. As of today, he is still recognized as one of the early founders of the state of Wyoming.

Capt. (the Reverend) Charles H. Russell entered the army from his parish at Williamsport, Maryland, and became captain of Company I of the First Maryland Calvary. On the night of September 14, Russell successfully negotiated the Confederate lines and delivered a message from Colonel Miles to General McClellan. Russell was subsequently promoted to major on October 9, 1862, and testified before the Harpers Ferry military commission. Russell completed his service on December 31, 1863, and returned to his parish at Williamsport.

Colonel William P. Maulsby, commanding officer of the First Infantry Regiment of the Maryland Potomac Home Brigade, was with the force in Harpers Ferry that Miles surrendered. Maulsby was subsequently paroled, testified before the Harpers Ferry military commission, was exchanged, and returned to duty. He participated in the battle of Gettysburg, where he was wounded and commended, and then participated in the battle of the Monocacy. At the close of the war, Maulsby returned to Frederick, Maryland, where he had practiced law and owned a newspaper before the war. Maulsby resumed his law practice and rose to become a judge in the Maryland court of appeals.

We now turn to Capt. Henry Cole, commanding officer of Cole's Cavalry in the Maryland Potomac Home Brigade. When we last left Captain Cole, he had succeeded in penetrating Confederate lines to deliver a message from Colonel Miles to General McClellan that informed McClellan that Miles could hold out only forty-eight hours unless relieved. McClellan asked Cole if he could get back to Miles with a message. The message was, don't surrender; help is on the way; reoccupy Maryland Heights if you can. Cole replied that he would try to get back. Here, the story becomes controversial. Some allege that he got back. Others insist that he did not. Unfortunately for us, Cole was not called as a witness before the Harpers Ferry military commission.

The only direct testimony before the commission regarding

Cole's return was that of Miles's aide, Lt. Henry M. Binney. The testimony was as follows:

> Question: Do you know what efforts Colonel Miles made to open communications with General McClellan?

> Answer: We heard reports of troops coming up, but nothing definite. For instance, we heard that General Wool was coming up with 20,000 men, and that General McClellan was coming up on the Virginia side with a large force, but nothing definite. On Sunday, Captain Cole, of the Maryland Home Brigade Cavalry, and Captain Russell of the First Maryland Cavalry, offered to open up communications with our army if there was any in Maryland. We had heard that Frederick had fallen into the hands of the enemy. Colonel Miles gave his consent, and they went; with what result I do not know. I have never heard anything of them since. We have been given to understand that they did get through to General McClellan, and represented the state we were in at Harpers Ferry. They never came back again.[2]

It was also testified that Miles, after he was mortally wounded, was heard to remark that he wondered where McClellan was, and why no attempt had been made to save the garrison. If Miles had received McClellan's message from Cole, he certainly would have known where McClellan was, and that relief was imminent. Thus, such comments by Miles could only be interpreted as an attempt to deceive his listeners. Miles was a God-fearing man and knew that his wounds were fatal and that he was within hours of his death. It is hard to believe that, under such circumstances, he would have intentionally lied. All in all, it seems most probable that Miles never received Cole's message.

By the time of Harpers Ferry, Cole was already creating a reputation as a dashing cavalryman, and he continued to enhance such reputation until the end of the war. When the four companies of the Potomac Home Brigade Cavalry were consolidated into a battalion, Cole was promoted to major and put in command. When the battalion was expanded into a regiment in 1864, Cole was again put in command and promoted to colonel. Cole finished the war as one of Maryland's greatest heroes and as such is remembered today. The military installation at Olney, Maryland, is today named the "Colonel Henry A. Cole Military Reservation."

The future of Capt. Samuel Means of the Loudoun Rangers was not bright, even though he and his rangers escaped with the cavalry on the night of September 14. In the prewar years, Means, a German Quaker and native of Loudoun County, Virginia, had been a well-to-do businessman with wide interests in Waterford, Virginia, and Point of Rocks, Maryland. Means, like most of his German Quaker neighbors, was pro-Union. At the outset of the war, Secretary of War Edwin Stanton had personally requested Means to see if he could recruit his Loudoun County neighbors to form a unit to fight for the Union. The understanding was that such a unit would be independent and would be kept in the vicinity of its own territory. Means succeeded in recruiting two companies of cavalry and was appointed their captain. Means himself had no military experience, and the unit was generally poorly trained and disciplined and indifferently equipped. The rangers were normally subordinated directly to the senior commander in the area, who in September 1862 happened to be Colonel Miles.

In September 1864, the army attempted to transfer the rangers away from their home area to a command in West Virginia. Means strenuously objected and resigned in protest before Secretary Stanton ruled in favor of the rangers.

Means was without a job, had lost most of his fortune, and could not go home because of Confederate forces in his area. He was already known as a heavy drinker and now became a complete alcoholic. He died in Washington, D.C., a broken man. In April 1865, shortly before the end of the war, Confederate colonel John Singleton Moseby completed the destruction of the Loudoun Rangers as an organized force.

Now let us turn to the victors at Harpers Ferry. The three besieging forces were headed by Generals Jackson, McLaws, and Walker. Major General Thomas Jonathon ("Stonewall") Jackson was wounded on May 2, 1863, at the battle of Chancellorsville. On May 10, at the age of thirty-nine, he died of pneumonia as the result of an amputation. Jackson had the good fortune to suffer his wound and death at the peak of his greatest victory, and thus his name became immortalized.

Major General Lafayette McLaws was never to occupy a higher rank than the one he occupied at Harpers Ferry. He continued to serve under his friend James Longstreet until December 1863, when the two had a final falling-out. In order to save McLaws from a court-martial, President Jefferson Davis had him transferred to the army of Joseph Johnston. McLaws survived the war unscathed and returned to Georgia, where he served as an insurance agent, tax collector, and postmaster. He died in Savannah in 1897 at the age of seventy-six.

Brigadier General John G. Walker was promoted to major general on November 8, 1862, and transferred to the Trans Mississippi Department, where he remained until the end of the war. Walker was considered one of the most capable, admired, and beloved by his men of all the Confederate generals, but because of the remote area in which he served he achieved little publicity or postwar fame. After the war, Walker fled first to Mexico and then to England, but by the late sixties he returned to Texas. He eventually settled near Winchester, Virginia, and, during President Grover Cleveland's administration, was appointed consul general to Bogota, Columbia. Walker died of a stroke in Washington, D.C., in 1893 at the age of seventy-one.

Major General A. P. Hill, a Jackson division commander and the man who accepted the surrender of Harpers Ferry, was promoted to lieutenant general and corps commander after Jackson's death. Hill had been one of the most highly regarded generals of the Army of Northern Virginia, but as corps commander he passed the limits of his capabilities and performed less well. Hill was killed in action before Petersburg in April 1865 at the age of forty.

Brigadier General Joseph B. Kershaw participated in almost every major battle in the East and, in addition, accompanied Longstreet to the battle of Chickamauga in 1863 and Gen. Jubal Early on his invasion of Maryland in 1864. All in all, Kershaw saw as much or more action than any other Confederate general. Kershaw was promoted to major general in May 1864 and finished the war unscathed. He returned to his native South Carolina, practiced law, and became a judge. Kershaw died in 1894 at the age of seventy-two. Kershaw's co-victor in the battle of Maryland Heights, Brigadier General Barksdale, was mortally wounded on July 2, 1863, at the battle of Gettysburg, and died at the age of forty-two.

Colonel Thomas Munford, the gallant defender of Crampton's Gap, remained in the cavalry of the Army of Northern Virginia until the end of the war. He was promoted to brigadier general in November 1864 and completed the war unhurt. After the war, he returned to his profession of farming and died in 1919 at the age of eighty-seven.

Before we leave the victors of Harpers Ferry, it is appropriate to turn to the fate of the individual who was involved in the exchange of the first shots of the battle. This distinction belongs to Col. Henry Kyd Douglas of Jackson's staff, who ran into Colonel Downey of Miles's command at Boonsboro on September 10. In the exchange of gunfire, Douglas had his plumed hat shot off by Downey's men, but was otherwise unharmed. After Jackson's death, Douglas served on the staffs of five Confederate generals, and at the end of the war was with Lee at Appomattox in command of A. P. Hill's old Light Division. Douglas had been wounded six times during the war but finished intact. After the war, he practiced law, first in Winchester, Virginia, and then in Hagerstown, Maryland. Douglas died in 1903 at the age of sixty-five and is buried at Shepherdstown, West Virginia, not far from the Antietam battlefield that he rode over on the night of September 17, 1862.

We will now turn to the fate of McClellan's corps commanders who marched off with him to Antietam Creek in September 1862.

The senior man in the Army of the Potomac next to McClellan was Ambrose Burnside. On November 10, 1862, President Abraham Lincoln appointed Burnside as McClellan's replacement over Burnside's objections. Burnside served as commanding general until early 1863, when he was ordered to take charge of the Department of the Ohio. In the spring of 1864, Burnside, along with his Ninth Corps, was ordered back East to join Gen. Ulysses S. Grant in his final campaign to destroy Lee and seize Richmond.

During the two years following Burnside's Bridge, Burnside was to add Burnside's Wall, Burnside's Mud March, and Burnside's Crater to his reputation. Burnside's Wall was an obviously impregnable position against which he repeatedly flung his men. Burnside's Mud March was a late-season campaign wherein the army got stuck in the mud, and he had to call the whole thing off. Burnside's Crater was the crowning achievement of all. Burnside's men, before Petersburg, spent weeks tunneling under the Confederate position opposite them. They then filled the tunnel with gunpowder and blew it up, creating a huge gap in the Confederate line. Burnside's men then marched into the crater, were unable to get out the other end, and were slaughtered.

That did it. Burnside took a leave of absence while an investigation was conducted and then resigned in April 1865. Actually, Burnside was not as bad as he sounds. There were extenuating circumstances in every instance. Grant summed up Burnside in his memoirs as follows:

> General Burnside was an officer who was generally liked and respected. He was not, however, fitted to command an army. No one knew this better than himself. He always admitted his blunders, and extenuated those of officers under him beyond what they were entitled to. It was hardly his fault that he was ever assigned to a separate command.[3]

This was an evaluation that a saint could envy.

After the war, Burnside returned to his native Rhode Island where he was elected governor three times. He then served as his state's senator until his death in 1881 at the age of fifty-seven.

Joseph Hooker, the commander of the First Corps, was next in seniority to Burnside. Upon Burnside's transfer to the Army of the Ohio, President Lincoln appointed Hooker commanding general of the Army of the Potomac on January 26, 1863. Hooker introduced some useful reforms and innovations. He then came up with a brilliant plan to out-finesse Lee from his defensive position before Fredericksburg. Hooker then proceeded to lead the Army of the Potomac into its biggest defeat of the war, at Chancellorsville, where he was soundly defeated by a Confederate army less than half the size of his own.

Hooker was relieved as commanding general of the Army of the Potomac on June 28, 1863, just days before Gettysburg, and transferred to Gen. William S. Rosecrans's Army of the Cumberland in the West. Hooker served ably as corps commander in the West until he failed to receive a promotion that he thought was his due and, at his request, spent the last months of the war in the backwoods.

Hooker was summed up in Grant's memoirs as follows:

> Of Hooker I saw but little during the war. I had known him very well before, however. Where I did see him, at Chattanooga, his achievement in bringing his command around the point of Lookout Mountain and into Chattanooga Valley was brilliant. I nevertheless regarded him as a dangerous man. He was not

subordinate to his superiors. He was ambitious to the extent of caring nothing for the rights of others. His disposition was, when engaged in battle, to get detached from the main body of the army and exercise a separate command, gathering to his standard all he could of his juniors.[4]

Hooker retired from the army on October 15, 1868, and died suddenly at Garden City, New York, on October 31, 1879, at the age of sixty-five.

McClellan's Second Corps commander was Maj. Gen. Voss Sumner. Sumner died in Syracuse, New York, of pneumonia on March 21, 1863, at the age of sixty-six.

Commander of the Fifth Corps, Fitz John Porter, participated in the battle of Antietam under a cloud. The charges of disobedience of orders leveled at him by Gen. John Pope had been held in abeyance pending the resolution of the current crisis. Now that the crisis was over, Porter's prosecution was to proceed. Porter was relieved from duty on November 10, 1862, and his court-martial began in December. On January 10, 1863, it rendered its verdict. Guilty! It recommended that Porter be dismissed from the service and never again be allowed to hold a position in the government. The verdict was endorsed by Lincoln, and Porter was cashiered on January 21, 1863.

Porter spent much of the rest of his life trying to overturn the verdict. In 1879, an army review board not only ruled that Porter was blameless, but praised his actions. However, neither of the next two Republican presidents would endorse the board's decision. However, in 1886, Democrat president Grover Cleveland did endorse the review board's decision, and Porter was restored to the rank of colonel in the regular army at the age of sixty-four. Two days later, Porter, his reputation now restored, retired. He died in 1901 at the age of seventy-nine.

General William Buel Franklin, McClellan's Sixth Corps commander, repeated his performance in the very next major battle of the Army of the Potomac, the battle of Fredericksburg. In the battle, Burnside had his army organized into "grand divisions," with Franklin commanding the grand division on the left. Burnside's intent, as verbally expressed to Franklin, was for Franklin to make the main effort, coincident with an attack on the right. However, Burnside followed up this verbal order with confusing written orders to Franklin—and

Franklin chose to rely on those, rather than on Burnside's known intentions. Consequently, as Franklin conducted a limited attack on the left, the troops on the right, unsupported, continued to be wasted, attacking a nearly impregnable position. The Congressional Committee on the Conduct of War, investigating the matter, found Franklin to blame.

Franklin waited for five months for orders and was then transferred to the Army of the Gulf in Louisiana. There, he became a central figure in yet another debacle.

It is interesting to compare Franklin's performance at Fredericksburg with Jackson's at Harpers Ferry. Jackson's orders as expressed in Special Order 191 were, like Franklin's, poorly expressed and ambiguous. Actually, they never called on Jackson to go to Harpers Ferry at all. However, Jackson clearly understood that Lee's objective was the capture of the garrison of Harpers Ferry, and he acted accordingly, regardless of the wording of the order.

After the war, Franklin achieved great success managing the Colt's Firearms Manufacturing Company in Hartford, Connecticut. Franklin died in Hartford on March 8, 1903, at the age of eighty.

General Jesse L. Reno, the commanding general of McClellan's Ninth Corps, was killed at the battle of South Mountain on September 14 at the age of thirty-nine. General Joseph Mansfield, commanding general of McClellan's Twelfth Corps, was killed at the battle of Antietam on September 17 at the age of fifty-nine.

Now we come to George B. McClellan himself. On November 9, 1862, he was relieved of command of the Army of the Potomac and sent home to New Jersey to await further orders. Such orders never came. In 1864, he was nominated by the Democratic Party as their candidate for president, to run against Lincoln. Had the war not turned in the favor of the Union before the election, it is entirely possible that McClellan would have been the seventeenth president of the United States.

After the war, McClellan headed several engineering firms. In 1878, he ran for and was elected governor of New Jersey. McClellan died in Orange, New Jersey, on October 29, 1885, at the age of fifty-nine.

The name George Brinton McClellan was not to die with its owner. It was to live on in the person of George Brinton

McClellan, Jr., who was born in 1865, the year the war ended. The young McClellan proved to be a prodigy like his father and achieved fame in his own right. He graduated from Princeton at the age of twenty, became president of the New York City Board of Aldermans at the age of twenty-eight, a U.S. congressman at the age of thirty, and in 1904, mayor of New York City at the age of thirty-eight. The younger McClellan lived until 1940 and died during the presidency of Franklin D. Roosevelt.

Before leaving the elder McClellan, let us look at three snapshot evaluations of him made by three major players in the Civil War, all of whom knew him well. The first is by Gideon Welles, Lincoln's Secretary of the Navy. It is from Welles's diary entry for September 3, 1862, which happens to be in the midst of the events described in this book. It reads:

> McClellan is an intelligent engineer and officer, but not a commander to lead a great army in the field. To attack or advance with energy and power is not in him; to fight is not his fate. I sometimes fear his heart is not earnest in the cause; yet I do not entertain the thought that he is unfaithful. The study of military operations interests and amuses him. It flatters him to have on his staff French princes and men of wealth and position; he likes to show, parade and power. Wishes to outgeneral the Rebels, but not to kill and destroy them.[5]

The next evaluation is by Gen. W. T. Sherman and is from a letter he wrote to his wife on October 27, 1864, after McClellan had fallen from power.

> I believe McClellan to be an honest man as to money, of good habits, decent, and of far more than average intelligence, and therefore I have never joined in the hue and cry against him. In revolutions men fall and rise. Long before this war is over, much as you hear me praised now, you may hear me cursed and insulted.[6]

The last evaluation is by General Grant, and is from his memoirs written just before his death in 1885. In these, Grant provided evaluations of the leading Union players of the war. Some of his comments were good, some were bad, but all were incisive. When it came to McClellan, Grant refused to make an evaluation. He simply stated that "McClellan was one of the mysteries of the war."[7] And he has so remained to this day.

Unlike McClellan's opponent, Robert E. Lee, not many public entities are named after him. However, there is one that would be close to his heart if he were alive. It is the George B. McClellan Gate, the entrance to the Arlington National Cemetery, where many of the veterans of his beloved Army of the Potomac are buried.

Next, we come to Henry Halleck, general in chief. In the spring of 1864, President Lincoln appointed U. S. Grant as general in chief of the armies. However, he retained Halleck, the bureaucrat *par excellence*, in Washington, under the new title, "chief of staff." Lincoln now had what he wanted—a smooth-functioning high command with Grant handling the fighting and Halleck handling the trivia and minutiae. Halleck had no postwar career, as he remained on active duty in the army until his death. His final assignment was commanding officer of the Division of the South, headquartered at Louisville, where he died in 1872 at the age of fifty-seven.

We will leave General Halleck with a snapshot evaluation of him provided by secretary of the navy Gideon Welles in the summer of 1863.

> In the whole summer's campaign I have been unable to see, hear or obtain evidence of power, or will, or talent, or originality on the part of General Halleck. He has suggested nothing, decided nothing but scold and smoke and scratched his elbows. Is it possible that the energies of the nation should be wasted by the incapacity of such a man?[8]

Confederate brigadier general Augustus Toombs, defender of the bridge at Antietam Creek, was wounded but recovered. He resigned from the service in March 1863, returned to Georgia, and reentered politics. For the remainder of the war, he was a major critic of President Davis and his policies and a defender of states' rights. At war's end, he narrowly avoided arrest and fled—first to Cuba, and then to France. He returned to Georgia in 1867 and again became a power in state politics, although he never again held office because he did not apply for a pardon or take an oath of loyalty to the Union. He died, an unrepentant rebel, on December 15, 1885, at the age of seventy-five.

Major General Jeb Stuart, Lee's cavalry commander, was mortally wounded at the battle of Yellow Tavern on May 11, 1864, and died at the age of thirty-one.

Of Stuart's three brigade commanders, we have already mentioned the fate of Colonel Munford. The other two, Generals Fitz Lee and Wade Hampton, both survived the war and had illustrious postwar careers. Lee remained in the cavalry of the Army of Northern Virginia until the end and was with his uncle at the surrender at Appomattox. He was elected governor of Virginia from 1885 to 1890 and then became president of the Pittsburgh and Virginia railroad. He was appointed consul general to Cuba in 1896, and during the Spanish American War of 1898, was appointed major general in the U.S. Army Volunteers. He served in the war with distinction and at its end was appointed military governor of Havana. Lee retired from the U.S. Army in 1901 with the rank of brigadier general. Lee's military career thus began and ended in the U.S. Army, with a four-year hiatus in the Confederate army. Lee died in Washington, D.C., in 1905 at the age of seventy. He is buried with other Confederate heroes in Hollywood Cemetery in Richmond. Thus, in death, Lee returned to the Confederacy for the final time.

Wade Hampton, during the remainder of the war, further enhanced his reputation as a fine combat commander who always led from the front and was always in the thick of the fighting. In the final phases of the war, he was promoted to lieutenant general and transferred to the army of Joseph Johnston in an attempt to stem Sherman's invasion of his (Hampton's) native South Carolina.

At the outset of the war, Hampton had been one of the wealthiest men (if not the wealthiest man) in the South. At the end, his home and plantations lay in ruins, and he was never able to fully recoup his fortune. However, he set out on a brilliant political career, where he was always known for his honesty and forthrightness. He was elected governor of South Carolina in 1876 and then represented his state with distinction in the U.S. Senate until his death in 1902 at the age of eighty-four.

Robert E. Lee's family was possibly rooted in America's beginnings more than any other. His father was Henry "Light Horse Harry" Lee of Revolutionary War fame. His mother was a Carter, one of Virginia's most prestigious founding families. His wife was a direct descendent of Martha Washington and her grandson, Washington's adopted son.

At the outset of the war, Lee was a wealthy man. He lived in the palatial Custis-Lee mansion on the eleven-hundred-acre plantation on the Potomac that had been inherited by his wife. The mansion is less than two and a half air miles from the White House. One can only imagine what eleven hundred acres of waterfront property two and a half miles from the White House would be worth today.

But Lee lost it all during the war. The Federal government seized his property and converted it into a military cemetery, with graves so close to the house that it could never again be used as a residence. The end of the war found Lee and his family impoverished.

Lee was provided several lucrative job offers, but he preferred to spend the remaining years of his life educating young people to further national reconciliation. He accepted the low-paying position of president of tiny George Washington College in Jackson's old hometown of Lexington, Virginia. His five-year tenure there was highly successful. He proved to be as adept at education as he was as at being a general.

Lee aged rapidly after the war and died in 1870 at the age of sixty-three, a little more than five years after the end of the war. Upon his death, the trustees of George Washington College decided to rename the institution Washington and Lee University, and so it remains to this day. No one would have objected to this change more than Robert E. Lee, who would have considered it practically sacrilegious to link his name with that of his idol, George Washington.

Lee's fortunes took a favorable turn after his death. In 1870, his son initiated a legal action to recover the Lee plantation, contending that it had been illegally seized without due process of law. The suit wound its way up to the Supreme Court, which, in 1882, declared in young Lee's favor by a five to four decision. The title was returned to his family. However, by this time, the plantation was already evolving into the Arlington National Cemetery, the Valhalla of the nation's war heroes. Young Lee thus sold the plantation back to the government for the modest sum of $150,000.

Lee's reputation, which was already great at the war's end, continued to grow during his tenure as an educator and beyond.

Militarily, he began to be looked upon as one of the great captains of history. Even more important, he began to be ever more admired for the nobility of his character. He always put duty above person, was selfless, modest, considerate, and an exemplary family man. Historians could find few chinks in his moral armor. As time went on and fact evolved into myth, he appeared ever more saintly, until, in the public esteem, he was admitted into the pantheon of the nation's greatest heroes.

Lee's citizenship was not restored in his lifetime. It was not until 1975, more than a hundred years after his death, that it was finally reinstated by an act of Congress. The signing ceremony was appropriately held in Lee's old home, the Custis-Lee mansion, in what is now Arlington National Cemetery. President Gerald Ford presided over the signing ceremony on August 5, 1975. In his remarks he stated:

> As a soldier, General Lee left his mark in military strategy. As a man, he stood as the symbol of valor and of duty. As an educator, he appealed to reason and learning to achieve understanding and to build a stronger nation. The course he chose after the war became a symbol to all those who had marched with him in the bitter years toward Appomattox.
>
> General Lee's character has been an example to succeeding generations, making the restoration of his citizenship an event in which every American can take pride.[9]

Not bad for a rebel!

And last, we come to Gen. James Longstreet, second in command to Robert E. Lee. Except for a stint of about six months' detached duty to General Bragg in the West, Longstreet remained with Lee to the end. He was present with Lee at the final surrender at Appomattox in April 1865, still second in command.

Longstreet almost suffered the same fate as Jackson. In May 1864, a year after Jackson's fatal wounding by his own men, Longstreet was also accidentally shot by his own men. Strangely, the event took place almost within a stone's throw of Jackson's wounding. Although Longstreet's wound appeared to be more serious than Jackson's, he recovered.

After the war, Longstreet fell out of favor in the South by espousing the hated Republican Party and accepting important appointments from it. These included his appointment as minister to Turkey. Today, there are no monuments to Longstreet in the South.

At the age of seventy-six, widower Longstreet married a young woman of thirty-four. Longstreet died in 1904 at the age of eighty-two, but his widow lived on to 1962. Yes, 1962. Thus, Longstreet's life, more than that of any other participant of these fateful events of September 1862, tied the events of those distant days to the lives of those now living.

Notes

Abbreviations
OR—U.S. War Department, *The War of the Rebellion: A Compilation of the Official Records of the Union and Confederate Armies.* Series I.
BL—*Battles and Leaders of the Civil War.* Vol. II.

Chapter 1
1. Daniel H. Hill, "The Battle of South Mountain, or Boonsboro," BL, 576.
2. Jacob D. Cox, " Forcing Fox's Gap and Turner's Gap," BL, 586.
3. OR, Vol. 19, Part II, 381.
4. Ibid., 384.
5. Ibid., 378.
6. Ibid., 388.

Chapter 2
1. Grant, *Personal Memoirs,* 193.
2. George B. McClellan, "From the Peninsula to Antietam," BL, 551.
3. OR, Vol. 19, Part II, 183.
4. George B. McClellan, "From the Peninsula to Antietam," BL, 552.
5. Richard B. Irwin, "Washington Under Banks," BL, 542.
6. OR, Vol. 19, Part II, 601-602.

Chapter 3
1. OR, Vol. 19, Part I, 852.
2. Ibid., 522.
3. Ibid.
4. Ibid., 799.
5. OR, Vol. 19, Part II, 180.
6. Ibid.
7. Ibid., 188.
8. OR, Vol. 19, Part I, 534.

9. Ibid., 790.
10. Ibid., 757.

Chapter 4

1. Henderson, *Stonewall Jackson,* 145.
2. David Stephen Heidler, *Encyclopedia of the American Civil War: A Political, Social, and Military History,* 145.

Chapter 5

1. John G. Walker, "Jackson's Capture of Harpers Ferry," BL, 604.
2. Silas Colgrove, "The Finding of Lee's Lost Order," BL, 664.
3. Ibid.
4. John G. Walker, "Jackson's Capture of Harpers Ferry," BL, 607.

Chapter 6

1. Henry Kyd Douglas, "Stonewall Jackson in Maryland," BL, 622.
2. Ibid., 623.
3. OR, Vol. 19, Part II, 232.
4. Ibid., 233.
5. Ibid., 247.
6. Ibid., 249.
7. Ibid.
8. OR, Vol. 19, Part I, 791.
9. Ibid., 536.

Chapter 7

1. OR, Vol. 19, Part I, 534.
2. Ibid.
3. OR, Vol. 19, Part II, 254-55.
4. OR, Vol. 19, Part I, 520.
5. Ibid.
6. Ibid., 524.
7. OR, Vol. 19, Part I, Supplement, 819.
8. OR, Vol. 19, Part II, 267.
9. Ibid., 266.
10. Ibid.
11. Ibid., 268.
12. Ibid., 269.
13. Ibid., 257.
14. Ibid.
15. Ibid.

Chapter 8

1. Henry Kyd Douglas, "Stonewall Jackson in Maryland," BL, 623.
2. OR, Vol. 19, Part I, 525.
3. Ibid.
4. Ibid., 758.
5. Ibid.
6. OR, Vol. 19, Part II, 270.
7. Ibid., 277.
8. Ibid., 270.
9. Ibid., 272.
10. OR, Vol. 19, Part I, 823-24.

Chapter 9

1. OR, Vol. 19, Part I, 576.
2. Ibid., 544.
3. OR, Vol. 19, Part II, 606.
4. Ibid., 607.
5. Ibid., 280.

Chapter 10

1. Silas Colgrove, "The Finding of Lee's Lost Order," BL, 603.
2. "Special Order, No. 191," BL, 664.
3. Bailey et al, *The Bloodiest Day*, 38.
4. OR, Vol. 19, Part I, 45.
5. OR, Vol. 19, Part II, 281.
6. Ibid.

Chapter 11

1. Daniel H. Hill, "The Battle of South Mountain, or Boonsboro" BL, 564-65.
2. OR, Vol. 19, Part I, 720.
3. Ibid., 721.
4. Ibid., 596.
5. Ibid., 538.
6. Ibid., 954.
7. Ibid., 951.
8. *History and Roster of Maryland Volunteers*, 658.

Chapter 12

1. Allan Tischler, *The History of the Harpers Ferry Cavalry Expedition*, 161-65.
2. OR, Vol. 19, Part I, 758-59.

3. OR, Vol. 19, Part II, 608.

4. Ibid., 609-610.

5. Ibid., 289.

Chapter 13

1. OR, Vol. 19, Part II, 743.

2. Julius White, "The Capitulation of Harpers Ferry," BL, 613-14.

3. William B. Franklin, "Notes on Crampton's Gap and Antietam," BL, 596.

4. Henry Kyd Douglas, "Stonewall Jackson in Maryland," BL, 626.

5. Jacob D. Cox, "The Battle of Antietam," BL, 630-31.

6. OR, Vol. 19, Part I, 951.

7. Ibid.

8. OR, Vol. 19, Part II, 294.

9. Ibid.

10. Ibid., 305.

11. Ibid., 295.

12. Ibid.

Chapter 14

1. OR, Vol. 19, Part II, 307.

2. OR, Vol. 19, Part I, 30.

3. John G. Walker, "Sharpsburg," BL, 675.

4. OR, Vol. 19, Part I, 857.

5. OR, Vol. 19, Part I, 961.

6. OR, Vol. 19, Part II, 308.

7. OR, Vol. 19, Part I, 30.

8. Ibid., 217.

9. Ibid., 540.

10. Ibid., 548.

11. OR, Vol. 19, Part II, 310.

12. Ibid.

13. Ibid.

14. Ibid., 311.

Chapter 15

1. James Longstreet, "The Invasion of Maryland," BL, 671.

2. Bailey et al, *The Bloodiest Day,* 109.

3. Thomas M. Anderson, "Letter to the Editors of Battles and Leaders," BL, 656.

4. OR, Vol. 19, Part II, 322.

Chapter 16
1. Bailey et al, *The Bloodiest Day*, 141.
2. Ibid. 150.
3. OR Vol. 19, Part II, 312.
4. Ibid., 330.
5. Ibid.
6. Ibid.
7. OR Vol. 19, Part I, 181.
8. Bailey et al, *The Bloodiest Day*, 156.

Chapter 17
1. OR, Vol. 19, Part I, 644.
2. Ibid., 761.
3. Ibid., 593.
4. Ibid., 786-87.
5. Ibid., 795-800.

Chapter 18
1. OR, Vol. 51, Part I, 818.
2. OR, Vol. 19, Part II, 271.
3. OR, Vol. 19, Part I, 758.
4. OR, Vol. 19, Part II, 271.
5. Ibid., 272.
6. OR, Vol. 19, Part I, 752-53.
7. William B. Franklin, "Notes on Crampton's Gap and Antietam," BL, 596.
8. Daniel H. Hill, "The Battle of South Mountain, or Boonsboro," BL, 565.
9. James Longstreet, "The Invasion of Maryland," BL, 669.

Chapter 21
1. Silas Colgrove, "The Finding of Lee's Order," BL, 603.
2. OR, Vol. 19, Part I, 586.
3. Grant, *Personal Memoirs*, 657.
4. Ibid.
5. Henry Steele Commager, ed., *Living History: The Civil War*, 1276.
6. Ibid, 165
7. Heidler, 1276.
8. Carl Sandburg, *Abraham Lincoln: The War Years*, Vol. II, 335.
9. President Gerald R. Ford's Remarks upon Signing a Bill

Restoring Rights of Citizenship to General Robert E. Lee, Gerald R. Ford Library and Presidential Museum, http://www.ford.utexas.edu/library/speeches/750473.htm

Bibliography

Bailey, Ronald H. and the Editors of *Time Life Books*. *The Bloodiest Day: The Battle of Antietam*. Alexandria, VA: Time Life Books, 1984.

Battles and Leaders of the Civil War. Vol. II. New York: Thomas Yoseloff, Publisher, 1956.

Civil War Times Illustrated Editors. *Great Battles of the Civil War*. New York: Gallery Books, 1984.

Commager, Henry Steele, ed. *Living History: The Civil War*. New York: Hess Press, 1950.

Freeman, Douglas Southall. *Lee's Lieutenants*. New York: Scribner, 1998.

Grant, Ulysses S. *The Personal Memoirs of Ulysses S. Grant*. New York: Konecky & Konecky, 1886).

Hearn, Chester G. *Six Years of Hell: Harpers Ferry During the Civil War*. Baton Rouge: Louisiana State University Press, 1996.

Heidler, David S. and Jeanne T., eds. *Encyclopedia of the American Civil War*. New York: W. W. Norton & Company, 2000.

Henderson, Lt. Col. G. F. R. *Stonewall Jackson*. New York: Konecky & Konecky, 1977.

Johnson, Curt and Mark McLaughlin. *Battles of the Civil War*. Singapore: Barnes & Noble, 1977.

Miller, Francis Trevelyan. *The Armies and the Leaders*. New York: Castle Books, 1957.

Norton, Henry. *Deeds of Daring or History of the Eighth New York*. Norwich, NY: Chenango Telegraph Printing House, 1889.

Sandburg, Carl. *Abraham Lincoln: The War Years*. New York: Harcourt, Brace, & World, Inc., 1939.

Swinton, William. *Army of the Potomac*. New York: Smithmark Publishers, 1995.

Taylor, Walter H. *Four Years With General Lee*. New York: Bonanza Books, 1962.

Thomason, John. *Jeb Stuart*. New York: Smithmark Publishers, 1930.

Tischler, Allan L. *The History of the Harpers Ferry Cavalry Expedition*. Winchester, VA: Five Cedars Press, 1993.

U.S. War Department. *The War of the Rebellion: A Compilation of the Official Records of the Union and Confederate Armies*. Series I, Vol. 19, Part I. Harrisburg, PA: National Historical Society, 1971.

U.S. War Department. *The War of the Rebellion: A Compilation of the Official Records of the Union and Confederate Armies*. Series I, Vol. 19, Part I, Supplement. Harrisburg, PA: National Historical Society, 1971.

U.S. War Department. *The War of the Rebellion: A Compilation of the Official Records of the Union and Confederate Armies*. Series I, Vol. 19, Part II. Harrisburg, PA: National Historical Society, 1971.

U.S. War Department. *The War of the Rebellion: A Compilation of the Official Records of the Union and Confederate Armies*. Series I, Vol. 51, Part I. Harrisburg, PA: National Historical Society, 1971.

Vernon, W. F. *History & Roster of Maryland Volunteers, War of 1865*, Vol. 2, Baltimore: Guggenheimer, Weil, & Co., 1899.

Waugh, John C. *The Class of 1846*. New York: Warner Books, 1994.

Index